AF412116

Female View

Women Fashion Photographers from Modernity to the Digital Age

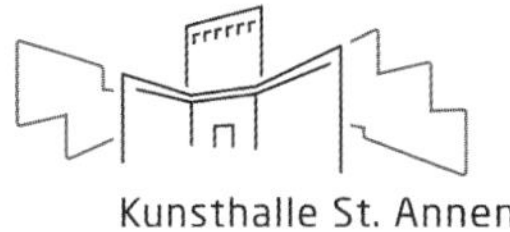

HATJE CANTZ

Content

Female View –
A Perspective

The medium of photography is a distinctive index of time: it constantly reflects technical and social developments, and, by its public use, political changes as well. This also applies to fashion photography. It picks up on social transformation and sometimes even shapes it.

The exhibition *Female View* draws attention to women in fashion photography, many of whom were pioneers of their genre whose works have provided trend-setting impulses. Following through in their professions with determination, they moreover embody a decidedly modern image of women.

By focusing on female photographers, the exhibition pinpoints industries commonly associated as "feminine" or "interesting for women", such as art, culture, and particularly fashion, and it exposes how they are still marked by structural inequality even today, for instance in terms of public perception or pay. The exhibition offers ample evidence that the imbalance is by no means based on artistic grounds. All of these women have played decisive roles in the artistic formation of fashion photography since the early 20th century: It is about time for a dedicated show to make their independent aesthetic achievements accessible to a broad public for the first time.

Many of the presented artists were or are not only fashion photographers, but also documentary photographers who know very well the political and social conditions in which they were or are active. Their photos are contemporary history documents that reveal a lot about social life at the particular time – for example in the 1940s: Women had to work, and materials were scarce, so clothing had to be practical and durable. In the German Democratic Republic, fashion photography often took place underground. At the same time, there were the official fashion magazines such as *Sibylle.* The spirit of today is captured by the photographers from the generation of the digital natives. The world we live in is globally networked, and photographs, including fashion images, are uploaded and posted synchronously millions of times over. Our image perception is becoming faster, and so are the fashion trends.

The artists, the curator of the exhibition, and the authors involved in this catalogue develop the perspective and at the same time address the viewers with the question: "Does the 'female view' exist?"

For Kunsthalle St. Annen, this is an opportunity to once again present itself as a place where diversity and the hidden are put into focus. Perception and recognition of the "other" are prerequisites for equality and for a society that is open to its own many perspectives.

In the past years, Antje-Britt Mählmann, the director of Kunsthalle St. Annen, has stood for this. As the curator of this innovative exhibition, she was the one to pull everything together. After the exhibition opening, she will be leaving our Hanseatic city for great challenges offered by other cultural venues. She will definitely leave her traces in Lübeck's local cultural landscape.

I thank all those who contributed to the success of this exhibition with loans, all the participating artists, the entire team involved in the project, and the friends and sponsors of Kunsthalle St. Annen. In addition to the Possehl Foundation, the foundation Friedrich Bluhme und Else Jebsen-Stiftung, and the foundation von Keller-Stiftung Lübeck, I extend my thanks to the foundation Karin und Uwe Hollweg Stiftung from Bremen.

Monika Frank
Senator for Culture and Education for the Hanseatic City of Lübeck

Antje-Britt Mählmann

Female View

Women Fashion Photographers from Modernity to the Digital Age

Fashion photography produced by women, often unduly neglected, is the focus of the exhibition *Female View*. Countless female photographers have worked for influential magazines such as *Harper's Bazaar* and *Vogue*, shaping the medium, the style of their time, and other artists over many decades. Quite a few of them had previously modelled for other photographers and knew the job from both sides of the camera. Up to now, many exhibitions on fashion photography have revolved around the male view of the female body presenting the clothing. But the viewers of these images are usually women. This is an issue that ties in with the fashion industry on a broader level, too: while the business as such is largely geared to female target groups, the executive boards are still overwhelmingly staffed by male leaders. Although many of the photographers on display have created iconic images and unique style trends, they are not widely known to the general public today. The aim of the exhibition is to map out the "female gaze" in fashion photography from the 1930s up to the present.

The varying body images and fashions also allow tracing the social and political changes through the decades. Today's production of fashion images is more diverse than in the 20th century, for instance. The present gaze is no longer directed exclusively at images advertised as ideal. Concepts such as beauty, gender, cultural participation, and identity are increasingly being called into question. The selection of the photographs extends to reflect the wider scope of contemporary production.

Female View contextualises the transformation of the photographic image and its spread in the media in historical and social terms: from fashion magazines to the exhibition space, from coffee-table books to video installations and to the present digital self-staging in the increasingly prevalent social media. The development since the 1930s until today is presented along a few selected artistic positions. These photographs serve to highlight the role of women, stylistic devices, the distribution and locational spread of fashion photos, and their aesthetics in their particular temporal context. While for instance Europe and the USA were the internationally leading fashion centres in the 20th century, today's fashion and its visual cosmos are more global than ever.

From the 1930s to the 1950s

A prologue within the exhibition offers an introduction to fashion photography of the 1930s and 1940s. The US-American photographer **Lee Miller** was an assistant to Man Ray in Paris, and she worked for magazines such as *Vogue* and *Harper's Bazaar* at the same time. Miller moreover documented the horrors of World War II and the holocaust for the American *Vogue* while she continued working as a fashion photographer in London.

Prior to World War II, the highly successful Berlin fashion photographer Else Ernestine Neuländer known as **Yva** hired an assistant for her studio: young Helmut Newton, who would later become one of the world's most famous photographers. Because of her Jewish background, Yva was banned from working in Nazi Germany from 1938 on, and she was deported in 1942 and murdered probably in the Sobibor extermination camp. The photographer **Ingeborg Hoppe** also had to fear persecution and restrictions during the Nazi dictatorship due to her part Jewish descent, but she managed to go undercover as an employee at Urs Lang-Kurz's studio. Hoppe opened her own studio in Stuttgart after the end of World War II and worked for numerous German magazines.

Unlike Yva, who was under professional ban as a Jew, the Paris-trained German fashion photographer **Regina Relang** became a member of the Nazified press association of the German Reich in 1939. Her photos were published in the contemporary German fashion magazines, which served primarily for propaganda and promotion of the National Socialist German Reich abroad. From 1946 on, Relang created memorable fashion photographs, including those amidst World War II ruins in Munich. Relang worked as a fashion photographer until the 1980s. Her photos of Dior's New Look in the streets of European metropolises, for instance, are particularly appealing and touching documents of the period. **Charlotte Rohrbach** likewise worked within the Nazified press as a photographer and continued her fashion photography after World War II.

Like Yva, the Austrian photographer **Madame d'Ora** (Dora Kallmus) came from a Jewish family. She had established a photo studio in Vienna in 1907 and operated it together with her colleague Arthur Benda. In 1925, she moved her studio to Paris and worked as a portrait and fashion photographer. When the Germans occupied France, she had to give up the studio and flee from Paris. She returned to a devastated post-war Vienna in 1946, where she engaged in documentary photography and in coming to terms with the collective war experiences.

The fresh start in the fashion and creative industries was generally marked by the challenge of coping with the trauma of the war and the material limitations of the post-war period. The painter and photographer **Lillian Bassman** and her husband Paul Himmel also initially turned to the photographic documentation of the war and its consequences for civil society. Bassman later became better known for her fashion photographs and, in her position as creative director at *Harper's Bazaar*, she was formative for the fashion photography community of the 1940s to the 1960s. **Louise Dahl-Wolfe** also took numerous photographs for the major fashion magazines, preferably in the open air, in the metropolises of the world.

From the 1960s to the 1980s

The 1960s and 1970s brought new opportunities for women to express themselves, including in the arts. The French photographer and filmmaker **Sarah Moon** was an international haute couture model in the 1960s, when she started to take photos of her female colleagues for fun. Her talent was soon "discovered", and today she is among the internationally most sought-after fashion photographers. Her artistic, occasionally near abstract images are reminiscent of earlier photographers of the 1920s to 1950s, although unlike them Moon frequently uses colour as an important compositional element.

The Australian June Newton, on the other hand, who worked under the pseudo-nym of **Alice Springs**, specialised primarily in black-and-white photography. From the 1970s on, she frequently worked together with her husband Helmut Newton in the international world of fashion. Springs had in common with many of the other female photographers on exhibit that she also modelled, mostly for her husband.

The Cold War presented a special situation particularly for photography in the divided Germany. Like all artistic and journalistic activity in East Germany, fashion photography was subject to specific governmental regulations. Alter-native lifestyles and images were either "hidden away" within official creative work, or they were relegated underground. Women photographers such as **Sibylle Bergemann** recorded the alternative fashions of the rebellious sub-culture and, at the same time, worked for the official fashion magazine *Sibylle*.

Ute Mahler, who often works together closely with her husband, is another of the exhibited artists to walk the narrow line between fashion and documentary photography.

Charlotte March from Hamburg was one of the West German photographers who started to breach outdated conventions of representation in the 1960s. Her photos show models in miniskirts, in postures of athletic movement, and occa-sionally in perspective views from below – thereby simultaneously depicting modernisation processes in society in general.

From the 1990s to the present

The works by the Paris-based portrait and fashion photographer **Bettina Rheims** are rebellious in a glamorous way. She links high gloss and feminine beauty to questions of sexual identity and self-determination. The subversive potential within her clean and glamorous aesthetics is revealed in the dialogue between photographer and model. Like Rheims, **GABO**, who lives in Branden-burg, is primarily interested in the inner expression of her models. For her, portraits and fashion photography belong intrinsically together.

Frankfurt-born **Ellen von Unwerth** also very succinctly merges apparently con-trasting perceptions of femininity in her oeuvre. One of the most high-profile fashion photographers today, Ellen von Unwerth became known in 1989 through a campaign for *Guess* with the then still unknown model Claudia Schiffer. Un-werth's photographic signature is characterised by playful and frequently provocative depictions of sex and glamour. Tongue in cheek, she brushes aside political correctness to expand the visual and identity-political limits of the medium. She also moves with the times in terms of the media, for example, in her appearance as herself in the Netflix series *Emily in Paris* in the year of the exhibition. In addition, she already has well over 600,000 followers on Instagram.

In the digital age

The progress of social networks and digitalization today continues to advance the intense massification of fashion photography initially sparked by the print media. Traditional areas of fashion, by dint of their exclusivity and luxury previously strictly limited to the chosen few, have been overtaken by democratisation processes that make digital image production accessible to any smartphone user. With the ever easier public access to fashion self-representations, gender stereotypes are also being increasingly challenged in the current digital image culture. Young people sharing outfits on the internet are further stepping up the pace compared to print media.

Many young women work along the boundaries of artistic and feminist representation and fashion imagery. The photographer **Liv Liberg** from Amsterdam, for example, produces fashion spreads for several major magazines and also, specifically commissioned by clients, for Instagram. Liberg's favourite model is her sister Britt, whose edgy look lends a distinctive expressiveness to the photos.

Amber Pinkerton is a young photographer from Jamaica, who currently lives in London and publishes in alternative fashion magazines such as *VICE* and *i-D*. Many of her pictures have the look and feel of documentary photography, and they deal with the diverse lifestyles and fashionable self-representations of the different communities in Jamaica and in London.

Nadine Ijewere is also based in London and of Nigerian-Jamaican roots. Her photos question the norms and stereotypes she encountered in fashion images in her childhood. She casts the models for her shoots herself.

Moscow-born **Elizaveta Porodina** likewise sets her own standards of interpretation in beauty and fashion. She studied clinical psychology prior to her career as photographer. Today her artistic and poetic images are published in international fashion magazines.

All of the present-day female fashion artists mentioned here also produce motion pictures and video works, and they present their images digitally, on websites, on Instagram, and through other digital media. The contemporary section of the exhibition *Female View* chiefly addresses questions of identity, individuality, and image production.

A female view?

The photographers presented here have one thing in common: Their work is inextricably linked to political events and prevailing trends. Besides being fashion photographers, several of them are also chroniclers and critical observers of their time, as is manifest in the documentary focus of their works. Others take an approach to fashion presentation through portraiture. A number of them are former models. They are the ones who are particularly familiar with the feeling and meaning of standing in front of the camera. Even if it is not possible to separate the "female gaze" from socially dominant norms of masculinity and femininity, it is still obvious that most of the photographers in this exhibition managed to break with norms of female work and (self) representation. Many of them harness gender clichés in a playful manner, upending on their own terms and finding new and surprising ways to challenge or circumvent them.

Nadine Barth

What Is A Fashion Image? —
A Reflection

Flipping through a *Vogue* magazine today will bring forth an encounter with a blast of colourful fashion images. Almost the entire first third of any copy, however, consists of ads for fashion, luxury, and beauty brands. And even in the following sections, the shifts between editorial spreads and advertisements, some covering several pages, are hardly discernible. The overall effect is an ingenious system targeted at making people want to buy the new looks. Fashion magazines are catalogues of items from the world of commerce. Whether in a campaign or an editorial shoot, the fashion image has a commercial context; its essence is defined by its inherent commodity character. The fact that the image tends to disguise its character, to flirtatiously own up to it, or to downright deny it is only a part of its marketing. Over time, the fashion image has developed strategies to deal with this "burden", in all kinds of different manners: playful, offensive, artistic, aggressive, restrained, subtle. Fashion images have a powerful ally, too: the spirit of the age, the zeitgeist.

Fashion images are dependent on the time of their making. Collections are designed and produced, sample pieces are photographed, and the shots make it into a fashion magazine. Half a year to a year passes from the moment an idea is conceived to the printed page. It takes a few more months for the readers to process what they have seen and to hopefully adopt the style. The fashion image comes across as avant-garde because it anticipates something that will be lived in the future, after the purchase. It thus moves on a timeline between the vision of the designer and the manifestation in society and is thus very close to the here and now.

How does a fashion image come into being?

Typically, fashion editors plan what to cover in a particular issue. They create a mood board, write down keywords, order collection pieces from the designers, book the photographers, the models, hairstylists, and the make-up artists. They discuss suitable places for the production with the photographers – in the studio or on location. By the time of the shoot, the team will have grown to about ten people including the assistants, with up to fifty people being involved in large productions. In the end, the image will be the result of the joint endeavours of all these minds – even if some contribute the ideas while others do the legwork. The designer responsible for the creation of a collection will certainly be present in person for campaign shoots, but not for editorial photo productions. So this is where the decisive transformation of an artistic vision into a photographic image takes place: a transformation that is indeed necessary, as the curator and lecturer Ulrich Lehmann points out. "Fashion only exists in representation. Clothing is elevated from its material properties to an aesthetic idea through its representation as an image in the media. It is only through this process that most clothing can become fashion in the first place. And the most common agent in this process is fashion photography."[1]

This leads us to the question of an image's predominant reference. An "image" in the traditional sense is defined as a depiction (signifier) with reference to the concept of what is depicted (signified). The Greek *eikon* in classical antiquity referred to the external perceptible appearance. Plato distinguished between the "natural image" (*eikon physei*), a mirror or shadow image, and the "artificial image" (*eikon techné*) that was formed for example by a craftsperson, a sculptor, or a painter. The natural image's reference to reality is clear: the mirror image in the water is a reflection of the face looking into the water. The artificial image's reference lies in the artist's vision, in the creative imagination. Here, the relationship between the image and what is depicted is more complex. The image is a part of reality because it is made of "tangible" materials, but its reference leads into a spiritual world, the ideas of which find their way into the visual object. Reality is "copied", "imitated", and to a certain degree "falsified".[2]

With the advent of photography, the natural image took on an expanded meaning. Photographs were to all intents and purposes understood as depictions of reality. This caused great amazement, but also a certain fear. Is it real what I see in the print? It is two-dimensional, after all, and it has undergone a complicated technical process. And how did the world get into the camera in the first place? The choice of method and framing, then the aperture and the focal length, perhaps a filter, to name but a few, are aspects through which a photographer takes influence on the image of reality. Ultimately, it is more a subjective than an objective view. The German art historian Alfred Lichtwark no longer saw the photographic work as a mere depiction, but rather as an interpreted idea of an object turned image.[3]

The first extant photograph is considered to be by Joseph Nicéphore Niépce, taken from the window of his study in Le Gras in the 1820s. He used a tin plate coated with bitumen dipped in lavender oil and then exposed it for eight hours. Landscape and street photos using the so-called daguerreotype process followed, and soon people moved into the focus of photography, too. In the 1850s and 1860s, Charles Reutlinger's studio on Boulevard Montmartre in Paris specialised in photographing clients in a carte-de-visite or carte-cabinet format. Columns or painted backgrounds were used to create the impression of an exclusive world. Meanwhile, at the court of Napoleon III, the Tuscan noblewoman Virginia Oldoini, Contessa de Castiglione, discovered the new medium and staged herself with great creativity to have her photos taken by Adolphe Braun or the prestigious Parisian studio Mayer & Pierson. Eventually, she had assembled some 400 elaborately created fashion photos of herself, some of them extravagantly coloured.[4] Fifty of these photos were exhibited in 2000 at the Metropolitan Museum of Art in New York under the title: "*La Divine Comtesse*" – *Photographs of the Countess de Castiglione*.

From the 1850s and 60s, it would still take several decades for fashion photos to find their way into magazines. Illustrations – whether painted, drawn, etched, or engraved – predominated in the early fashion magazines of the 18th century. Launched in 1770, *The Lady's Magazine* is considered the first of its kind, joined in 1785 by *Cabinet des Modes* from Paris and in 1792 by *Journal des Dames et des Modes.* In Germany and Austria, *Journal des Luxus und der Moden* was first published in 1786. These early editions were loose sheets with articles on fashion, art, theatre, music, literature, gardening, furniture, travel, history, and politics.[5] The invention of autotype, a halftone printing process, replaced wood engraving; text and images could then be printed together. A pioneer in the genre, *La Mode Pratique*, was the first magazine to print a fashion spread in 1892.[6]

The two dominating fashion magazines of the early 20th century – *Harper's Bazaar*, founded in 1867 and part of the Hearst Corporation since 1913, and *Vogue*, established in 1892 and taken over by Condé Montrose Nast in 1909 – soon also bought into fashion photography. Gradually, the elaborate illustrations produced according to the art trends of their time were being replaced by photographs.

Photography with its focus on realistic depiction introduced a new objectivity to women's magazines: Edward Steichen staged harlequin dresses by the Parisian designer Paul Poiret for *Art et Décoration* in 1911, and in 1913 Baron Adolphe de Meyer published his first fashion photo for the French *Vogue*: the portrait of art collector Gertrude Vanderbilt Whitney.

Whereas the visual arts of the time used the medium of photography in a highly experimental manner – Futurism's motion studies, Dadaist collages, or cross-fades and photograms in Surrealism, to name a few – the fashion photos in the 1910s and 20s were rather traditional: A carefully illuminated set at the studio resulted in a "simplified neoclassical image formula"[7]. Condé Nast even instructed his photographers to produce the truest possible depiction of the clothing "with precise sharpness and technical perfection". He clearly gave preference to the realistic art style of the "natural image" from classical antiquity. Photographers such as Horst P. Horst, Cecil Beaton, and George Hoyningen-Huene were far too obstinate for Nast's taste. What he was concerned with was the "correct description of the product for sale"[8].

It was not before the legendary art directors Alexei Brodowitch (at *Harper's Bazaar* under editor-in-chief Carmel Snow) and Alexander Liberman *(Vogue)* entered the scene that these instructions were waived. Extravagant sets, shots in the street, motion, even blurs were not only acceptable now but even explicitly welcome. From the 1930s on, female photographers started to be booked: **Louise Dahl-Wolfe** was part of the *Harper's Bazaar* team from 1933 to 1958, shooting 86 covers and a total of more than 600 pages for the magazine.

Frances McLaughlin-Gill was the first woman to sign a permanent contract with *Vogue* in 1943. Toni Frissell was the third American woman who, together with Dahl-Wolfe and McLaughlin-Gill, shaped female fashion photography in U.S. magazines during these years. Their pictures were elegant and feminine, yet full of life, and they addressed women's lives, presenting them in front of theatres or in art galleries, at picnics or at the beach.

Lee Miller brought a touch of Surrealism to the world of fashion pictures. She was discovered as a model by Condé Nast in 1927, but moved to Paris only two years later to become Man Ray's darkroom assistant and lover. Both of them experimented with solarisation and Sabattier effects. Miller used this technique around 1942 for various fashion photos at the London *Vogue* studio, such as in her famous *Corsetry, Solarised Photographs*. Gestures and lines interact masterfully here; the facial expression is one of ecstasy.

The fashion image increasingly detached itself from its counterpart, the signified, namely the clothing, and opened up to a world of attitude and feeling. Even today, the signifier, that is the fashion photo, absorbs currents of the times, makes suggestions for finding identity, and thus remains in a symbolic dimension.

In her essay "In Plato's Cave", Susan Sontag writes that photographs "do not seem to be statements about the world so much as pieces of it, miniatures of reality that anyone can make or acquire."[9]

The fashion image with its multiple reproducibility through its spread in the media, in magazines or online, has made the acquisition of these pieces of the world accessible to all. The fact that this world is a constructed one, a vision behind which "reality disappears"[10] does not detract from the aesthetic pleasure of the fashion image. Freely floating chains of fashion signifiers are simply beautiful.

1   Ulrich Lehmann, Introduction, in: *Chic clicks: Creativity and Commerce in Contemporary Fashion Photography*, Ulrich Lehmann and Jessica Morgan (ed.), Exhibition catalogue. Institute of Contemporary Art, Boston, Fotomuseum Winterthur, Ostfildern-Ruit 2002, T12.

2   See Plato, e.g. *Cratylus*, 424e, *Phaedrus* 235d, and *Protagoras* 267c.

3   Alfred Lichtwark, *Die Bedeutung der Amateurphotographie (The Importance of Amateur Photography)*. Offprint from the newspaper "Hamburgischer Correspondent" of 15 October 1893, Hamburg 1893, p. 9.

4   Timm Starl, *Icons of Photography. The 19th Century*, Freddy Langer (ed.), Munich 2002, p. 48.

5   Wiebke Koch-Mertens, *Der Mensch und seine Kleider (Man and his Clothes)*, 2 volumes, Part 1: *Die Kulturgeschichte der Mode bis 1900 (The Cultural History of Fashion up to 1900)*, Zürich 2000, p. 372.

6   Klaus Honnef, "Paradox par excellence, Die Mode und die Fotografie – ein beziehungsreiches Verhältnis (Paradox Par Excellence, Fashion and Photography – a Highly Interconnected Relationship)", in: *Modefotografie von 1900 bis heute (Fashion Photography from 1900 to today)*, Ingried Brugger (ed.), exhibition catalogue. Kunstforum Länderbank Wien, Vienna 1990, p. 14

7   Ingried Brugger, "Modebilder – Zeitbilder (Images of Fashion – Images of Time)", in: Exhibition catalogue. Vienna 1990, p. 7–9.

8   Nathalie Herschdorfer, Introduction, in: idem (ed.), *Zeitlos schön, 100 Jahre Modefotografie (Timelessly Beautiful: 100 Years of Fashion Photography)*, Munich 2016, p. 11.

9   Susan Sontag, "In Plato's Cave", in: idem (ed.) *On Photography*, New York, 1977, p. 4.

10 Paul Virilio, *The Aesthetics of Disappearance*, Berlin 1986.

Eugenie Shinkle

A Woman's Eye:
Fashion Photography, Femininity and Feeling

The phrase "female gaze" is a fairly recent addition to our cultural vocabulary. Put simply, it refers to the idea that a woman's gaze is categorically different (even 'opposite', as some have argued) to that of a man. In discussions of photography, it's frequently called on to support claims that images of women by women differ in specific and recognisable ways from those made by men.

But the gaze isn't the same thing as the eye's look. Rather than something that is under the control of the individual, the gaze refers to a subject's wider awareness of "being looked at". Photography is only one link in a long chain of institutions, discourses, and technologies that act together to construct both the gaze and the ideals of gender with which it's aligned. The male gaze – the convention against which the female gaze is often positioned – is embodied in cultural expectations about the way that women should appear and how they should behave in order to conform to shared standards of femininity. Such standards are shaped and formed in ways that are beyond the individual photographer's control.

Who better though, to understand the restrictions that society imposes on female selfhood than women themselves? Female fashion photographers are subject to the same unwritten codes of behaviour and appearance as the models they photograph; they deal with the same frustrations and insecurities that go along with the demand to look and act in certain ways. They understand what it means to live in a female body, to identify as feminine. This is not to claim that female photographers differ in essence from their male counterparts. It is, however, to acknowledge that they are positioned differently in relation to their subjects, to the industry in which they work, and to discourses of fashion more generally. To speak of a female *view* is to recognise a different way of representing femininity – one that incorporates a lived experience of female subjectivity and the conventions that define and delimit it.

All of the most significant shifts in Western notions of femininity that have taken place over the past century have been registered in fashion photography. Its emergence as a standalone genre early in the twentieth century coincided roughly with the beginnings of widespread women's suffrage. The brashness of the flapper era, the can-do attitude of the war years, the struggles for racial and gender equality throughout the 1950s and 60s, and, more recently, a growing awareness that gender itself is not a simple matter of male or female, but a continuum – all of these circumstances have been given expression in fashion photographs. Many of them are signalled clearly in changing fashions, but they are also perceived on a deeper, more visceral level, in shifting conventions of gesture, expression, and pose.

Our *feelings* about images – the bodily sensations or intensities that arise when we look at photographs – also play a significant part in their meaning. The term 'affect' is often used to describe these non-rational modes of encountering the world – less easily regulated responses like emotions and gut feelings. Typically, affects are experienced in an indirect, non-reflective way; often, they're difficult to explain or express in language. Nevertheless, they do not lack meaning. The rising warmth of a blush, for instance, is difficult to put words to, and impossible to control or rationalise, but no less meaningful because of this. For many years, these flows of feeling were dismissed as merely instinctive, and seldom taken into account in writing on photography and other disciplines. More recently, however, writers and thinkers in a wide range of fields – cultural studies, politics, and economics to name a few – have begun to explore the ways that affect, delivered by and through the body, shapes the way that we understand the world, images, and each other.

Our experience of fashion photographs is reliant on bodily empathy – our ability to grasp what another body feels even if we can't quite work out what its appearance means. Shifting notions of femininity are not just made visible in fashion photographs, in other words, they are also *felt* – by the model, by the photographer, and by the viewer too. The history of fashion photography is an account of transformations in the way that female subjects present themselves to the eye, and in the way that they inhabit their bodies. From the sculptural stillness of early twentieth-century fashion photographs towards more playful and powerful attitudes; from demure to girlish to womanly, and, more recently, to the deliberately awkward: each shift in the body's demeanour marks a change in the way that feminine subjectivity is lived, and the way that it is embodied in images of fashion.

***

The earliest photographs in this exhibition date from the late 1920s. Few women worked as fashion photographers before this time – 'technical' professions such as photography were not considered appropriate for well-bred young ladies. Pioneers like **Yva** and **Madame d'Ora** dared to push the boundaries of femininity simply by choosing to do the work that they did. Even so, Madame d'Ora's role was, in modern terms, primarily that of a stylist and art director. She rarely operated the camera, designating that task to her studio assistant and business partner Arthur Benda.

The fact that a woman could not only work as a fashion photographer, but that she could reach the top of her profession, was a signal of changing attitudes towards gender. The so-called 'flapper' era of the 1920s ushered in scandalously short skirts and levelled challenges at many of the social conventions that governed women's lives. Flappers smoked, they danced the Charleston, they kissed whomever they chose. Their counterparts in the fashion press, however, continued, for the most part, to exhibit a dignified stillness: leaping, gesturing, or appearing too animated were not yet part of the mainstream vocabulary of fashion photography. Even the 'fresh air' school of outdoor fashion photography – led by innovative image-makers like Toni Frissell and Martin Munkacsi – called for a certain amount of restraint. Taken in the 1930s, Yva's photograph of a model in a bathing suit exemplifies the uneasy relationship between emancipation and physical discipline. The swimming costume is daringly revealing for its time, and the model's athletic frame is the embodiment of streamlined, modern femininity. Her pose, however – arms angled overhead, back arched, and leg stretched behind her – is carefully contrived, an orderly and static representation of a body in motion.

Fashion photographs take shape around a contradiction – on the one hand, they are a timely reflection of the changing reality of women's lives; on the other hand, they consistently promote ideals and expectations that have little to do with this reality. So, although the early years of the twentieth century brought new freedoms, these were accompanied by new ways of regulating the fashionable subject. From the 1930s onward, for instance, women were under growing pressure to conform to an ideal female form that was widely circulated in the media. Urging readers to bring their own bodies and lifestyles into line with popular images of beauty and vitality, fashion photographs presented a carefully controlled kind of freedom. Conflicting messages such as these have become part of the language of fashion photography. Throughout the twentieth century, they manifested as an ongoing dialogue between modesty and excess, between relative androgyny and lavish femininity, between independence and restraint.

The austerity and no-nonsense attitude of the years surrounding WWII, for example, were countered, in the period following the end of the war, by the overtly feminine silhouette of Dior's New Look. Shot against a backdrop of bombed-out buildings in London, **Lee Miller's** 1941 photograph of a model in a Digby Morton suit – a simple, practical garment – reflects the reality of daily life under challenging conditions. No fairytale fantasies here: like Miller herself – who began her career as a model, but soon moved on to work as a photographer and later, as a war correspondent for *Vogue* – the women in her photographs were strong and capable.

In America, a similar resolve manifested in the way that fashion itself was manufactured and sold. Spearheaded by designers like Clare McCardell and Mildred Orrick, the 1930s and 40s saw the emergence of a rapidly growing market in ready-to-wear fashion. Couturiers in Europe had been creating *sportif* garments for wealthy customers from early in the twentieth century, but it was the American designers who forged the link between functional, affordable garments and a chic, modern image. Photographers like **Louise Dahl-Wolfe** were instrumental in creating this image. Her 1939 photograph of the socialite and model Lady Margaret Strickland is typical of her work: clad in fashionable sportswear with her hair wrapped in a turban, Strickland stands with cigarette in hand, the wind blowing her skirt suggestively between her legs. Along with confidence and self-possession, there's also a subtle nod to female sexuality in this image – a sly repudiation of the unblemished virtue which befitted a "respectable" woman.

With the end of WWII, however, fashion returned to a more stereotypically feminine outline. Dior's New Look – with its nipped-in waists and voluminous skirts – was a response to the austerity of the war years. It also signalled a return to a kind of classicism in posing – sinuous curves and stylised attitudes that made no attempt to emulate real life, but that referred only to the rarefied domain of fashion itself. The American photographer **Lillian Bassman** created some of her most memorable images in response to the structured undergarments required to create the wasp-waisted silhouette. Rather than photographing on a crowded set, Bassman worked alone with her models, often in domestic settings, away from the gaze of male photographers. As Bassman herself remarked in 2006, 'I think my contribution to the genre has been to photograph fashion with a woman's eye for a woman's intimate feelings.'

The sexual revolution and the civil rights movements that gathered strength from the 1960s onwards made space for more radical challenges to feminine ideals. In contrast to the distant, aristocratic image cultivated by 1950s models, highly publicised relationships with actors, photographers, and musicians left the public under no illusions about their 1960s counterparts' regard for old-fashioned virtues. In some respects, fashion photography's response to these changes was at odds with the freedoms that they represented: the sexual liberation of the 1960s, for instance, was embodied in the childlike silhouette of models like Twiggy and Penelope Tree. But the increasing popularity of girl-next-door beauties like Jean Shrimpton, and models of colour such as China Machado and Donyale Luna, was a sign of growing openness in an industry that had been, until that time, overwhelmingly white and middle-class. What's most remarkable about **Charlotte March's** 1966 photograph of Luna clutching her knees is not her folded limbs and her wide-eyed expression – it's the fact that she was on the pages of a mainstream fashion magazine.

It wasn't until the 1970s and 80s that the female sexuality hinted at in Dahl-Wolfe's 1939 image was more openly expressed in fashion photographs. The era of the so-called 'supermodels' embodied two apparently antithetical images of femininity – independent, self-possessed women who were also stereotypically feminine and openly sexual. A former model herself, photographer **Ellen von Unwerth** embraced this contradiction. Her work, she claimed, explored female sexuality in a manner different to that of a male photographer: "I understand the female body better, and I know from my own modelling days how you feel both constrained and free when you're in front of a camera." Her images capture the attitude of a generation for which having it all – family, a social life and a successful career, as well as cover-girl looks – was both an entitlement and an expectation that regular women struggled to meet.

By contrast, photographers like **Ute Mahler**, working in the GDR during the same period, used fashion photography as a way of pushing back against repressive ideologies. Mahler's photographs reflect her interest in documentary and portrait photography: her models are posed in everyday surroundings with little apparent regard for glamour or fantasy. Designer garments weren't widely available, and most of the outfits in her photographs were sourced from government clothing outlets or hand-sewn by the editors of the magazines for which she worked. Like those of many of her peers, Mahler's photographs were less about the latest fashions than they were about a politics of self-fashioning – a subtle but potentially subversive form of expression in an authoritarian state.

Though they don't always take the form of explicit political statements, fashion images are an important channel for generating and circulating affects that feed back into political discourse. Individual political views are shaped not just by shared values, but by body-based perceptions that circulate between subjects in less direct ways. Along with visible signs on the body's surface, qualities and perceptions such as these are expressed as feelings that bubble up, often unchecked, from its depths. Features such as pose, expression, and gesture can communicate specific messages, but they also invite the viewers of fashion images to inhabit new and less customary ways of experiencing female subjectivity.

Technology plays an increasingly important role in this sharing of affects. Fashion photographs have always been ephemeral things – designed to be admired, desired, and quickly forgotten – but they are no longer confined to the stillness of the magazine page. Now, they are also part of a constant stream of fast-moving electronic images that flicker in and out of our awareness. Today, the fashion photograph must engage audiences ever more forcefully – commanding attention with bold statements and powerfully invoked sensations.

The affects stirred up by contemporary fashion photographs are often strange and unexpected. Since the 1990s, fashion has promoted openly transgressive images of femininity – initially, in the alternative fashion press and, more recently, in mainstream publications too. Models are chosen for their character and personality rather than their conformity to rules of conventional beauty. Awkward, uncomfortable poses take the place of more graceful attitudes. **Liv Liberg's** younger sister Britt often models for her. In the photographs featured in this exhibition, Britt's slicked-back hair and minimal makeup accentuate her striking, androgynous looks. Garments sit uneasily on – and off – her body; her expressions range from deadpan to confrontational, her poses are deliberately artless and sometimes uncomfortable. Suggestions of 1950s glamour sit alongside references to punk, and to the lo-fi aesthetic of 1990s fashion photography. Like much recent fashion photography, Liberg's images have a strange timelessness and an undertone of anxiety.

Today, fashion photography draws on a mosaic of influences and time periods; it speaks to multiple subjects and invites many different gazes. Jamaican-born **Amber Pinkerton's** images reflect on the way that nuances of colour and class shape the experience of Black subjects. **Bettina Rheims'** portraits use the language of classical portraiture to depict individuals who choose not to live within conventional definitions of gender. **Nadine Ijewere's** images seem to belong to a world where age, gender, and even culture itself no longer have distinct borders. This levelling out is, in part, an effect of a rapidly changing global landscape – one that is more diverse and less culturally isolated, more aware of difference if not always more accepting. Ijewere's photographs, along with those of many of her contemporaries, bring indigenous heritages into dialogue with the signs and sensibilities of a more global culture. Fashion photography has long been in the business of selling dreams. Now, its subtext is more complex: not just the construction (and deconstruction) of gender identity, but the contradictions of living in a connected society. The photographers who push the boundaries of fashion photography today also aim to unsettle and to provoke, to celebrate difference while revealing our shared humanity. To ground the accelerated time scale of contemporary reality in the slower materiality of the body. To share their views and hopes for a world where gender is embraced as a fluid category and feminine subjectivity is lived in manifold forms.

Diana Weis

Becoming an Image:
(Fashion) Photography in the Post-Internet Generation

A surge of digital visualisations, focussed in particular on forms of expression for body and identity, was brought forth by the rapid spread of smartphone photography and the rise of social networks at the beginning of the 21st century. Posing for photos as an act of creative self-presentation became a formative cultural technique of the "Generation Selfie". Besides accessories, hairstyles, make-up, and further body modification practices such as tattoos, piercings, and cosmetic procedures, fashion, of course, has always been an indispensable essential for presenting one's own body in ever new variations. The frequent accusation of a narcissistic, self-absorbed generation in love with its own image[1] overlooks the political impulses of showing oneself, which have clearly reflected on the fashion industry in recent years.

At least since the beginning of the 20th century, the construction of identity through acts of expressive self-stylisation, including those outside the norms of social consensus on beauty and "good" taste, have been an integral part of youth and subcultures. Provocative style performances, such as those by the *garçonnes* of the 1920s or the *punks* of the 1970s, typically first caused a stir in the streets, were shortly after treated by the press as examples of moral decay among youths – and were finally received in a tempered form into the fashion mainstream.

The new wave of digital fashion images differs not only in the acceleration of processes characteristic of the net culture, but above all in a tremendously expanded scope of influence. Photos can now be shared and commented on with a broad public – worldwide, within seconds, and with little effort. Since fashion thrives on imitation, visual impulses and representation techniques have also circulated widely. Within just a few years, a complex and highly allusive image culture has emerged, with classic motifs of 20th century fashion photography being repeatedly referenced, modified, ironically twisted, or recontextualised.

Understanding the body as a medium

It is not surprising that the potentials of the net culture appeal to young women in particular. The concept of one's own body as a medium to be staged has already been part of their everyday lives even prior to the digitalisation wave. In addition, fashion and imagery, both traditionally attributed as feminine means of expression, are two spheres that came to coincide in the social media. The visual space of the internet is an evident expansion of what the cultural scientist and feminist Angela McRobbie termed *bedroom culture*[2]: a space safe at least from physical assault where identity models and their effects can be explored. Trying out makeup and different styles or outfits and copying poses of famous models are core components of such *bedroom* rituals. What distinguishes the new digital fashion images from previous forms of self-exploration with the camera is the awareness of the protagonists to be personally involved in a visual culture that is often perceived as ambivalent. The "own body and its decoration", writes media scientist Annekathrin Kohout, are "made into a political instrument" by these young women.[3]

The curator Marisa Olson introduced the term "postinternet" in 2011 to describe the aesthetic practices of a new generation of artists. Her focus was not on the appropriation of digital media formats or the availability of works on the net, but rather on the inherent ambivalence between simultaneous celebration and critique in dealing with the visual topoi of the net age.[4] It is often impossible to infer from the images themselves whether the medially transmitted gender norms, for example from commercial fashion photography, pop culture, or pornography, are merely being copied or deliberately criticized and deconstructed.

The appealing contrast between intimacy and deliberate display that characterises image production in the digital age is distinctly perceptible in the works of the Dutch artist **Liv Liberg.** She was ten years old when she started photographing her four years younger sister Britt in their mother's clothes – initially to imitate commercial fashion images from glossy magazines.[5] The portraits that she created over the years are powerful, some oppressive, others bizarrely strange, and they offer multilayered comments on being a girl and becoming a woman and the significance of fashion in this process.

Later on as a fashion photographer for editorials and advertisements, Liberg continues her playful engagement with forms of staging the self and the other, and the close, collaborative relationship between photographer and model remains formative for her works. In the "Lotta" series, Britt Liberg wears luxury brand clothes by Chanel with the same nonchalance with which she used to raid her mother's closet. The series title alludes to Lotta Volkova, the stylist and influential style icon among millennials, who worked together with Liberg on the project. Volkova became famous for her irreverent manner of mixing the codes of high fashion with trash elements and subcultural references. In an interview, she once remarked about her youth in post-Soviet Russia: "We had nothing, but we had the Internet."[6]

Meeting the gaze, claiming visibility

It is an intriguing concept to see the internet as a dynamic space of references and imagination, where not only boundaries between genres but also class boundaries between high and street culture dissolve. However, the external features of the represented bodies are far from having become irrelevant. White, young, and very slim, Lotta Volkova and Britt Liberg for instance belong to the type of women who are still predominantly depicted in commercial fashion images. This made it possible for them to use the medium of the image explicitly as a foil to play with the viewers' expectations.

The photographer **Nadine Ijewere,** who grew up in London as the child of Nigerian-Jamaican immigrants, had a completely different baseline. In an interview, she recounts that she used to miss seeing the skin colours or hair types of the women around her pictured in fashion magazines.[7] In recreating the poses of white models, she and her friends were struggling for visibility in a (visual) environment that had no place for them. She had yet to acquire the pictorial traditions that white artists like Liv Liberg were already bored with.

The art historian Kaja Silverman used the term *gaze regime* to refer to the regulating, normative, and controlling power of collective viewing habits. The gaze demands specific modes of representation in order to be able to see. Conversely, this means: Whoever wants to be seen must adhere to certain parameters of representation.[8] Young artists like Ijewere take their expressive power from the fact that they do not stop at questioning established structures – they simply sweep them aside. Instead of subjecting her models to the gaze regime of the mainstream fashion industry, Ijewere takes the liberty of setting her own gaze, her own experience, as the standard. The photo *Seashell* shows the smiling face of a young woman – with freckles, bright blue eye shadow, and a gap between her front teeth – precisely in the way Ijewere sees her: unique, strong, and beautiful.

Even though comparable emancipatory approaches already existed in the civil rights movement of the 1960s, it was not until the 21st century that net culture offered a stage for their dissemination that was independent of the gatekeeping of commercial fashion magazines. Social networks provided an easily accessible opportunity for young people, in particular, to demand visibility and to effectively change the gaze regime of the fashion industry to this day. The Jamaican born and raised photographer **Amber Pinkerton** points out the importance of social media platforms such as Facebook and Tumblr for her development as a photographer. Like many of her friends, she started as a teenager to document her eccentric outfits with her smartphone and to share the pictures online: "That was our own little culture"[9]. The marginalisation of black bodies in the media only became an issue for her after she had moved to London for her studies. Today, Pinkerton works mostly with black models, some of whom she finds in the streets of Kingston. In her fashion shoots, she continues the practice developed as a teenager for social media: to postulate her own image culture utterly unfazed by the exclusion mechanisms of the prevailing fashion photography.

Fashion bodies: hybrid identities

Fashion photography by its very nature is a hybrid medium that can be attributed neither entirely to the sphere of art nor to that of commerce. Far from downgrading the genre, this assessment rather substantiates the medium's outstanding relevance for social formation processes. At least since modernity, the role of fashion has also included pointing out alternatives to hegemonic ideas of femininity, masculinity, or social class. The medium of fashion photography made these offers of new identity concepts accessible to a broader public and through aestheticisation helped them gradually gain acceptance.

The boundaries between professional and private photography become increasingly blurred in digital image production of the internet age. However, the assumption of the new fashion images being more "democratic" because they turned "everyday people into models and their own stylists" soon proved to be a misunderstanding.[10] In terms of production depth, private social media presences are often on par with their professional counterparts. The art historian Wolfgang Ullrich observed that the "dichotomy between person and role" no longer exists in the age of selfies; instead, posing for pictures rather resembles the practice of actors who turn their own bodies into an "artistic device".[11] The reception dynamics of the internet shape the self-representations of the post-internet generation. Their indiscriminate scrolling through images of widely varying quality and origin has its reflection in their eclectic use of vestmental codes. The ideal of an integral and incorruptible identity, the core of which is displayed to the outside world by the means of fashion, has given way to a fragmented, brittle fashion/body hybrid that is perpetually open to interpretation according to the situation. The opportunities of access and participation the internet offers in its capacity as a prodigious cultural image memory cause reality and virtuality, just like authenticity and staging, to increasingly melt into each other, to the point that they are no longer to be regarded as opposite poles, but rather as parallel narrative strands intersecting in the infinity of image space.

1   See Bernd Heinzlmaier, *Performer, Styler, Egoisten: Über eine Jugend, der die Alten die Ideale abgewöhnt haben (Performers, Stylers, Egoists: About a Youth the Old have Weaned from Ideals)*, Berlin 2013, p. 177ff.

2   Angela McRobbie and Jenny Garber, "Girls and Subcultures", in: Stuart Hall and Tony Jefferson (ed.), *Resistance Through Rituals. Youth Subcultures in Post-War Britain,* London 1975, p. 210.

3   Annekathrin Kohout, *Netz-Feminismus. Digitale Bildkulturen (Internet Feminism. Digital Image Cultures)*, Berlin 2018, p. 50.

4   See Marisa Olson, "Postinternet: Art After the Internet", in: *Foam Magazine,* No. 29, Winter 2011, p. 59–63.

5   See Interview with Liv Liberg, in: *Novembre Magazin,* No. 15, December 2019, online: <novembre.global/magazine/britt-liberg-shot-by-liv-liberg> [8 December 2021].

6   See Interview with Lotta Volkova in *032c,* No. 30, June 2019, online: <https://032c.com/vetements-stylist-lotta-volkova-need-system> [8 December 2021].

7   See Interview with Nadine Ijewere, in: *Vogue Germany,* 2 June 2021, online: <https://www.vogue.de/kultur/artikel/nadine-ijewere-fotograf-in-interview-co-berlin-ausstellung> [8 December 2021].

8   Kaja Silverman, "Blickregime begegnen (Meeting the Gaze Regime)", in: Christian Kravagna (ed.): *Privileg Blick. Kritik der visuellen Kultur (Privilege of the Gaze. A Critique of Visual Culture)*, Berlin 1997, p. 41–64.

9   See Interview with Amber Pinkerton, online: <https://www.laramonro.com/words-with/amberpinkerton> [8 December 2021].

10 Monica Titton, "Mode in der Stadt. Über Street-Style-Blogs und die Grenzen der Demokratisierung der Mode (Fashion in the City: Street Style Blogs and the Limits of Fashion's Democratisation)" *Texte zur Kunst (Texts on Art),* Vol. 20., Issue 78, 2010, p. 93.

11 Wolfgang Ullrich, *Selfies,* Berlin 2019, p. 17.

Plates

Lee Miller

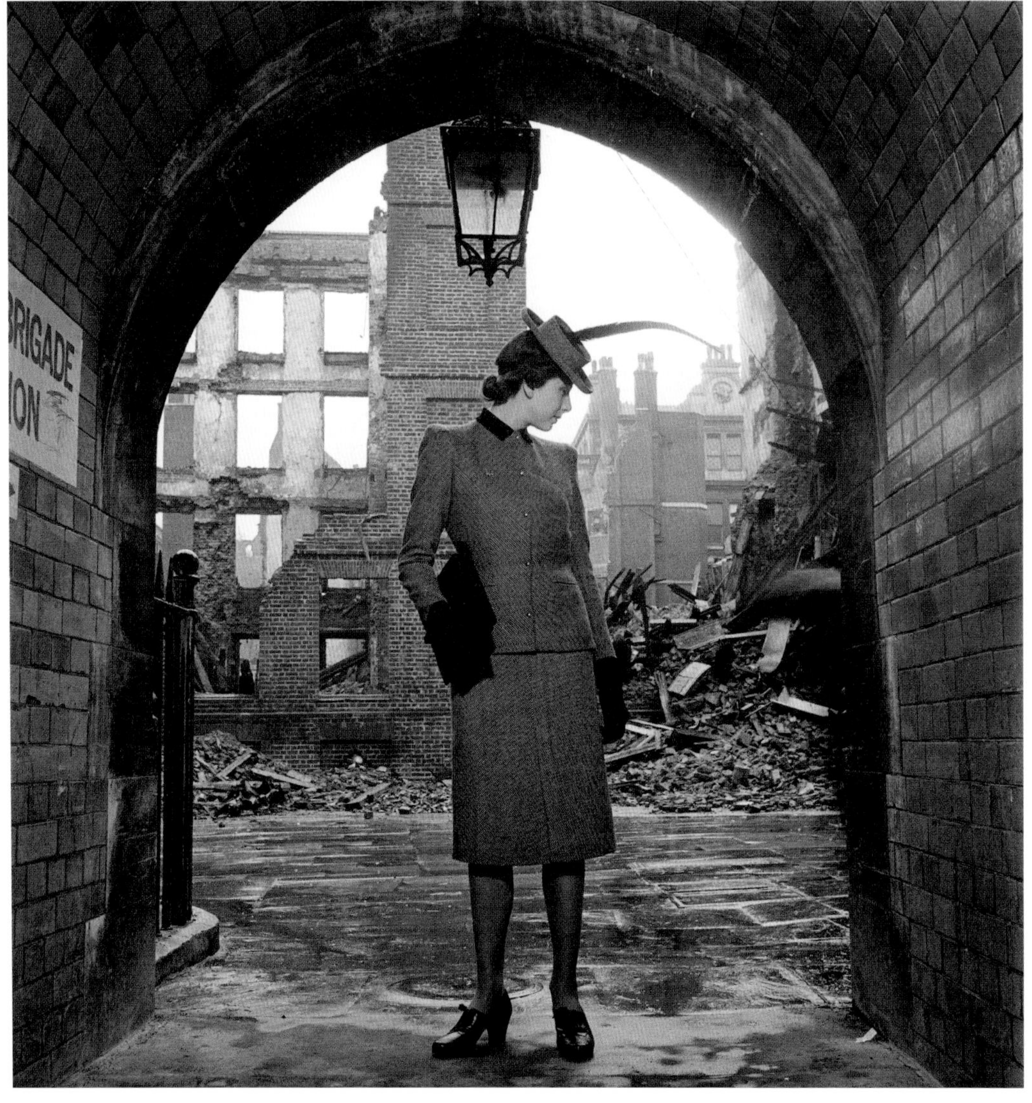

Lee Miller
Model [Elizabeth Cowell] Wearing Digby Morton Suit, 1941
Modern C-type digital print sourced from a scan of the vintage print or negative, 35.3 × 27.8 cm
Lee Miller Archives

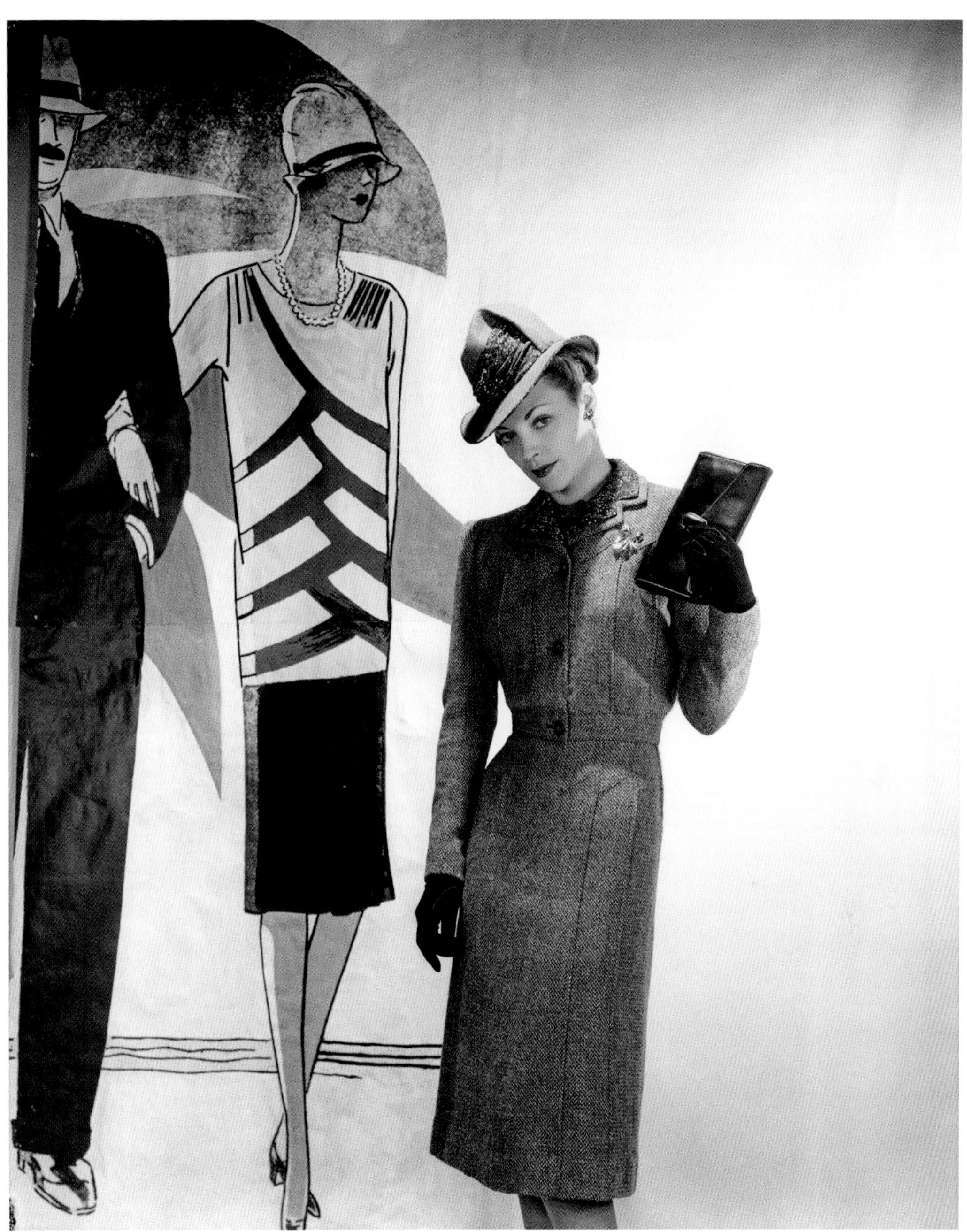

Lee Miller
The Lead, 1941
Modern C-type digital print sourced from a scan of the vintage print or negative, 35.3 × 27.8 cm
Lee Miller Archives

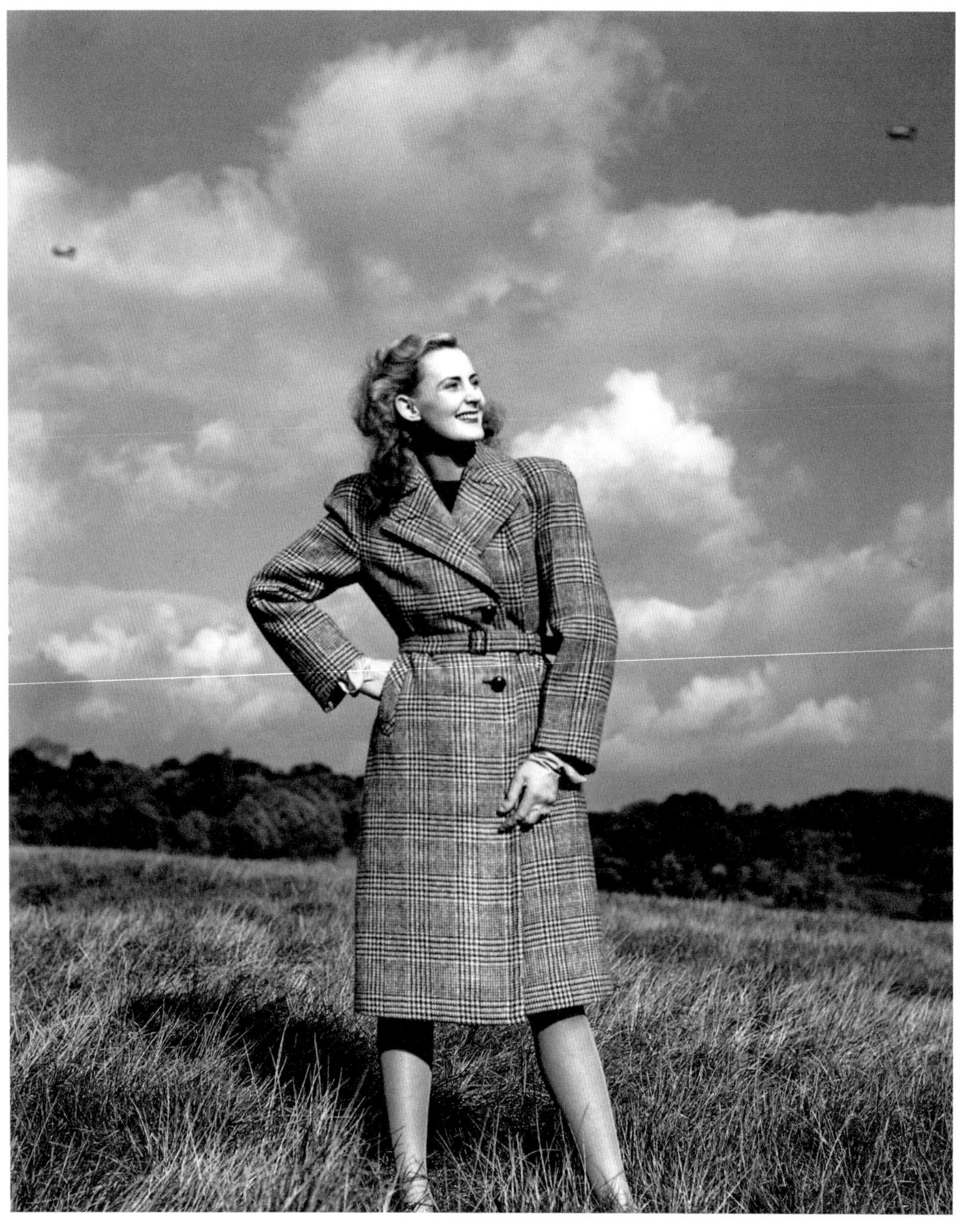

Lee Miller
Marlbeck Vogue Fashion Assignment, 1941
Modern C-type digital print sourced from a scan of the vintage print or negative, 35.3 × 27.8 cm
Lee Miller Archives

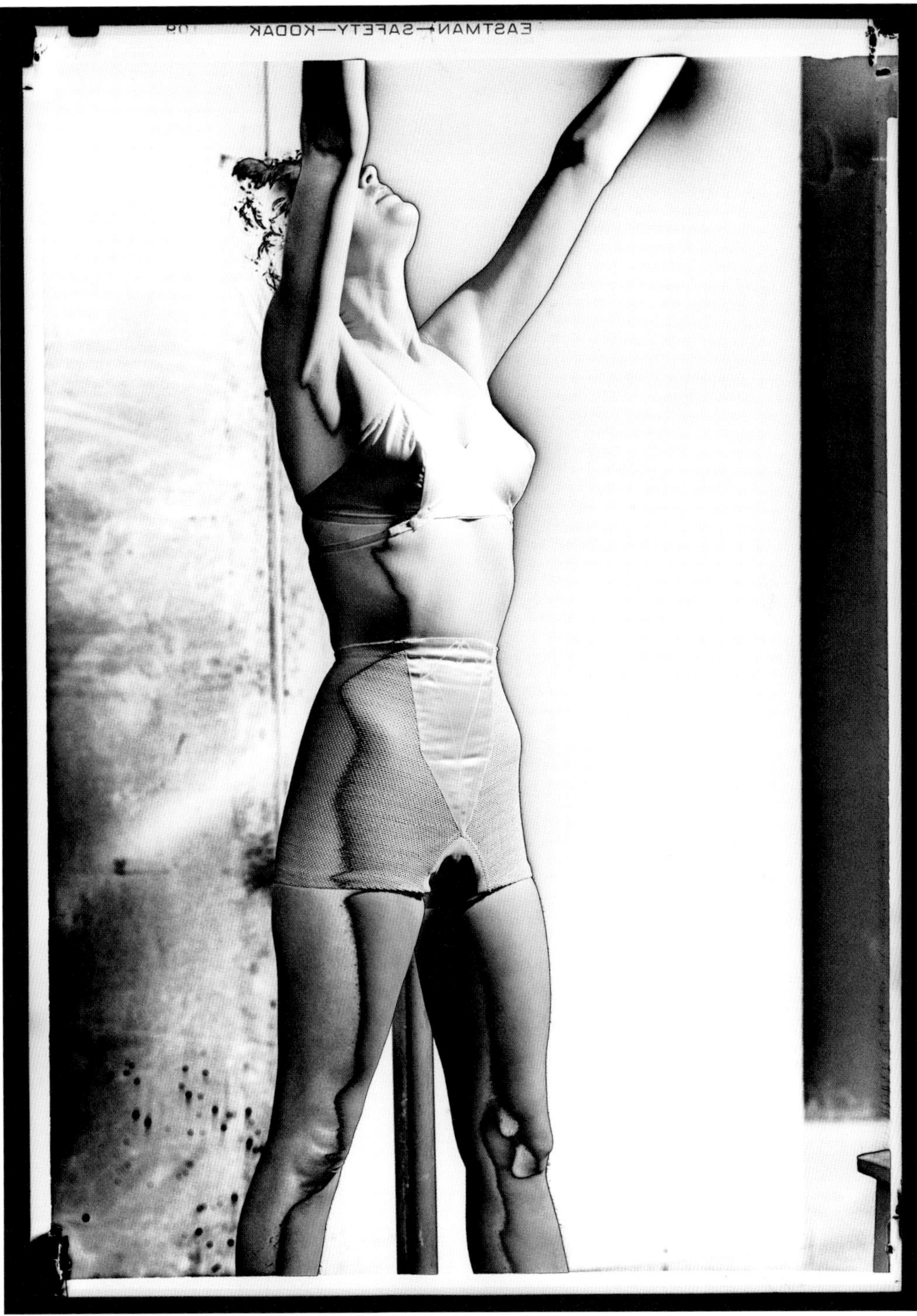

Lee Miller
Corsetry, Solarised Photographs, 1942
Modern C-type digital print sourced from a scan of the vintage print or negative, 35.3 × 27.8 cm
Lee Miller Archives

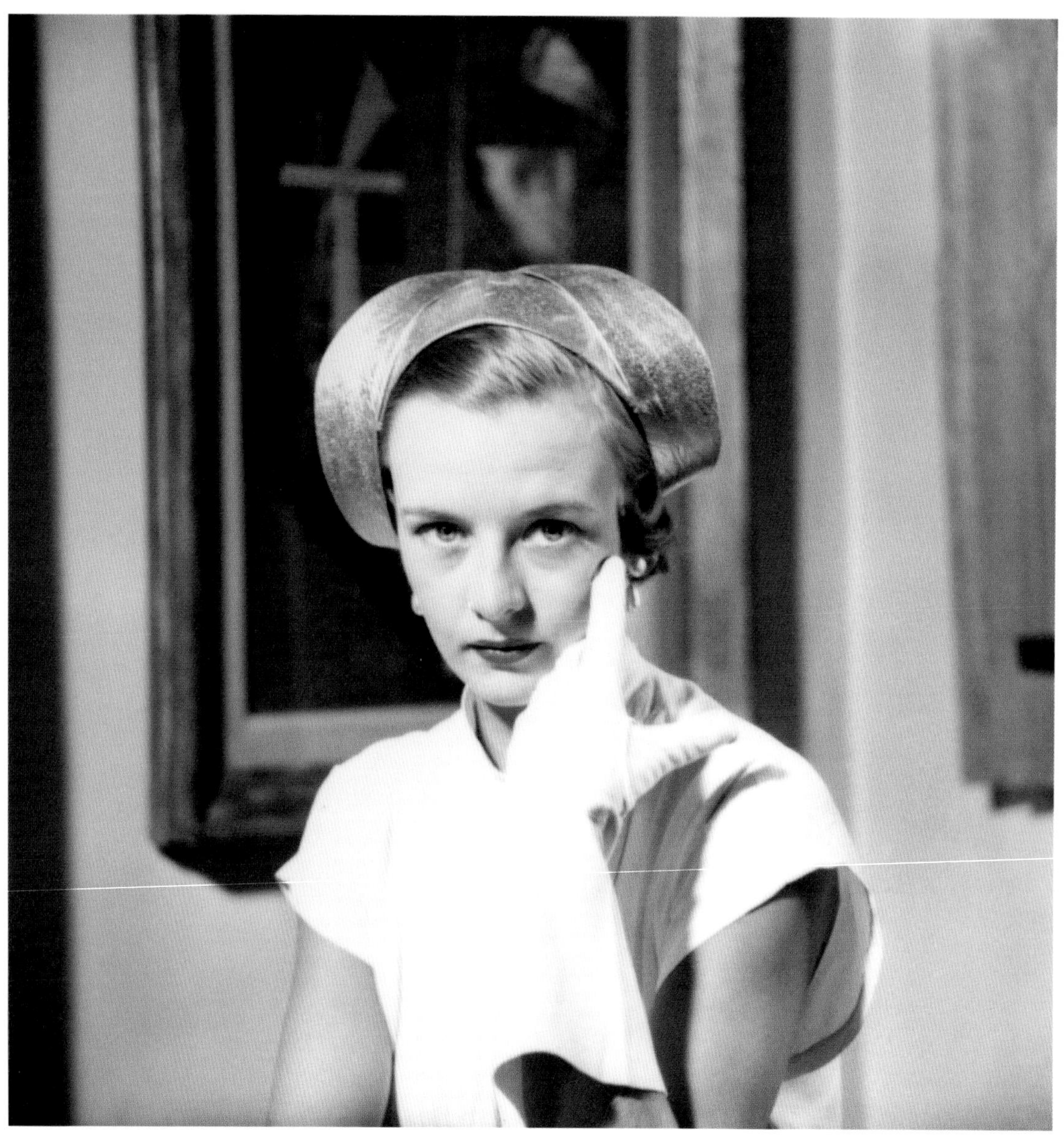

Lee Miller
Fashion Study with Hats and Gloves, 1949
Modern C-type digital print sourced from a scan of the vintage print or negative, 35.3 × 27.8 cm
Lee Miller Archives

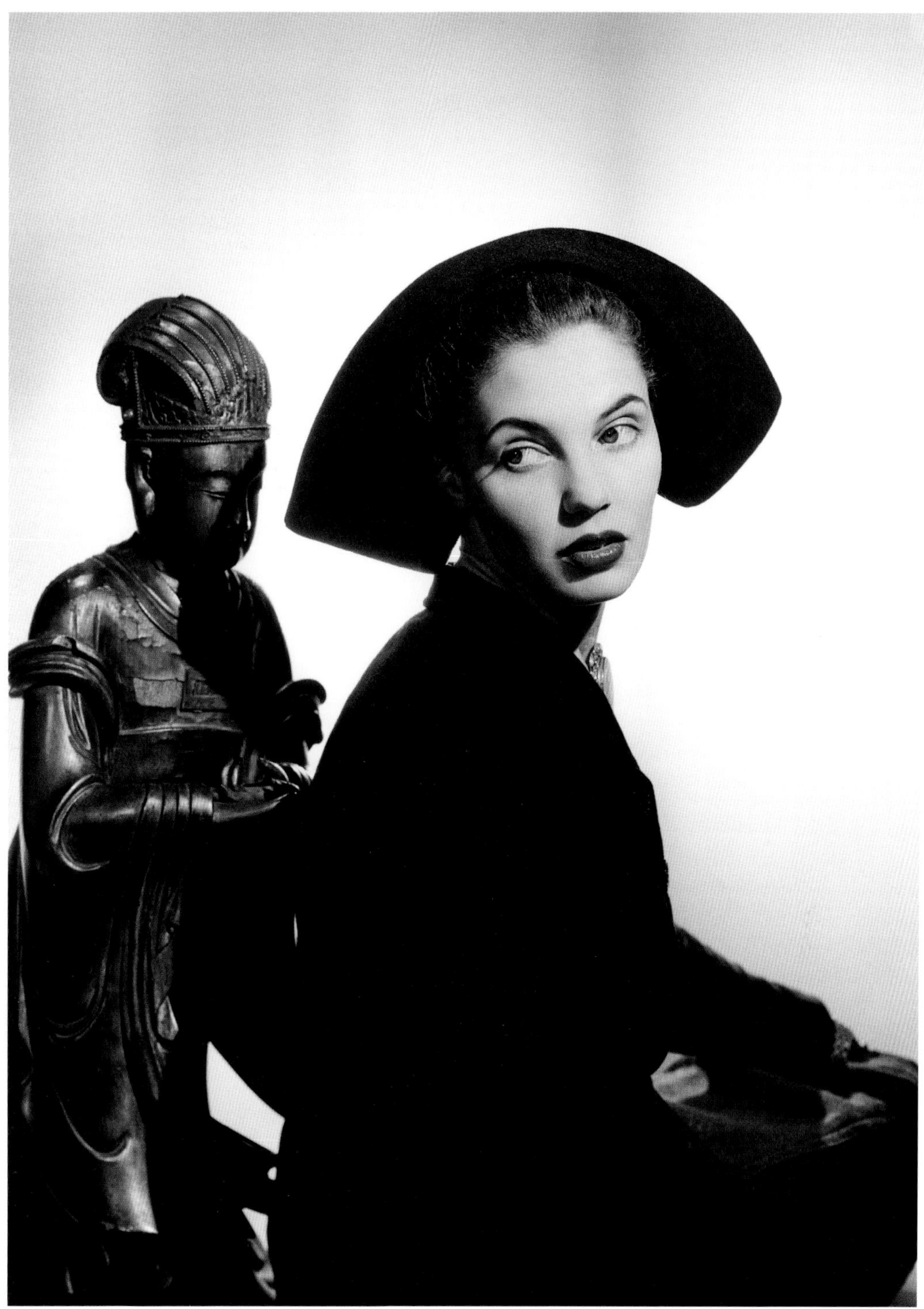

Lee Miller
Upward Bend, ERIK folds back his black felt brim to form a stylised Dutch bonnet..., 1942
Modern C-type digital print sourced from a scan of the vintage print or negative, 35.3 × 27.8 cm
Lee Miller Archives

Yva

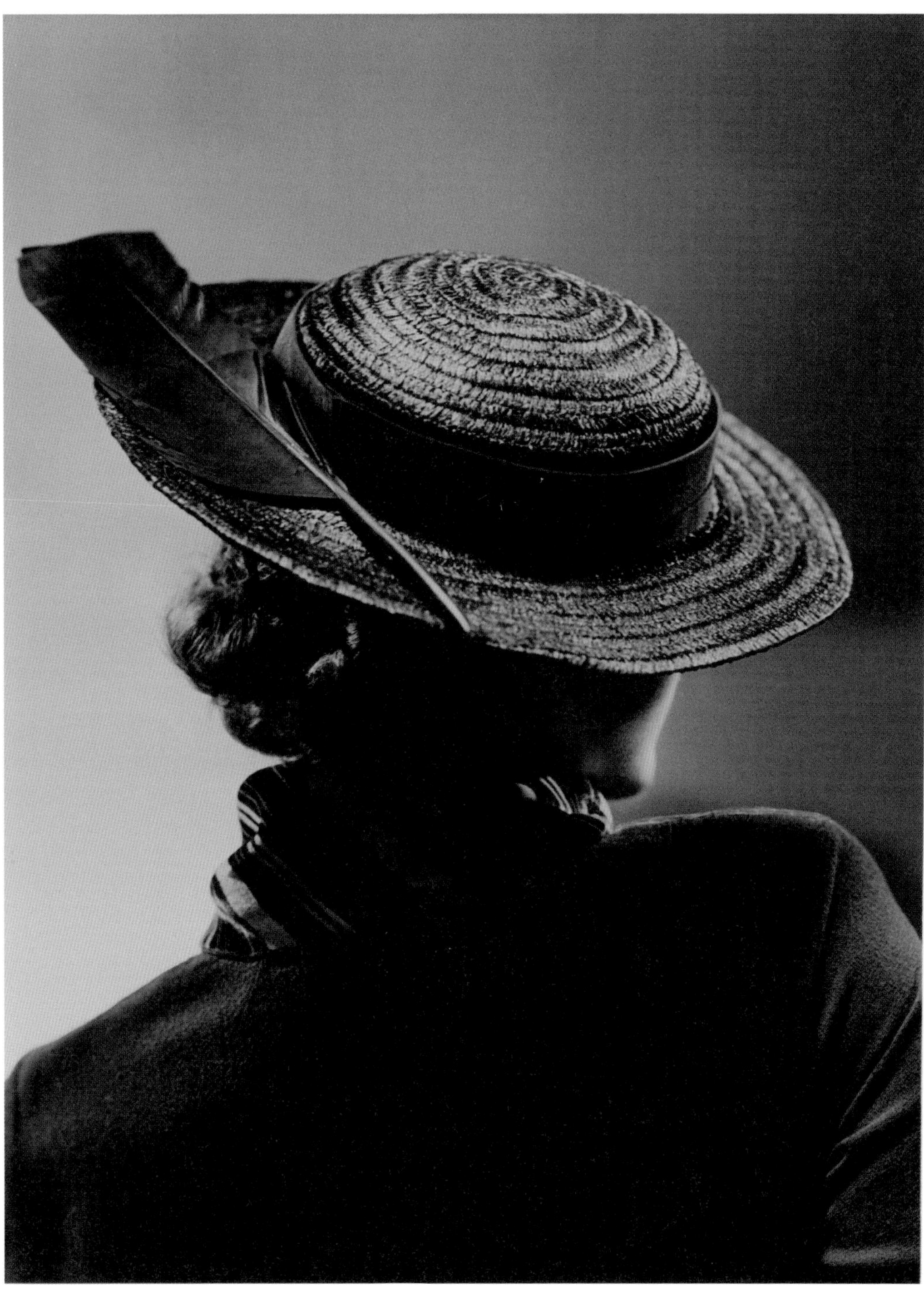

Yva
Flat Boater Hat of Coarse, Steel Blue Straw with Same-Coloured Feather, c. 1932
Gelatine silver print, 23.1 × 17.4 cm
Museum für Kunst und Gewerbe Hamburg

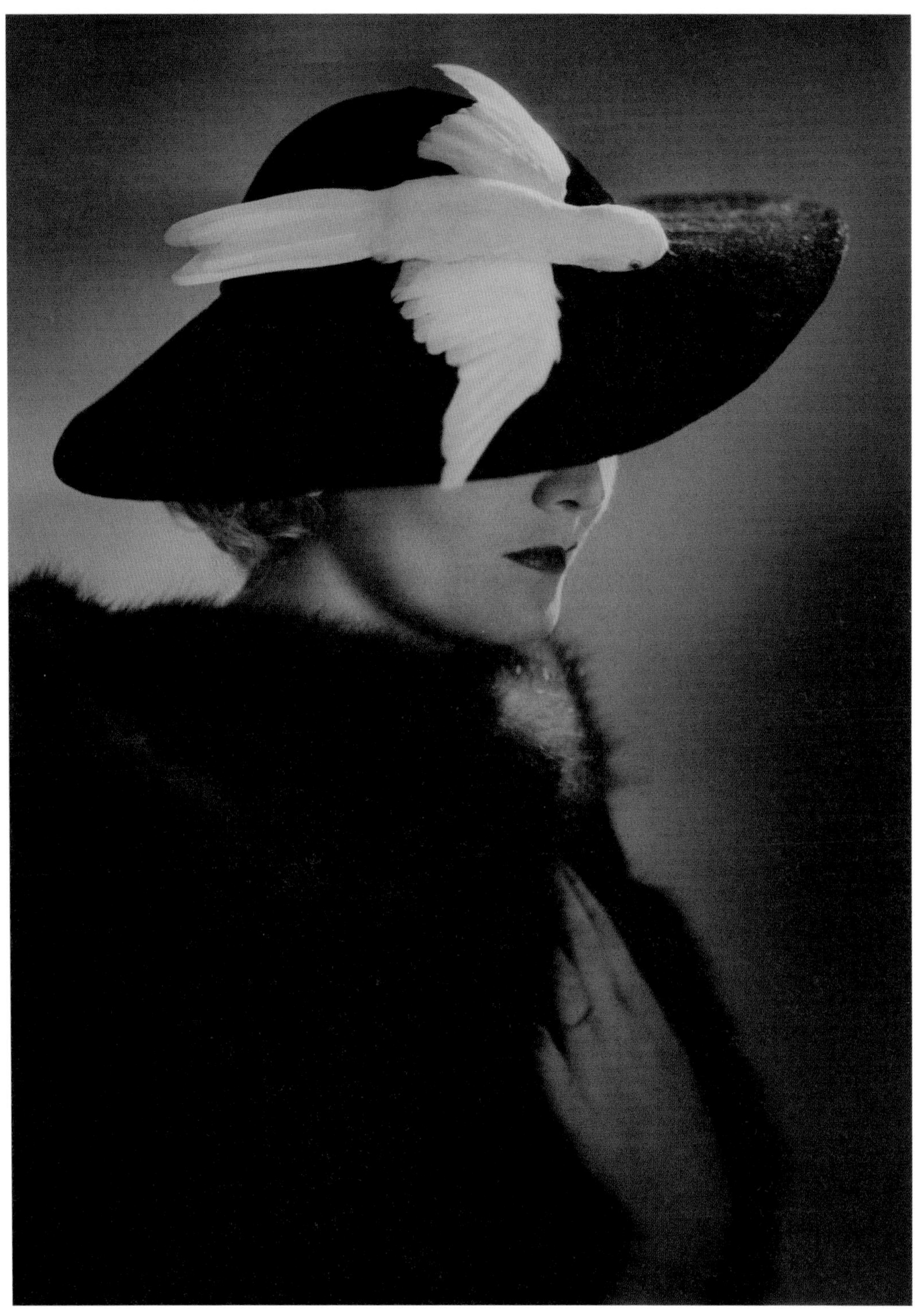

Yva
Elegant Black Velvet Hat with White Bird, 1925–38
Gelatine silver print, 23.9 × 17.5 cm
Museum für Kunst und Gewerbe Hamburg

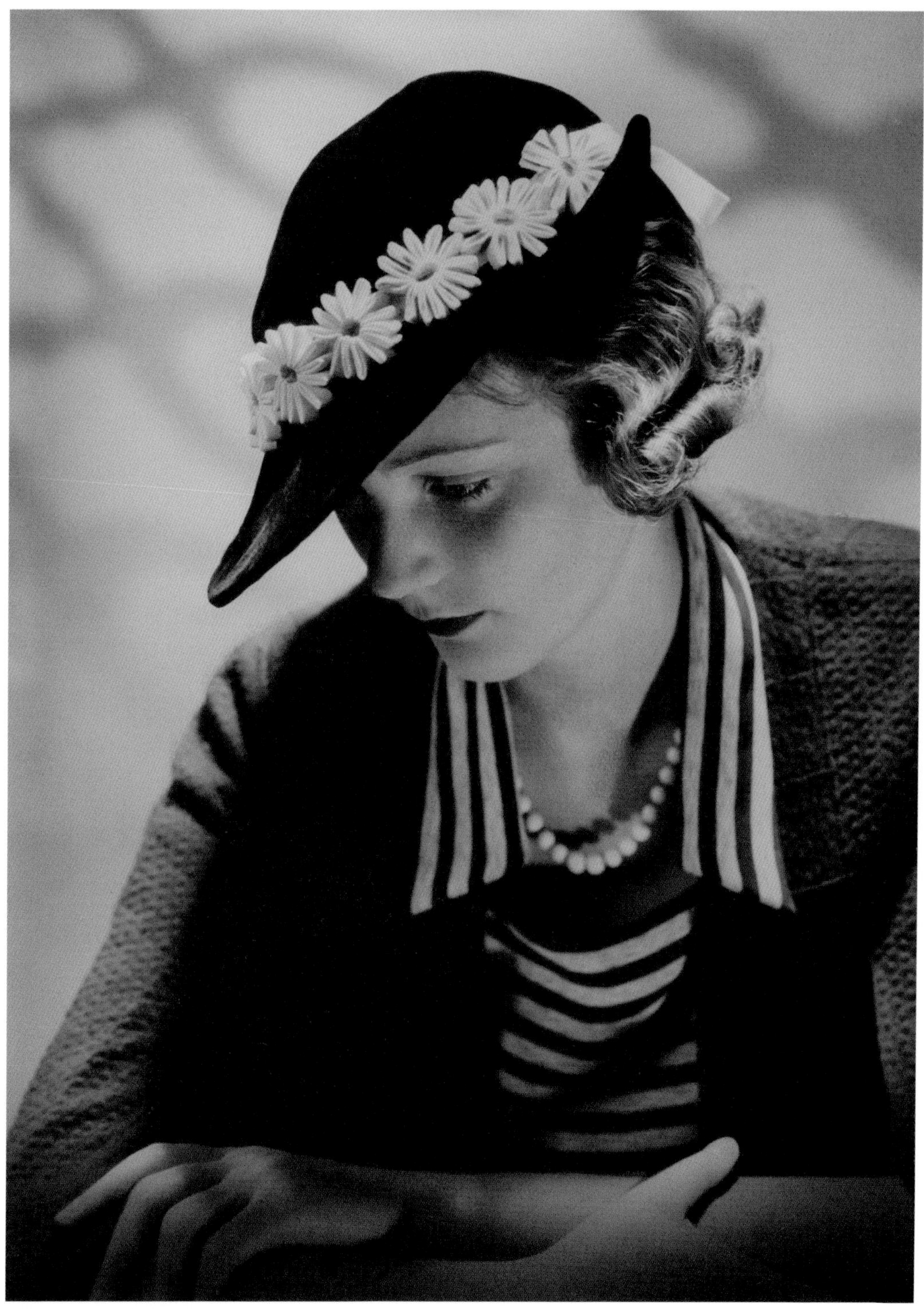

Yva
New-Fashioned Black Velvet Hat with Daisies of Grosgrain Ribbon, 1925–38
Gelatine silver print, 24.1 × 17.9 cm
Museum für Kunst und Gewerbe Hamburg

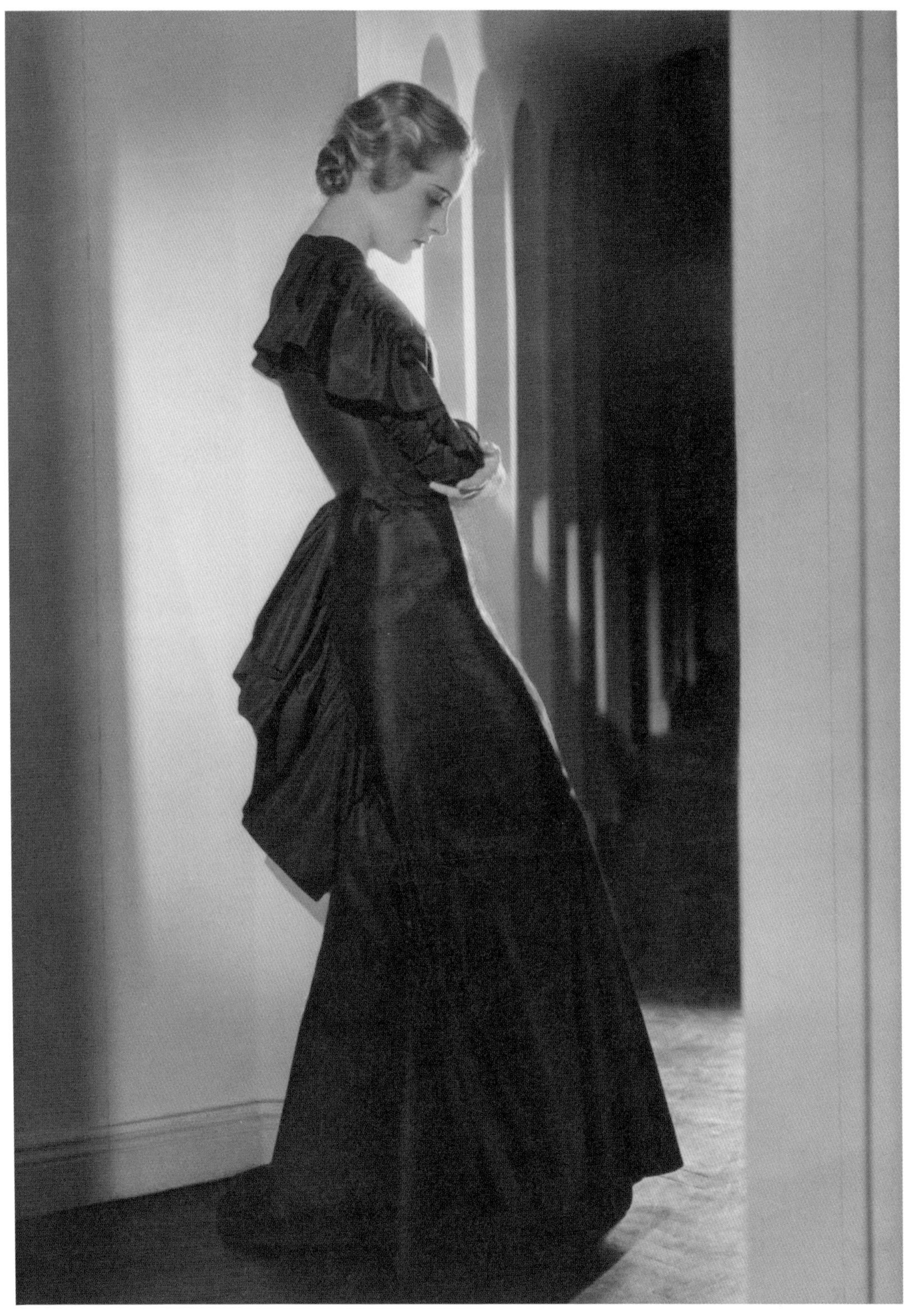

Yva
Elegantes Abendkleid (Elegant Gown), 1934
Gelatine silver print, 22.2 × 15.2 cm
Deichtorhallen Hamburg, F.C. Gundlach Collection

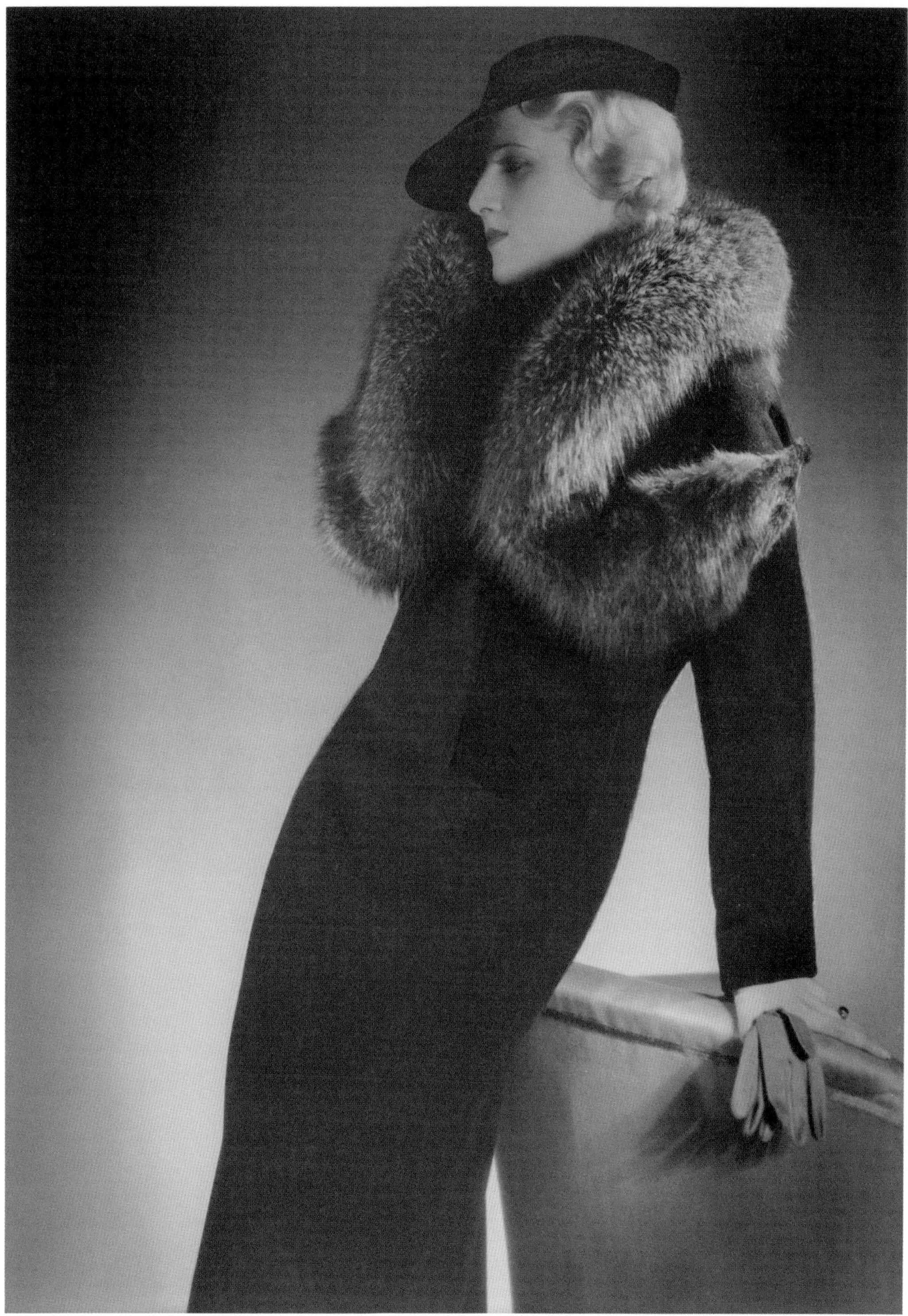

Yva
Elegant Black Wool Fox Coat, Silver Fox Collar, Hermann Hoffmann, c. 1934
Gelatine silver print, 22.2 × 15.2 cm
Deichtorhallen Hamburg, F.C. Gundlach Collection

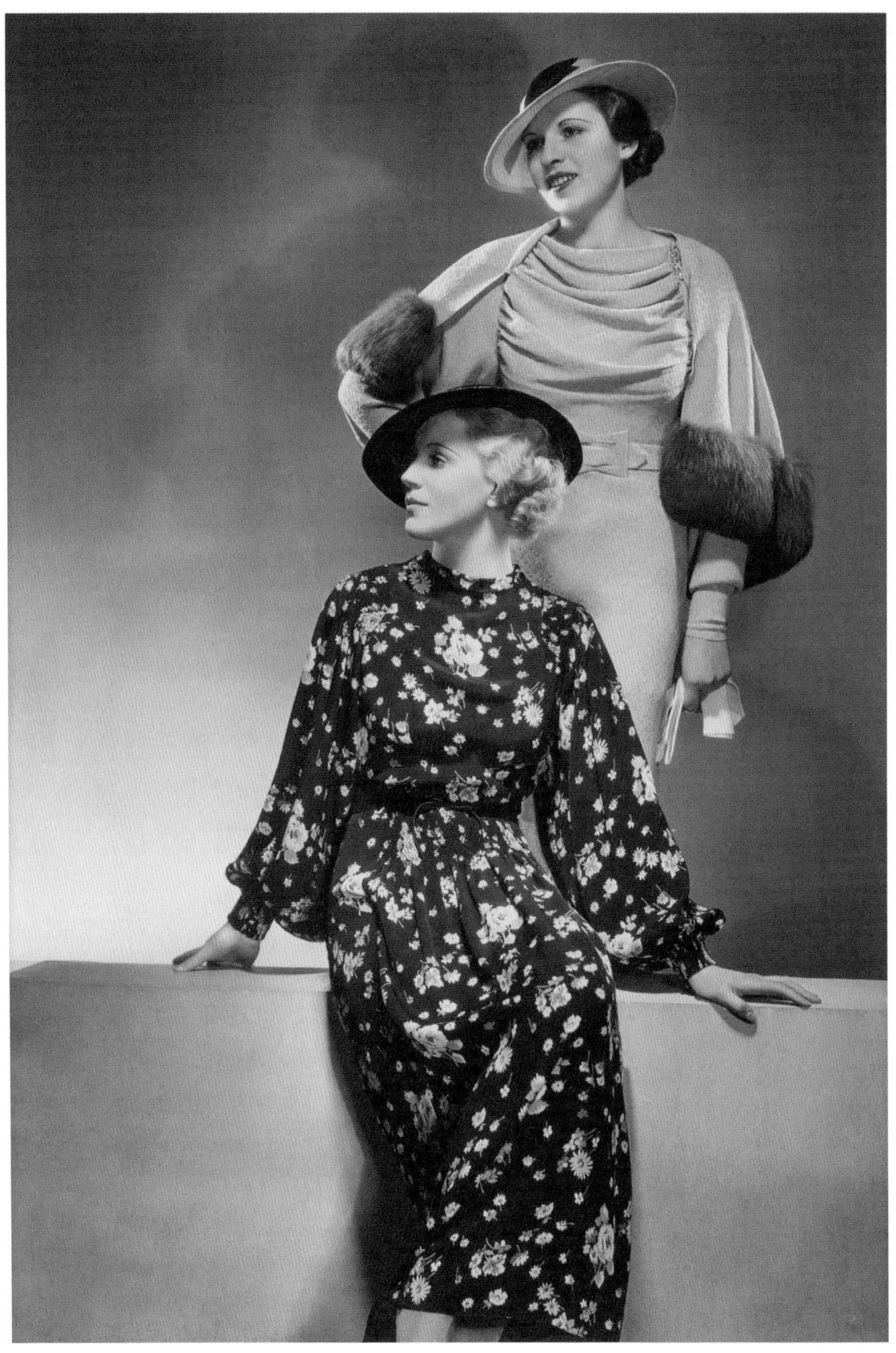

Yva
Untitled, 1930s
Gelatine silver print, 22.2 × 15.2 cm
Deichtorhallen Hamburg, F.C. Gundlach Collection

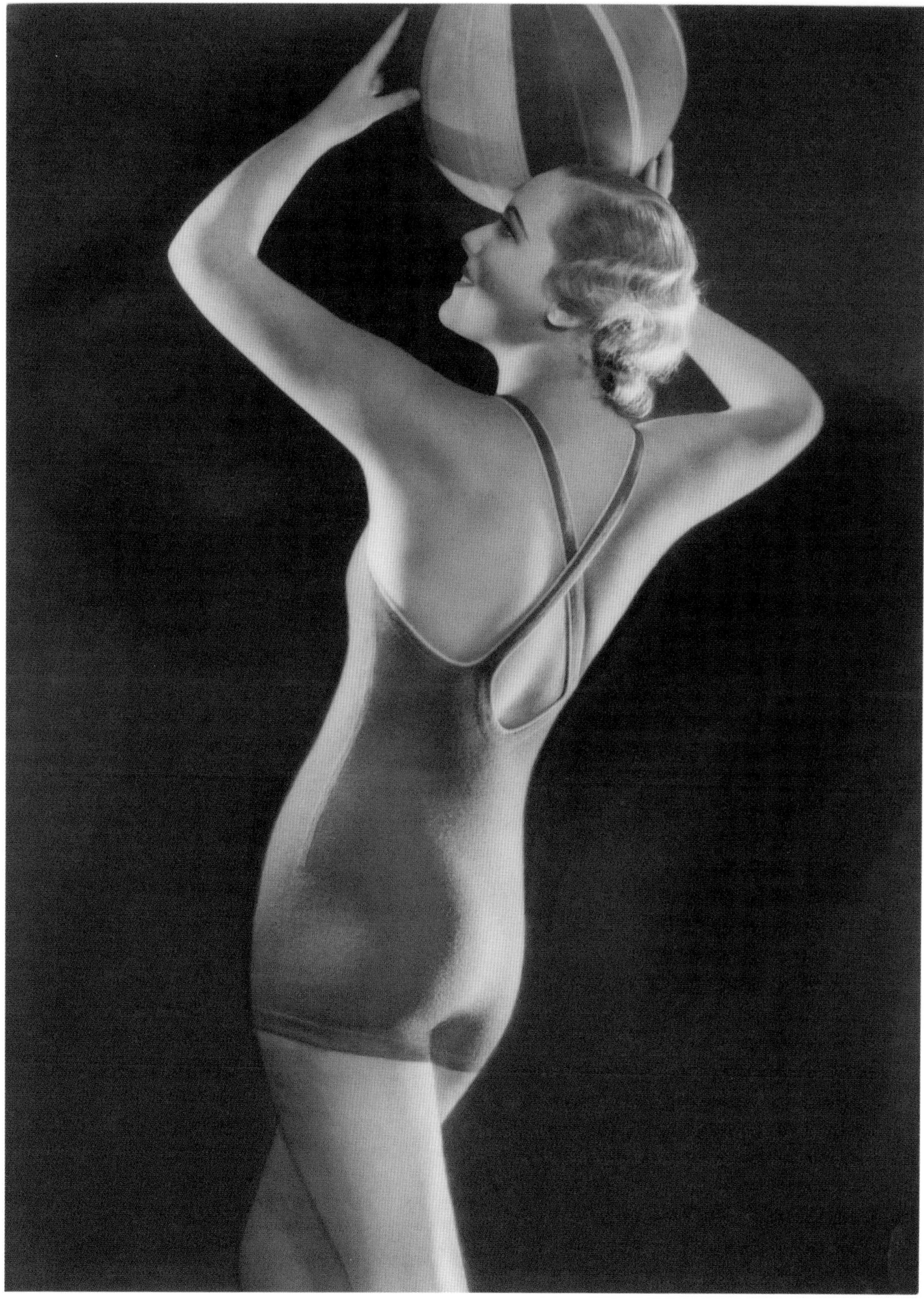

Yva
Badeanzug, Modell: Jantzen (Bathing Costume, Model: Jantzen), 1930s
Gelatine silver print, 22.6 × 16.5 cm
Deichtorhallen Hamburg, F.C. Gundlach Collection

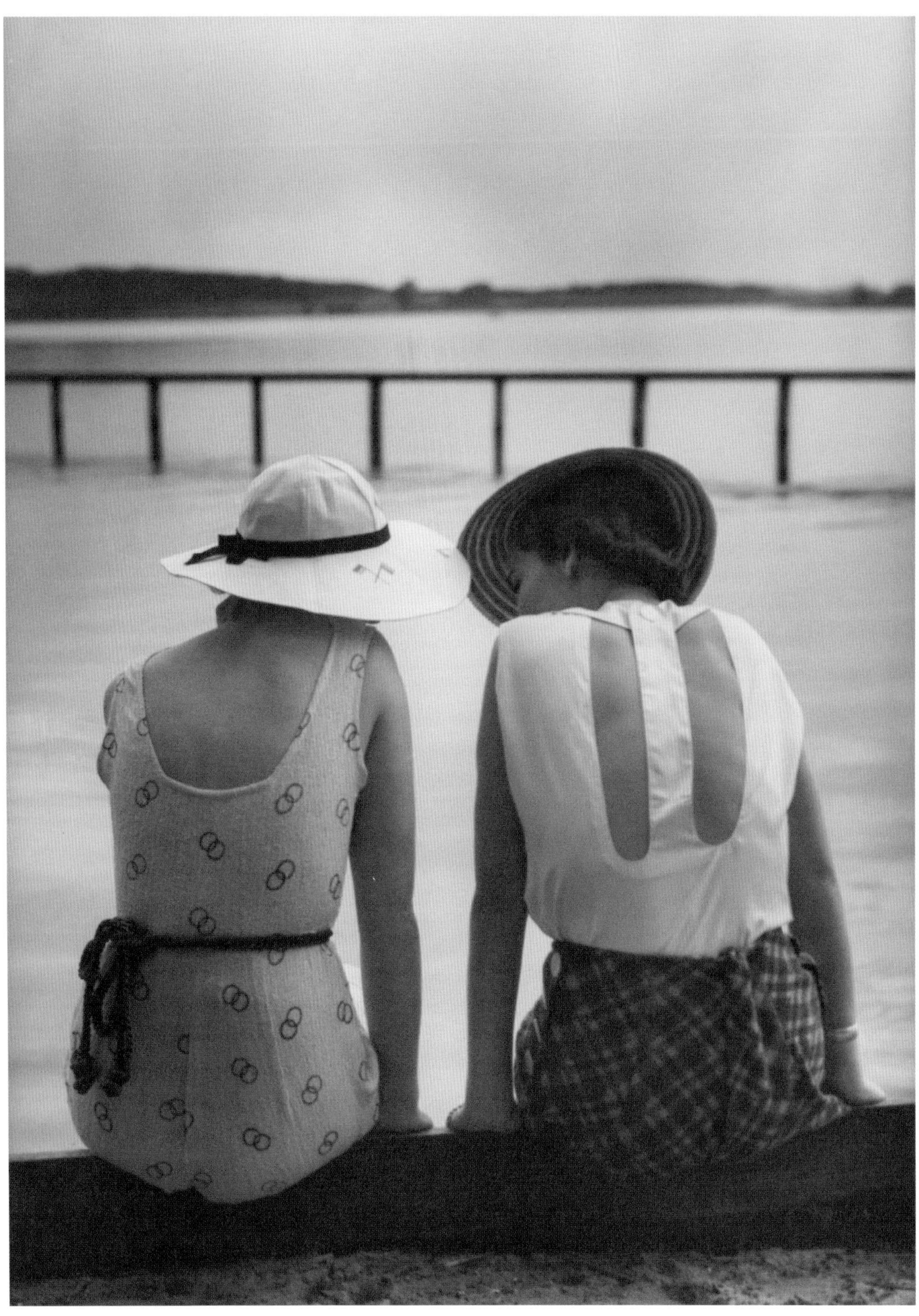

Yva
Two Women at the Shore (back view), c. 1936
Gelatine silver print, 16 × 22.5 cm
Deichtorhallen Hamburg, F.C. Gundlach Collection

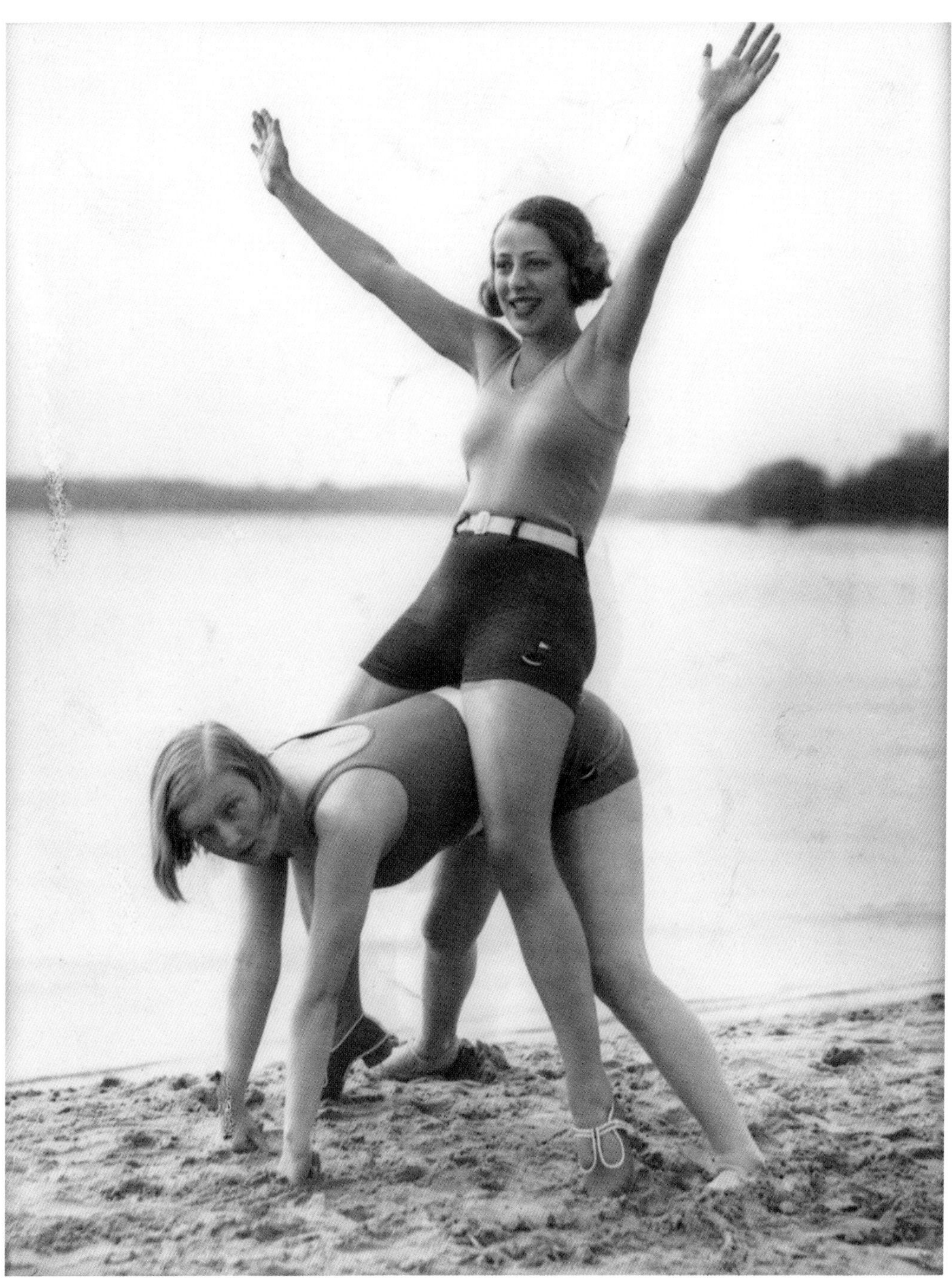

Yva
Untitled (Two women on the beach), c. 1930
Gelatine silver print, 22,8 × 17.7 cm
Deichtorhallen Hamburg, F.C. Gundlach Collection

Madame d'Ora

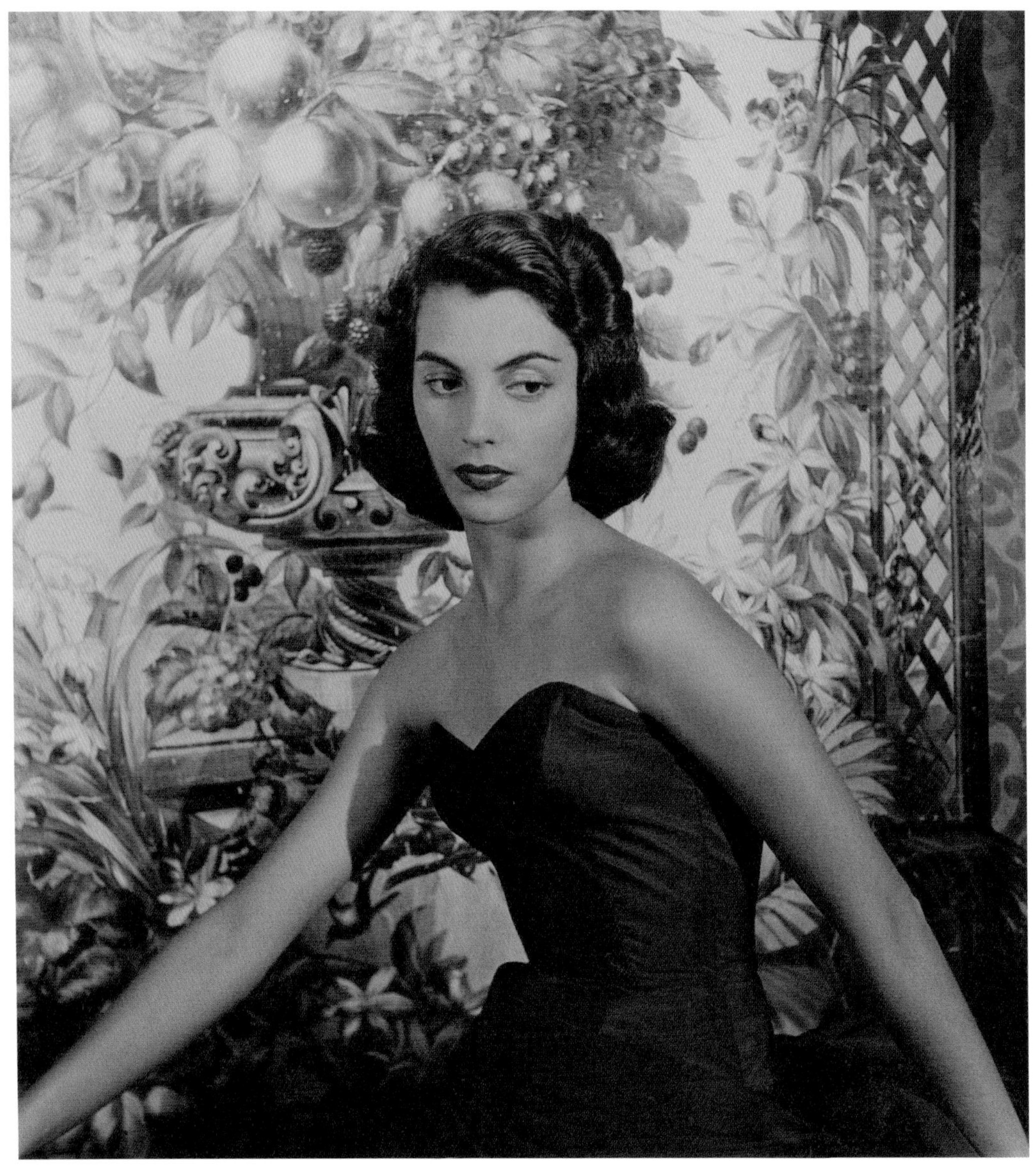

Madame d'Ora
Madame Nena de Gomez, 1950s
Gelatine silver print, 27.4 × 24.9 cm
Museum für Kunst und Gewerbe Hamburg

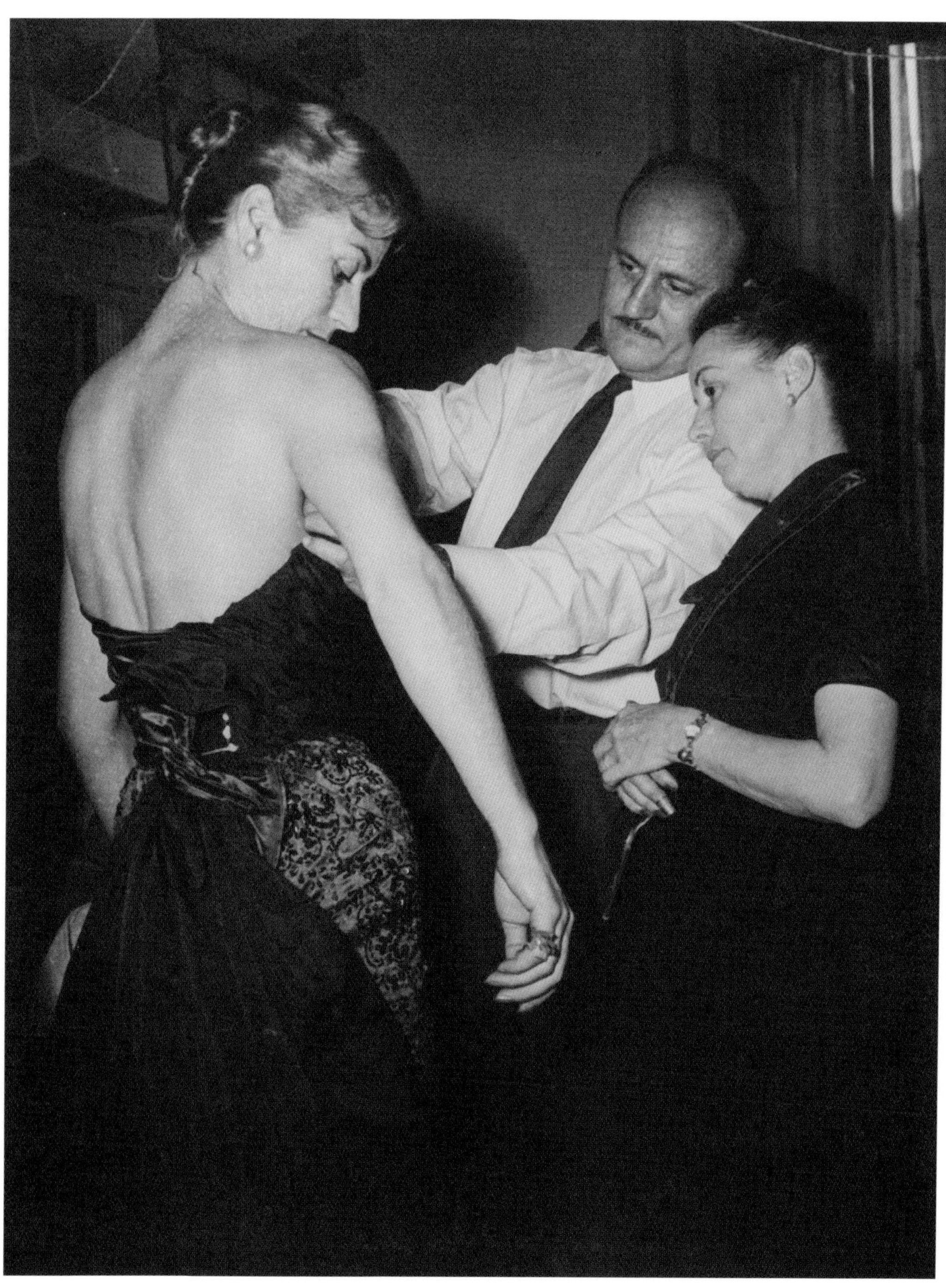

Madame d'Ora
Der Modeschöpfer Pierre Balmain bei der Anprobe (Fashion Designer Pierre Balmain at the Fitting), 1950s
Gelatine silver print, 12.4 × 9.5 cm
Museum für Kunst und Gewerbe Hamburg

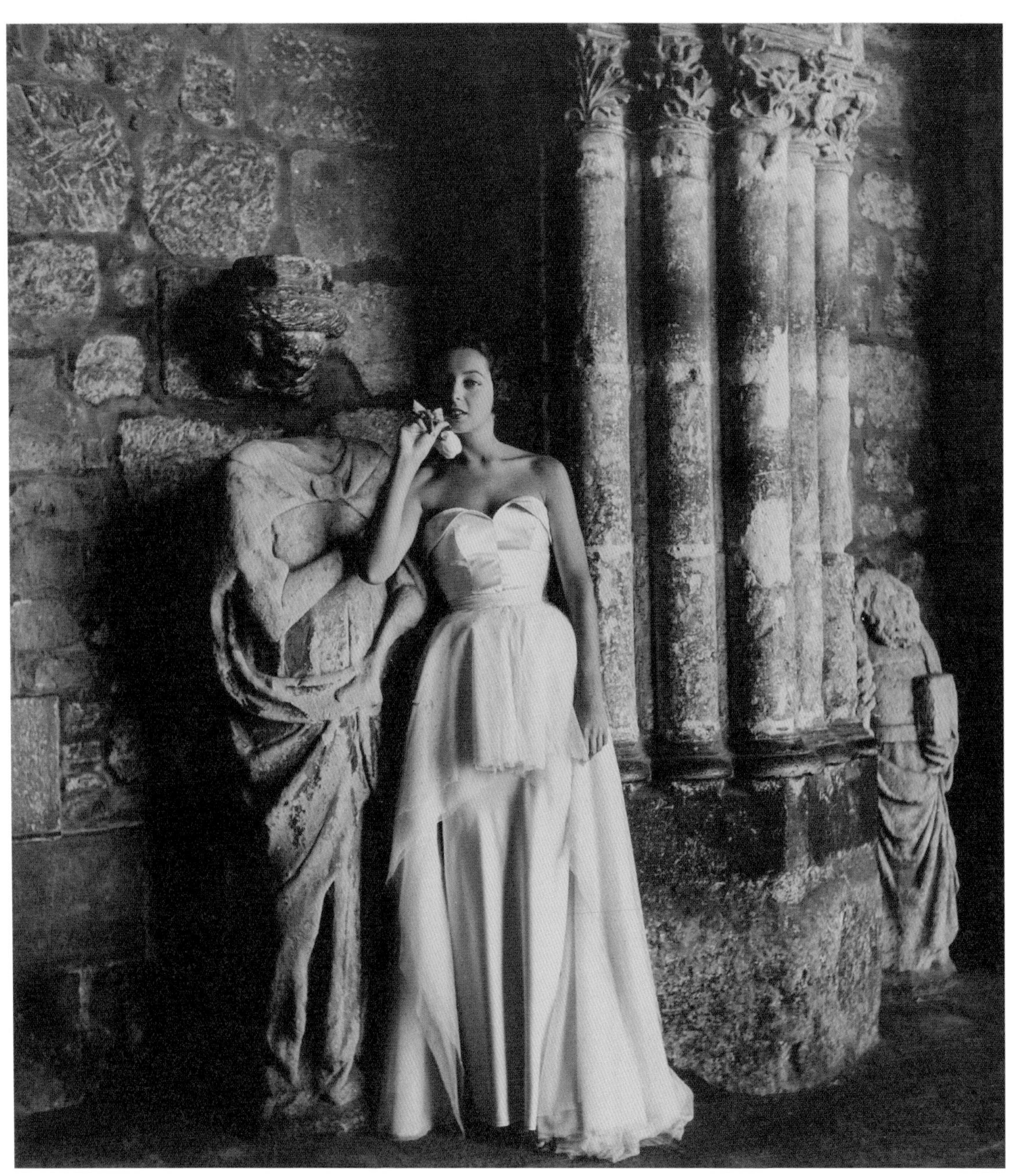

Madame d'Ora
Marie-Sol Leglise, Model Balenciaga, before 1957
Gelatine silver print, 24 × 21.5 cm
Museum für Kunst und Gewerbe Hamburg

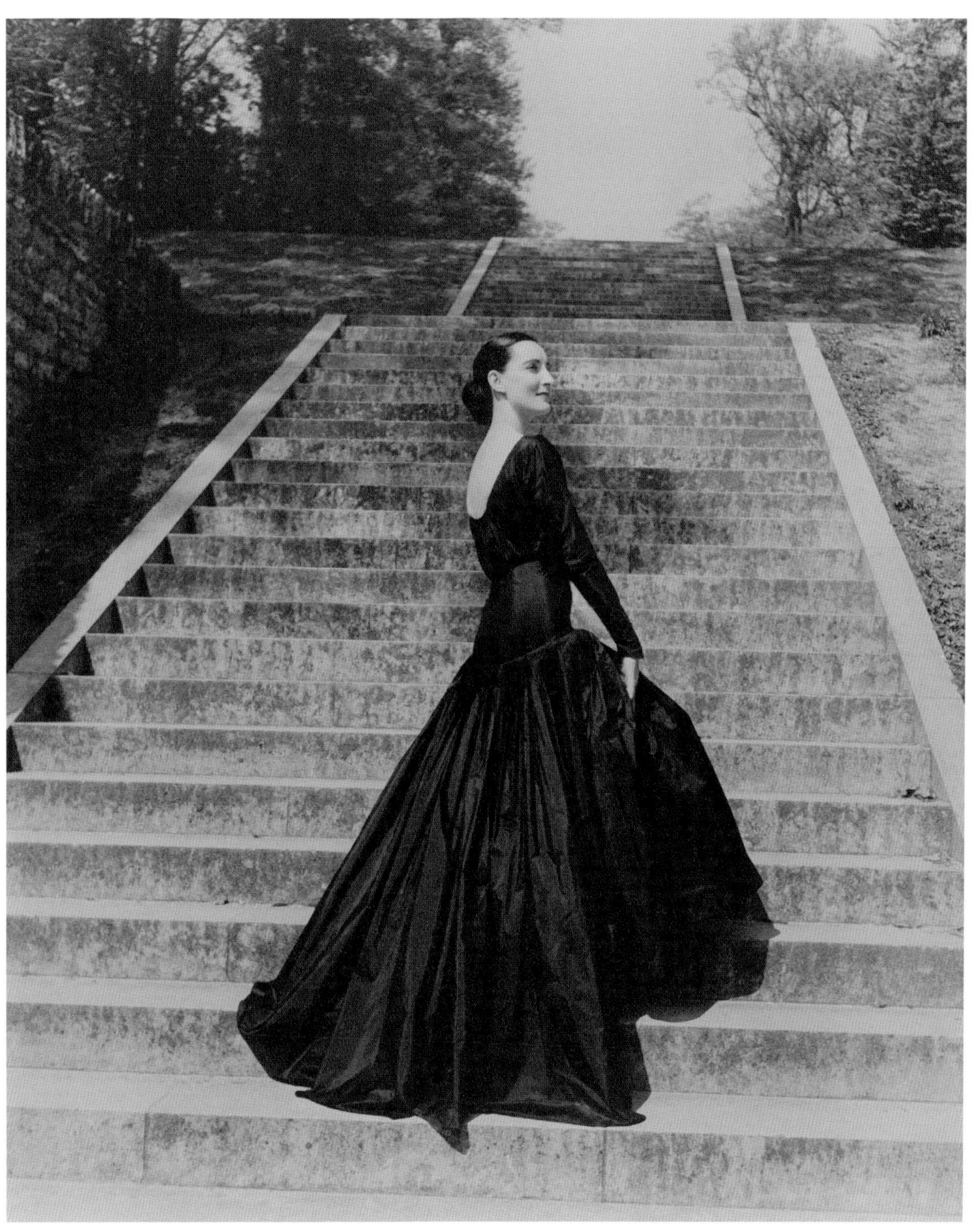

Madame d'Ora
Madame Rupert in einem langen schwarzen Kleid (Madame Rupert in a Long Black Dress), 1950s
Gelatine silver print, 29.4 × 24.1 cm
Museum für Kunst und Gewerbe Hamburg

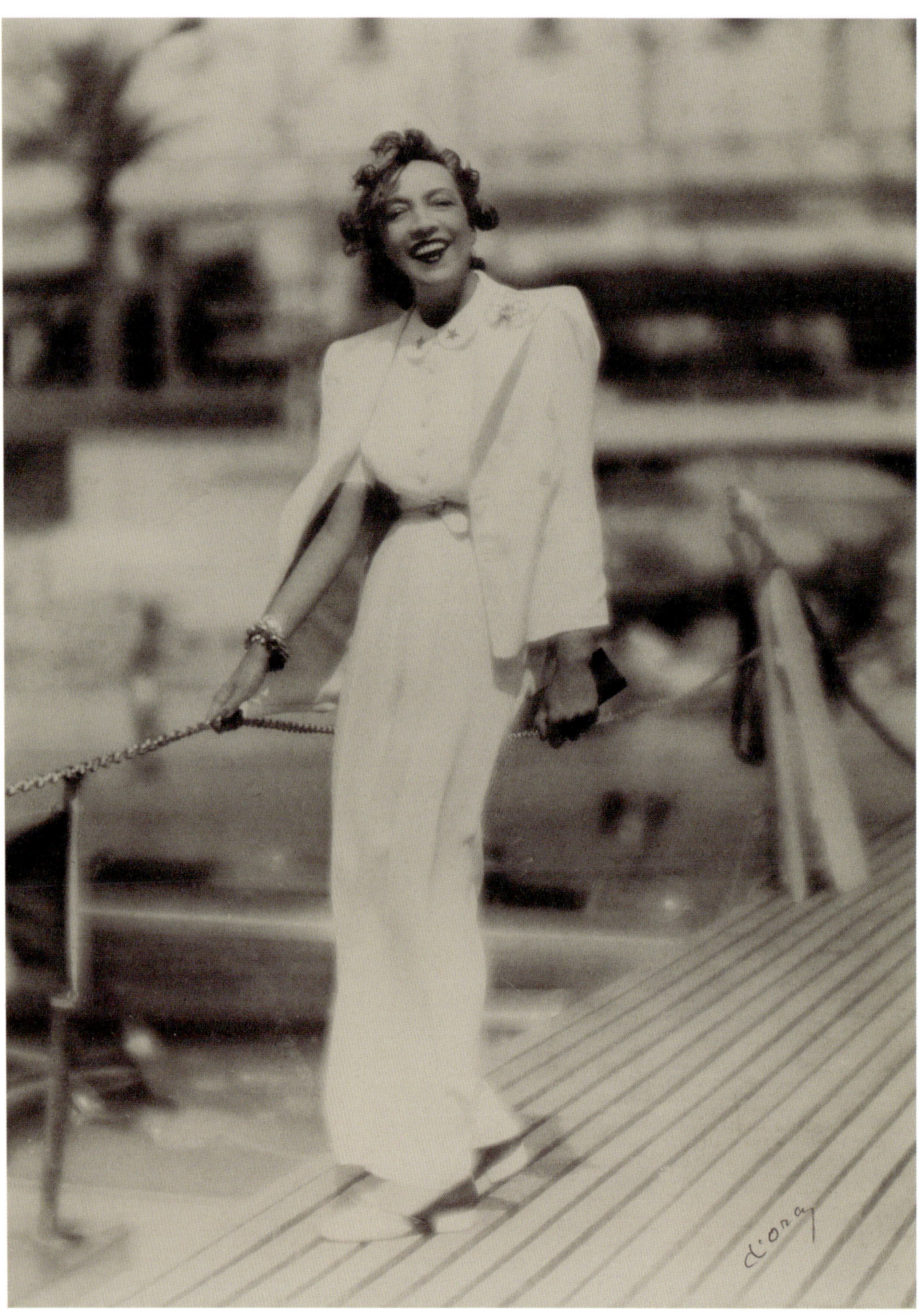

Madame d'Ora
Madame Mathis, 1955
Gelatine silver print, 26 × 19 cm
Museum für Kunst und Gewerbe Hamburg

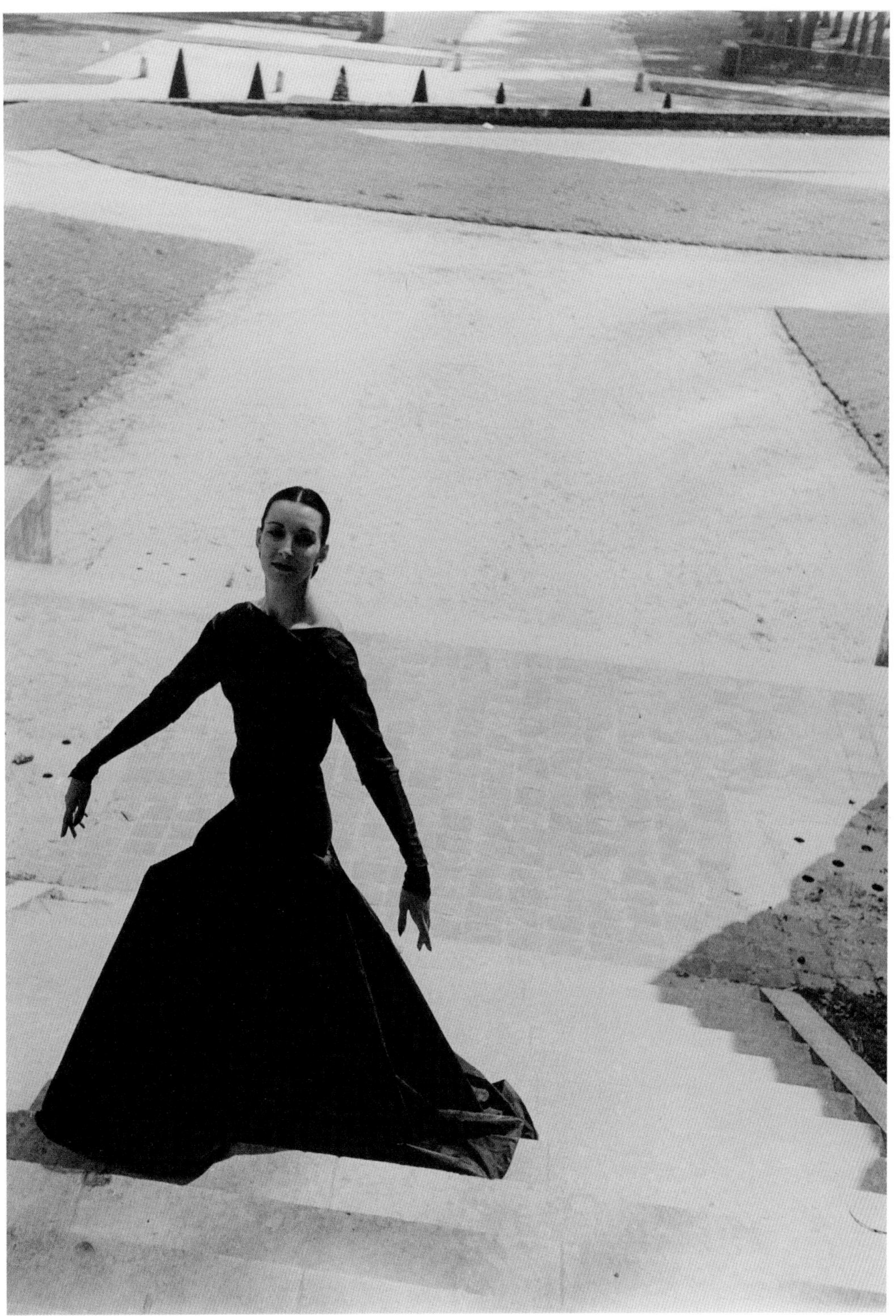

Madame d'Ora
Madame Rupert, c. 1953
Gelatine silver print, 34 × 24.2 cm
Museum für Kunst und Gewerbe Hamburg

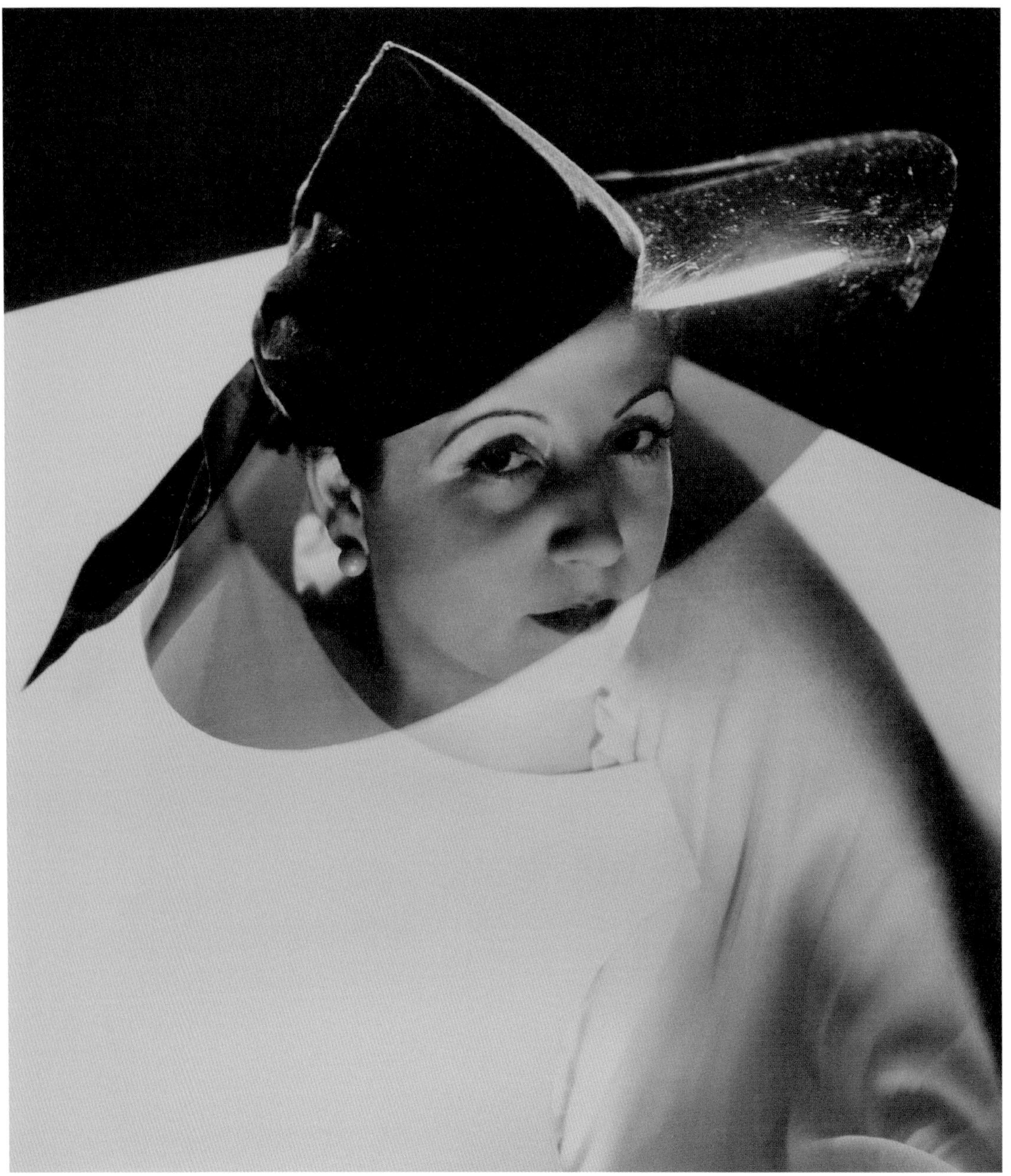

Madame d'Ora
Madame Agnès mit einem Hut aus Samt mit durchsichtiger Krempe
(Madame Agnès in a Velvet Hat with Transparent Brim), c. 1936
Gelatine silver print, 22.8 × 20 cm
Museum für Kunst und Gewerbe Hamburg

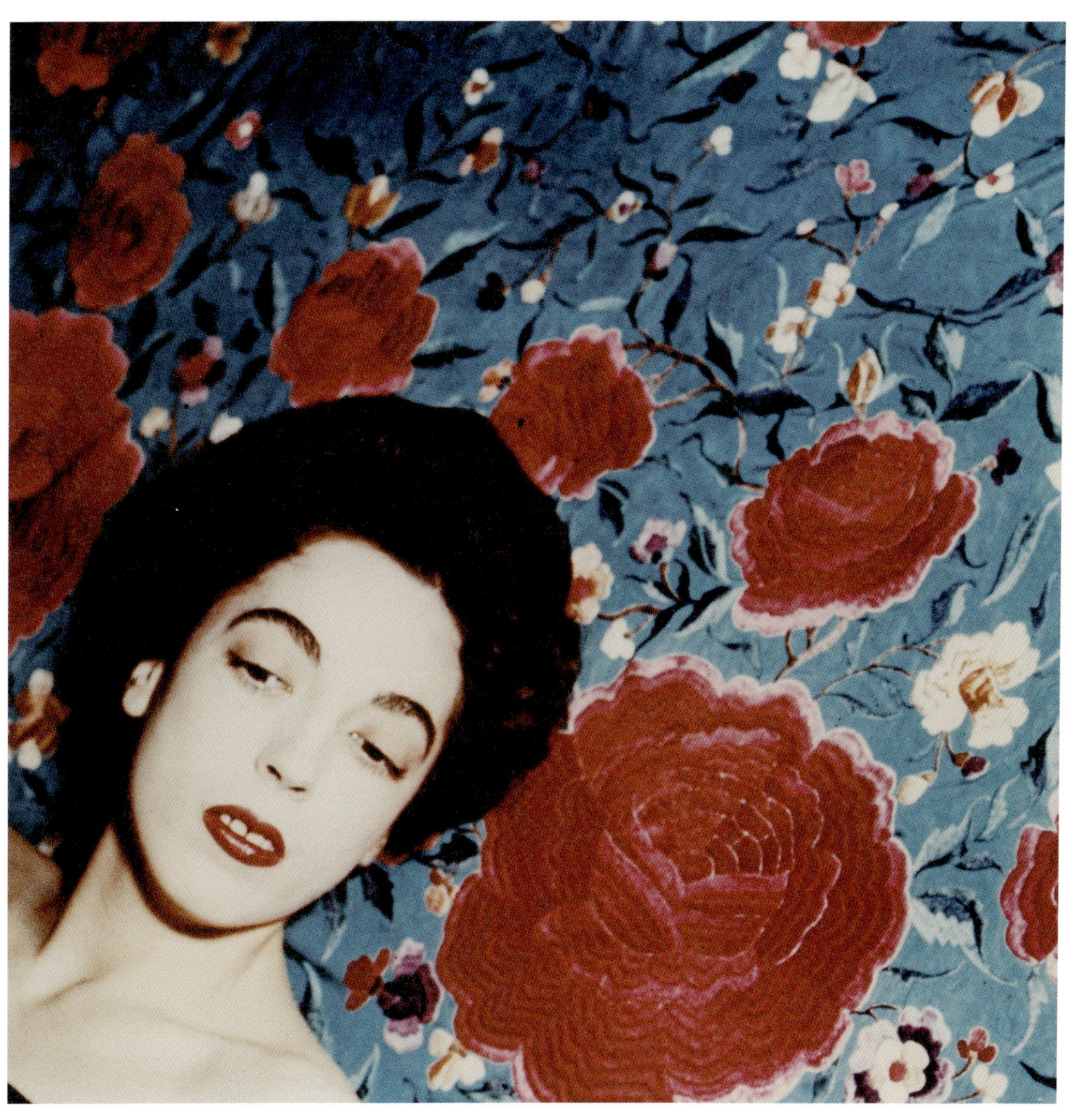

Madame d'Ora
Isabelle de Tinoco, 1950s
C-Print, 17.7 × 17.4 cm
Museum für Kunst und Gewerbe Hamburg

Charlotte Rohrbach

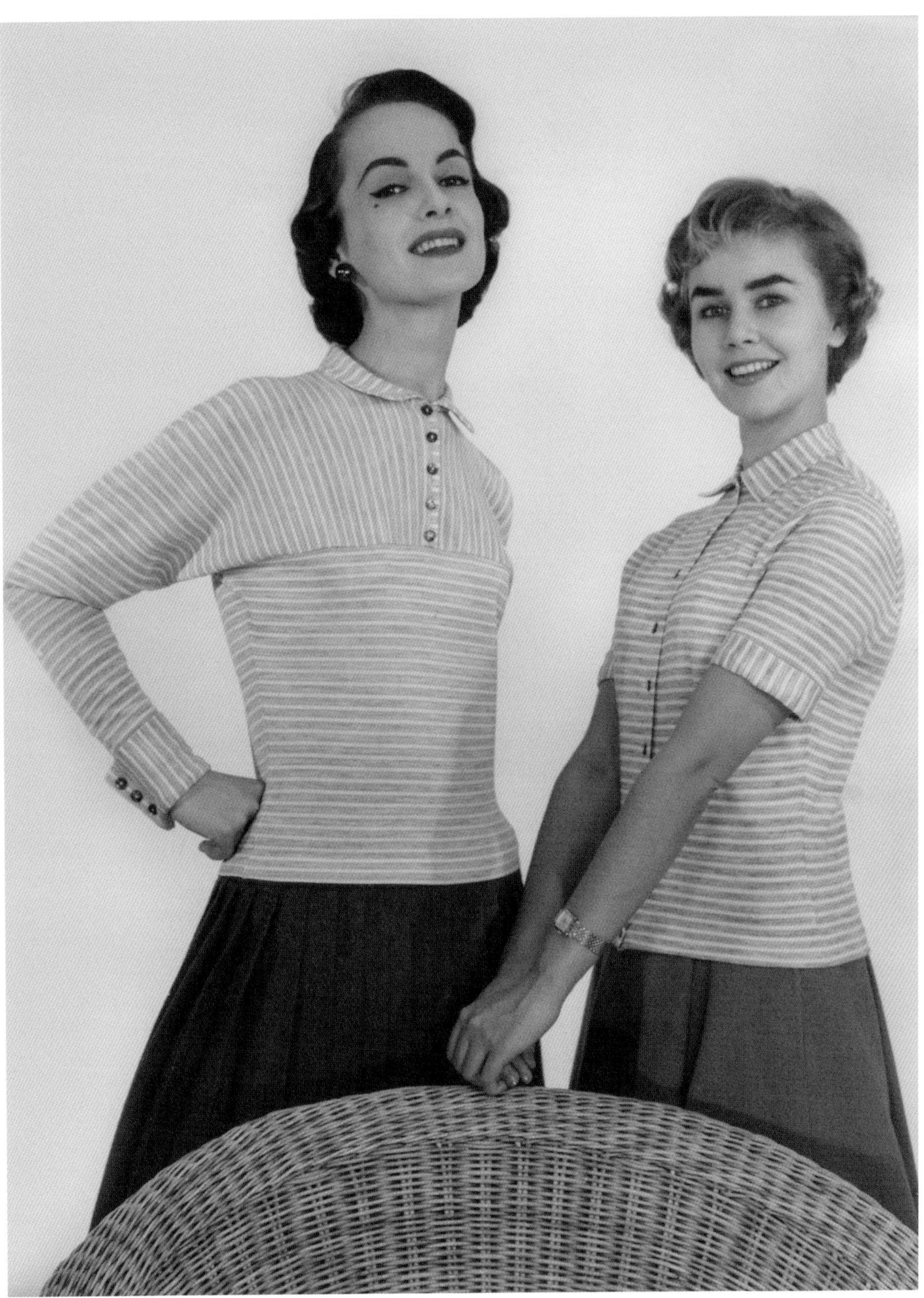

Charlotte Rohrbach
This Pleases the Young Lady: Little Jumpers for Office and Leisure, undated
Gelatine silver print, 30.4 × 22 cm
F.C. Gundlach Foundation

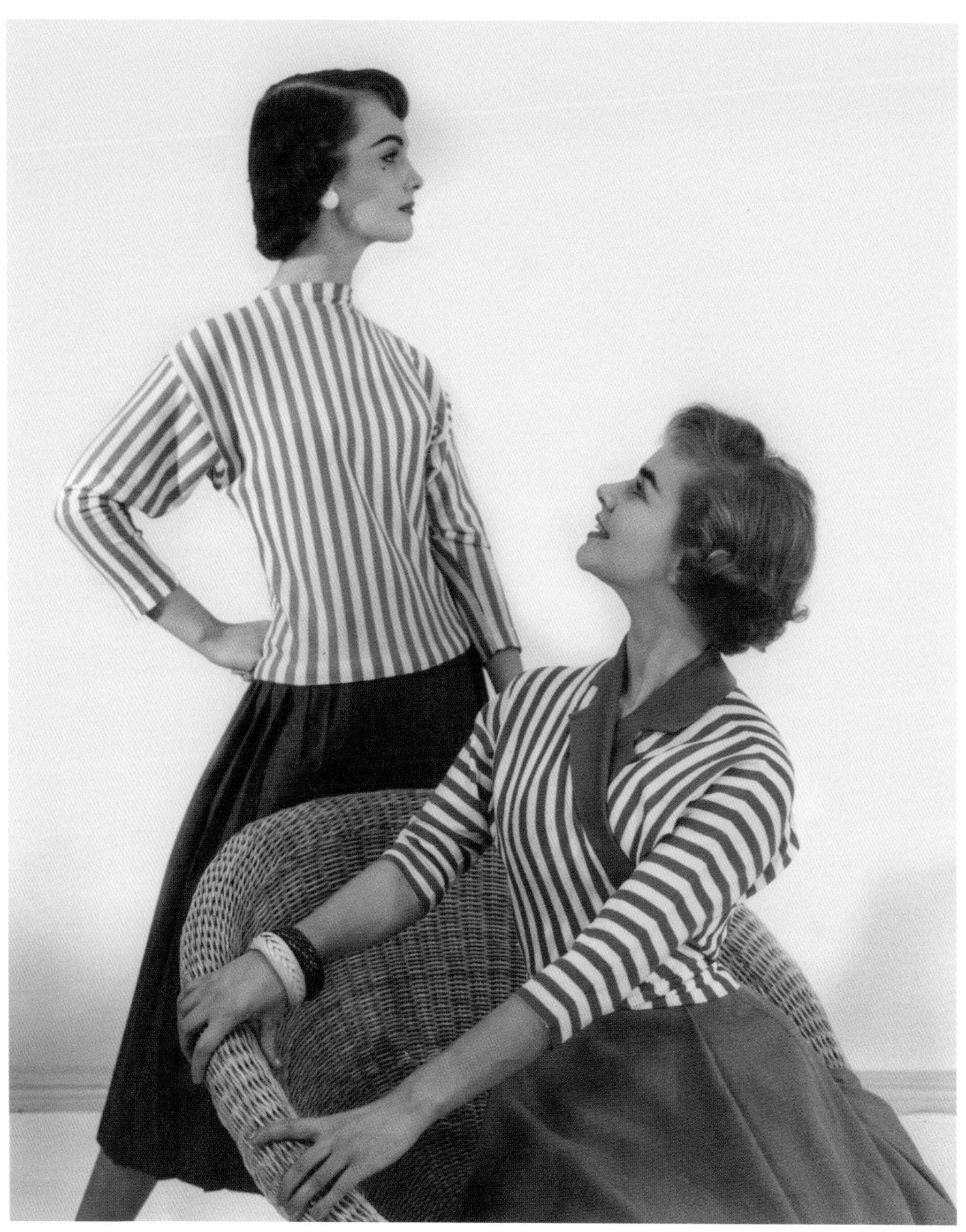

Charlotte Rohrbach
This Pleases the Young Lady: Little Jumpers for Office and Leisure, undated
Gelatine silver print, 29.4 × 24 cm
F.C. Gundlach Foundation

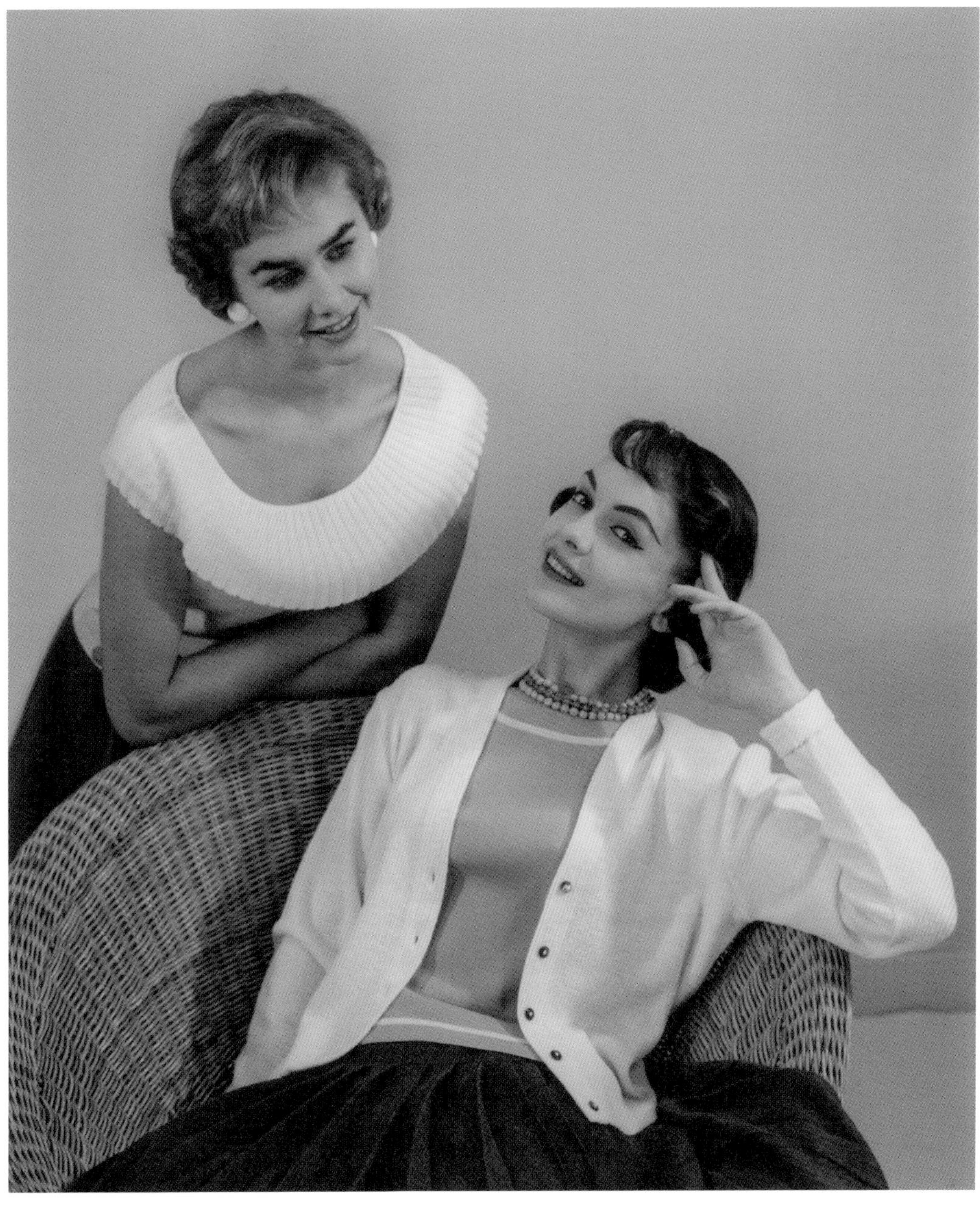

Charlotte Rohrbach
This Pleases the Young Lady: Little Jumpers for Office and Leisure, undated
Gelatine silver print, 28.5 × 24 cm
F.C. Gundlach Foundation

Ingeborg Hoppe

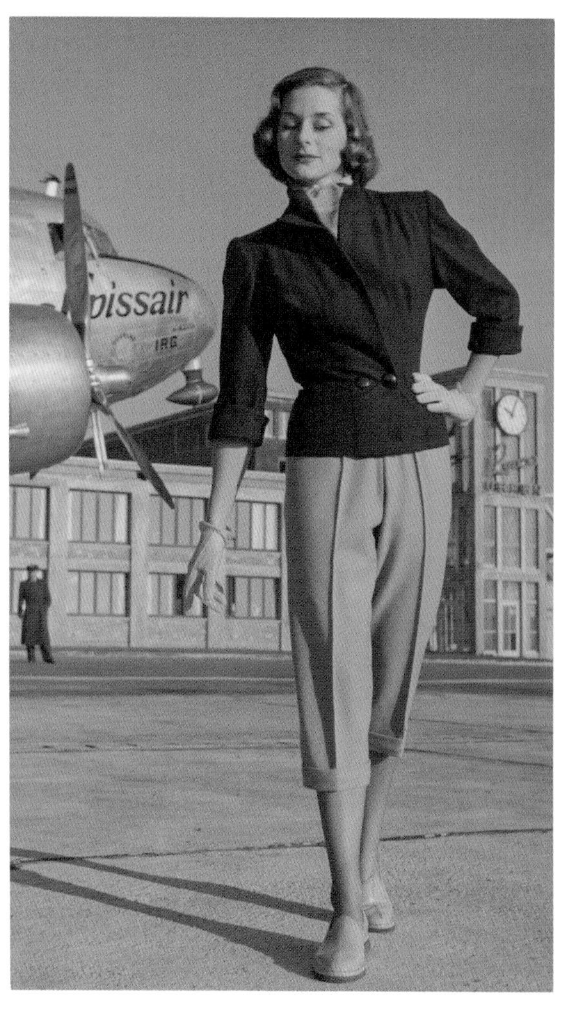

Ingeborg Hoppe
This Pleases the Young Lady:
In Anticipation of the Summer Trip, 1951/52
Gelatine silver print, 29.6 × 15.1 cm
Deichtorhallen Hamburg, F.C. Gundlach Collection

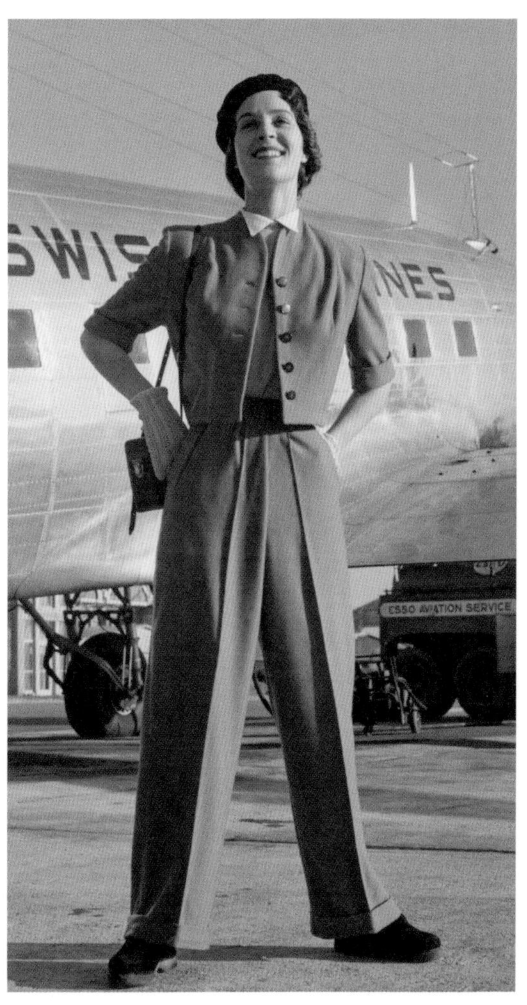

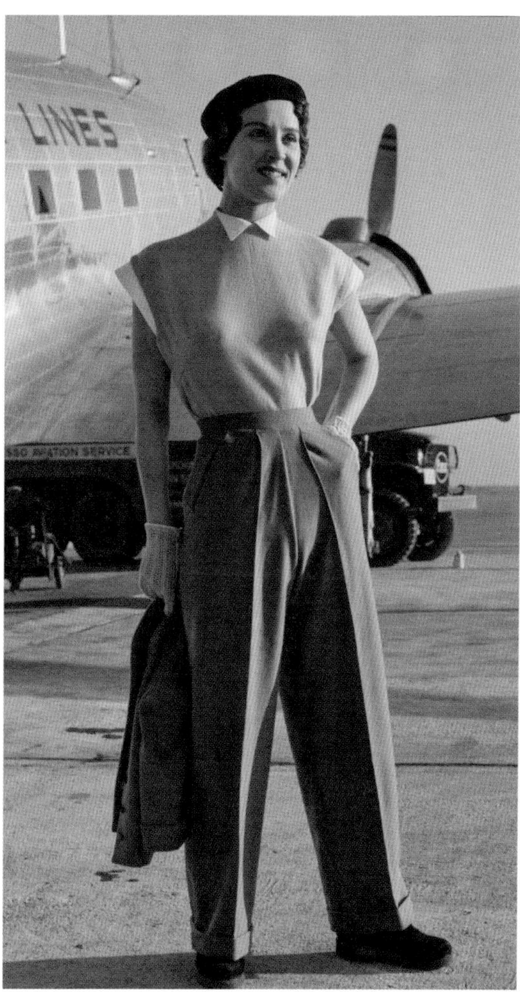

Ingeborg Hoppe
This Pleases the Young Lady:
In Anticipation of the Summer Trip, 1951/52
Gelatine silver print, 29.1 × 15.7 cm
Deichtorhallen Hamburg, F.C. Gundlach Collection

Ingeborg Hoppe
This Pleases the Young Lady:
In Anticipation of the Summer Trip, 1951/52
Gelatine silver print, 29.2 × 16 cm
Deichtorhallen Hamburg, F.C. Gundlach Collection

Regina Relang

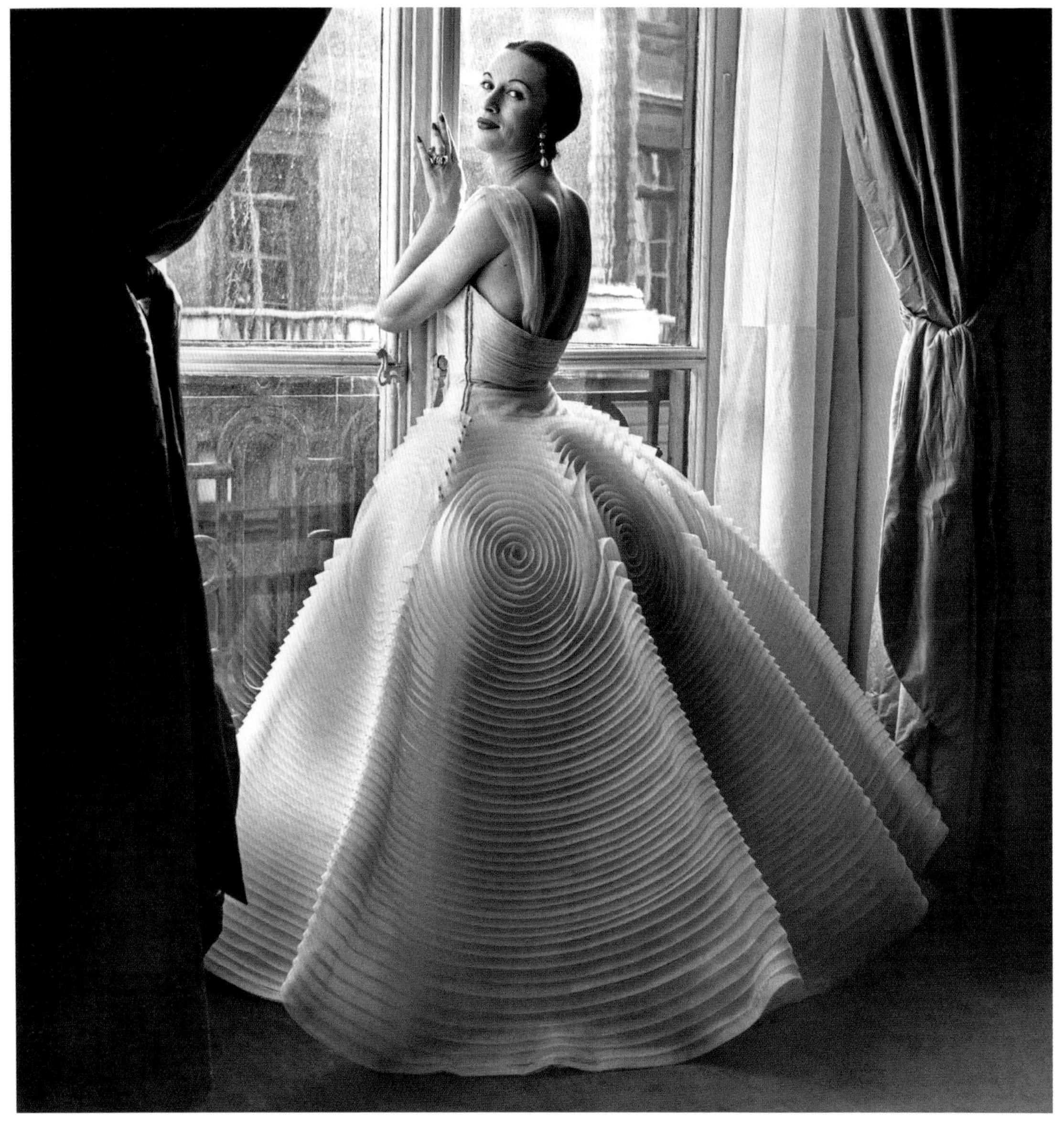

Regina Relang
Gitte, undated
Gelatine silver print, 29.5 × 28 cm
F.C. Gundlach Foundation

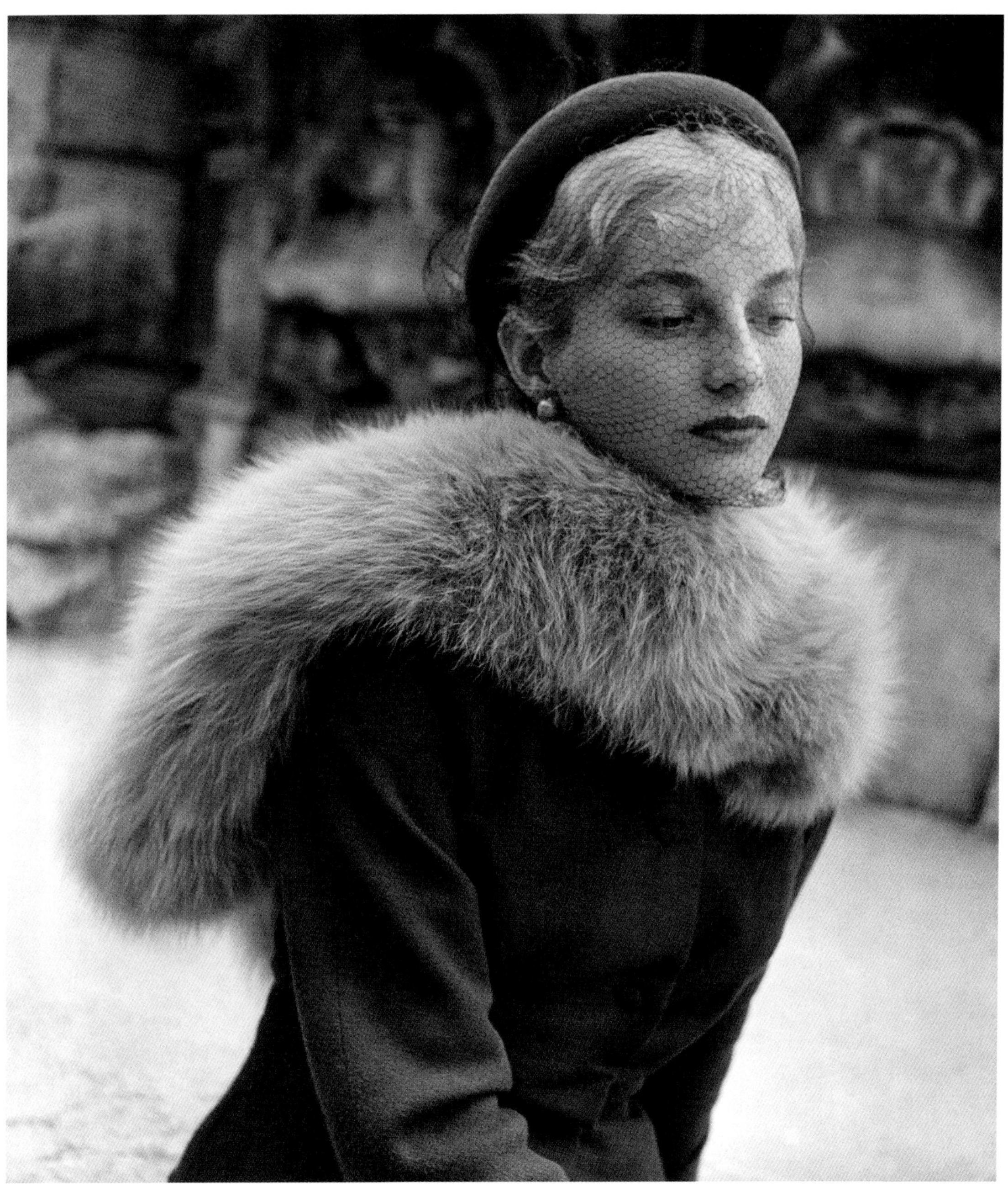

Regina Relang
Veils Are Still Being Worn, undated
Gelatine silver print, 27.9 × 24.3 cm
F.C. Gundlach Foundation

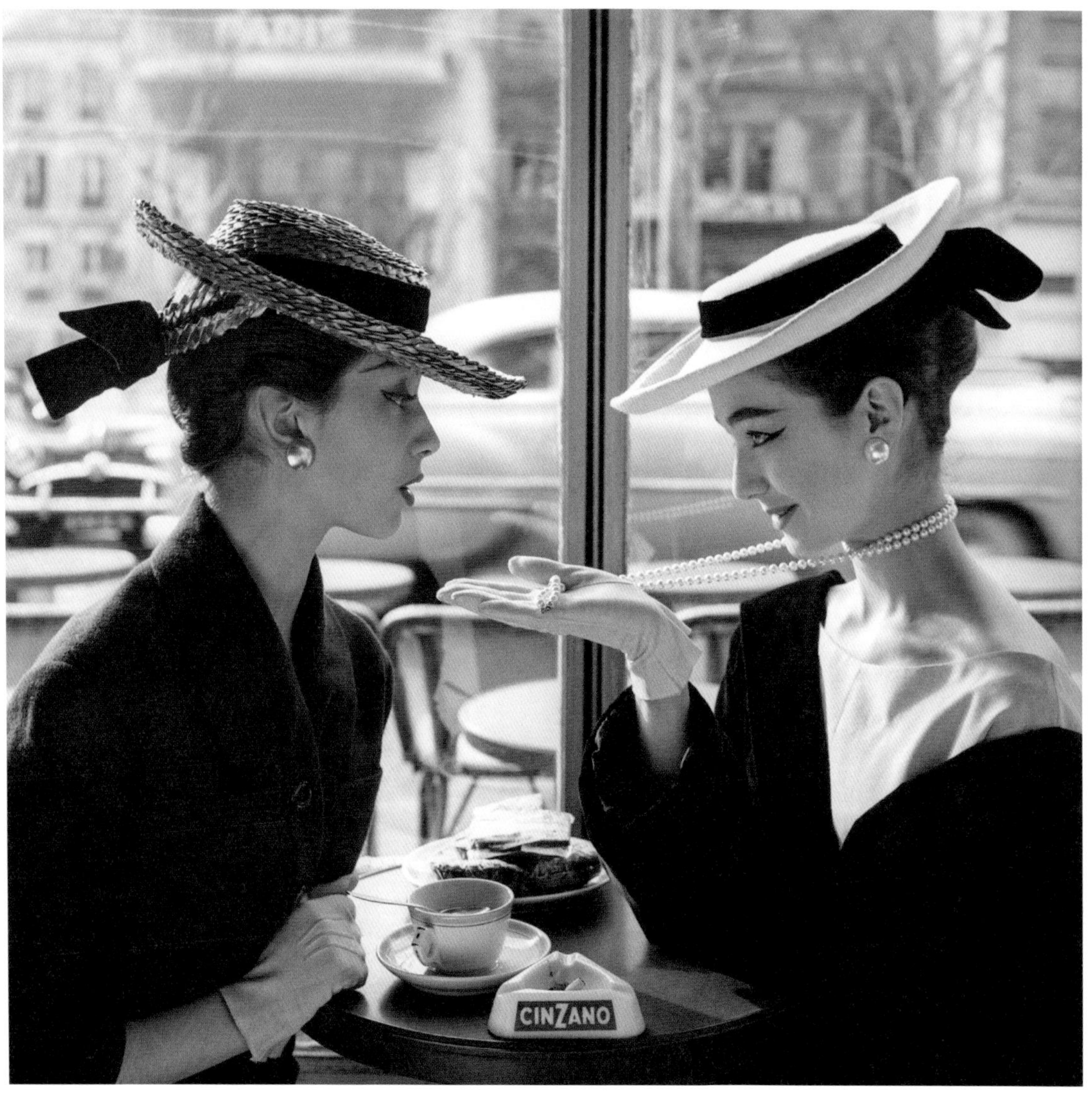

Regina Relang
Fashion Hats, undated
Gelatine silver print, 23.5 × 24.2 cm
F.C. Gundlach Foundation

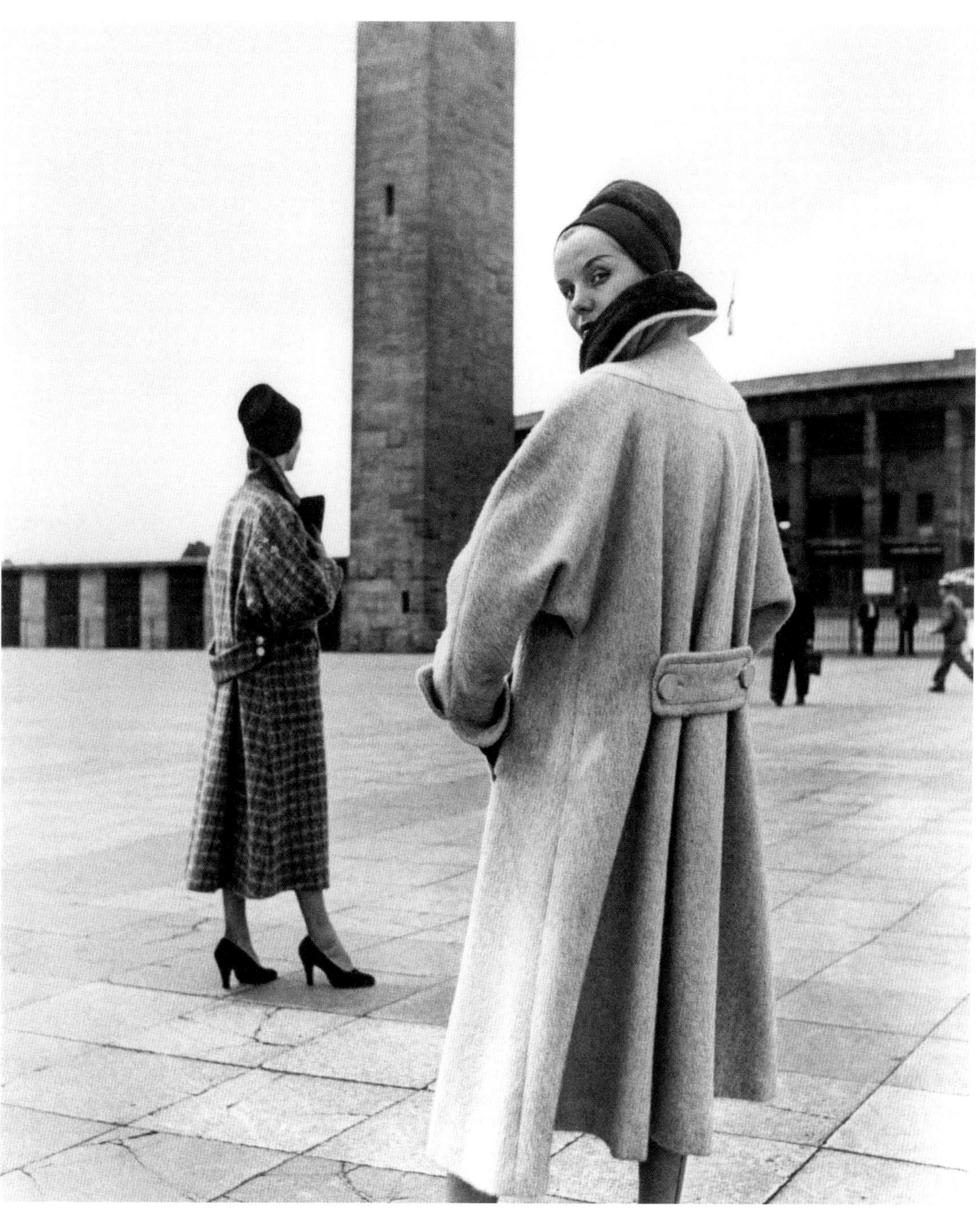

Regina Relang
Coats by Staebe-Seger Outside the Olympic Stadium, 1949/50
Gelatine silver print, 28 × 24 cm
F.C. Gundlach Foundation

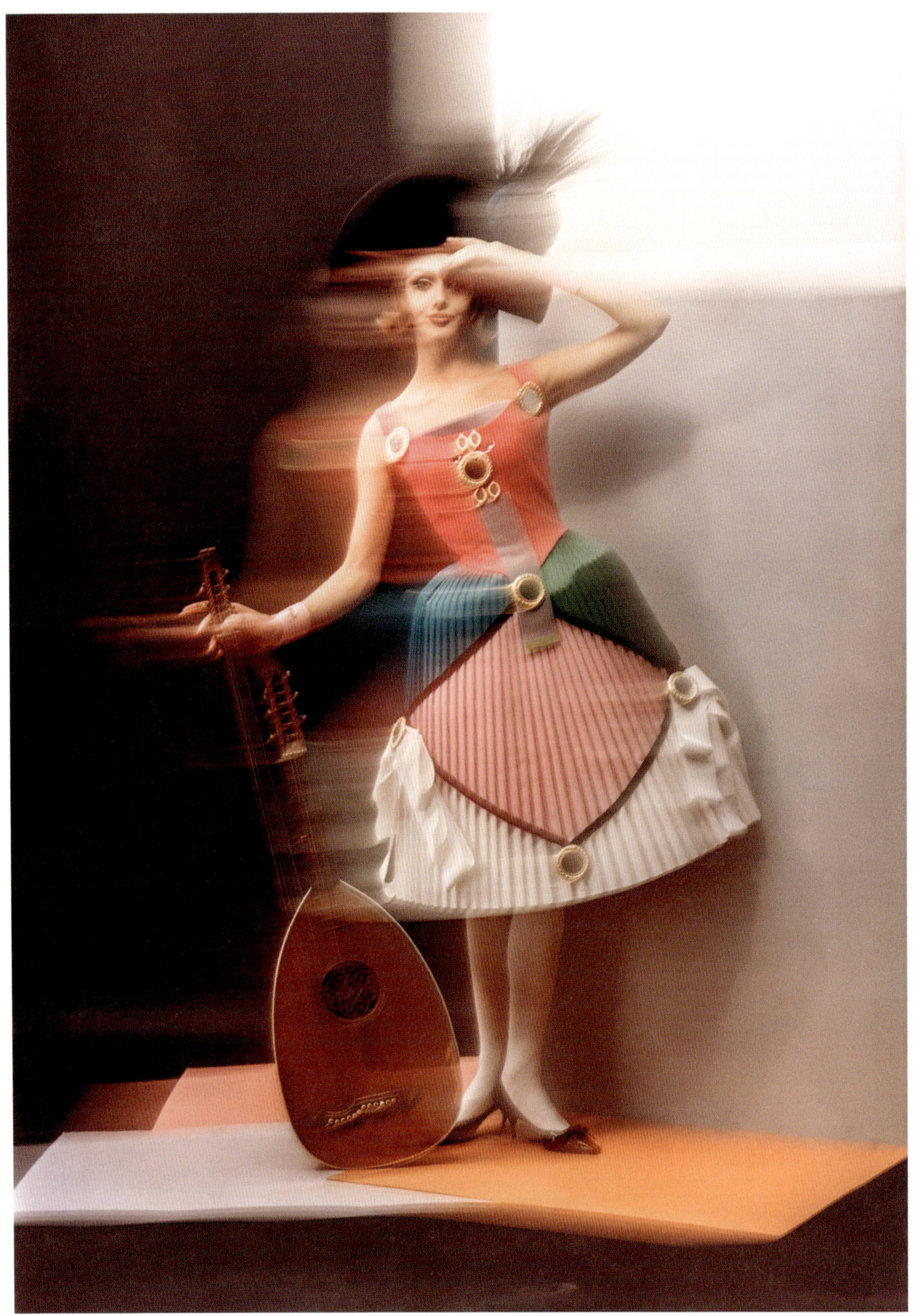

Regina Relang
Ina als Harlekin (Ina as Harlequin), 1973
C-Print, 49.5 × 35.2 cm
F.C. Gundlach Foundation

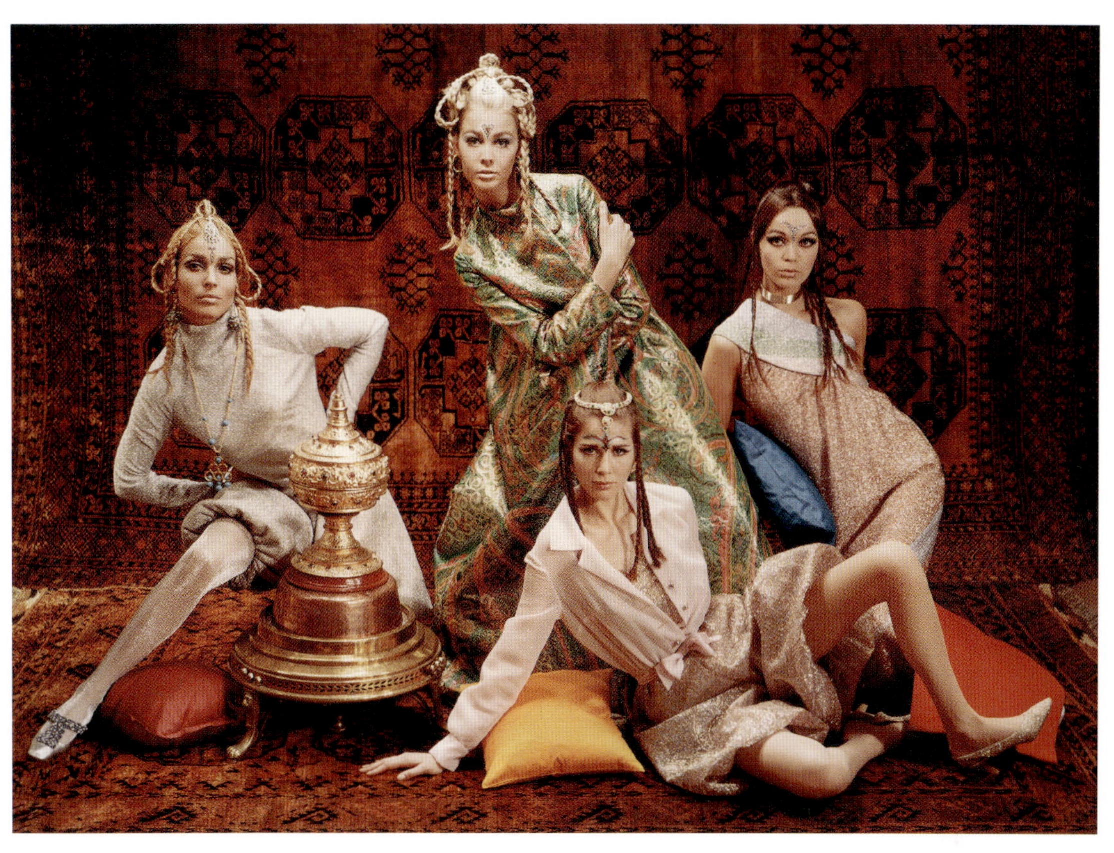

Regina Relang
Der neue Look (The New Look), undated
C-Print, 36.5 × 60.5 cm
F.C. Gundlach Foundation

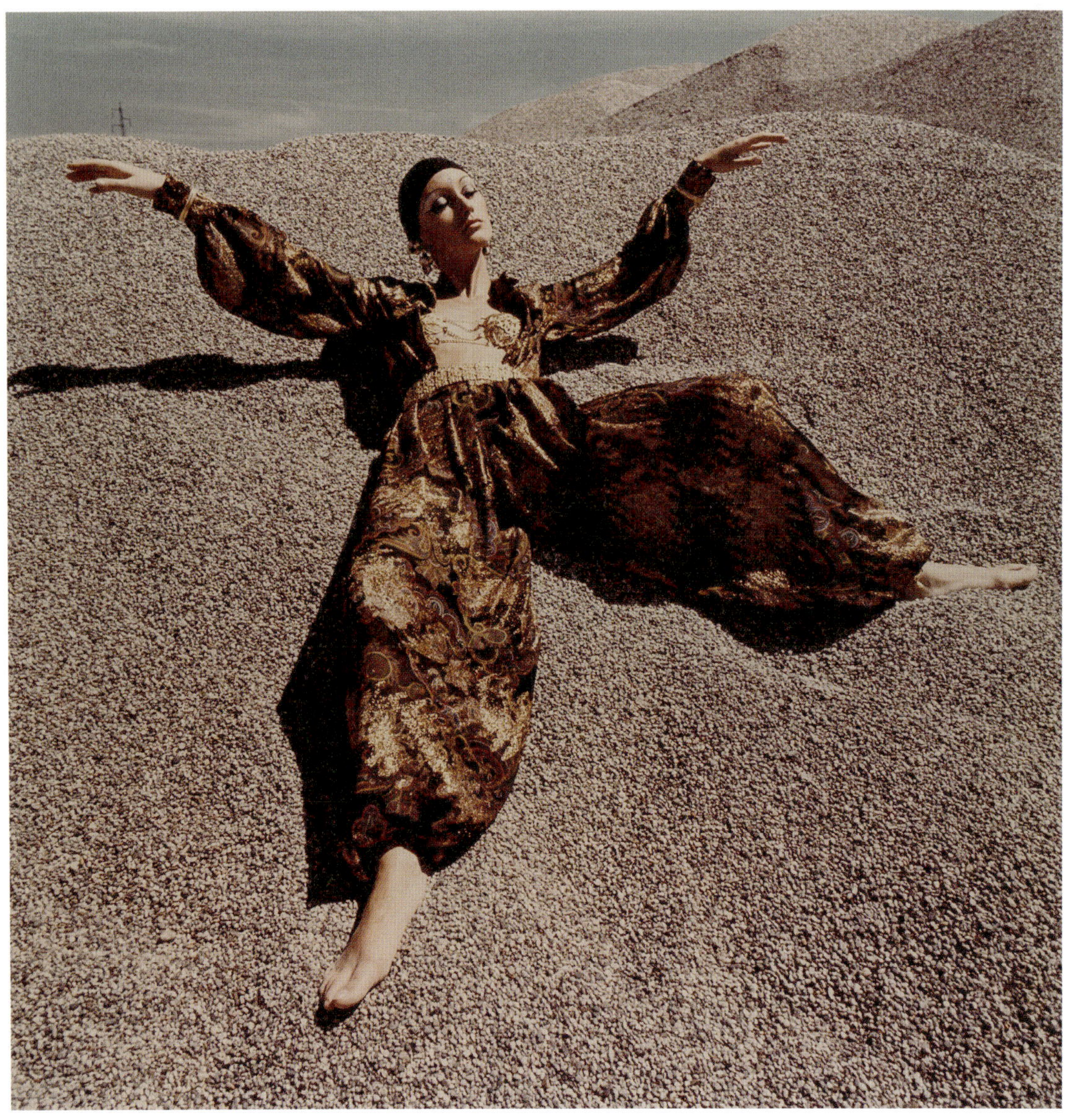

Regina Relang
Oriental Look, 1969
C-Print, 40.5 × 40.1 cm
Museum für Kunst und Gewerbe Hamburg

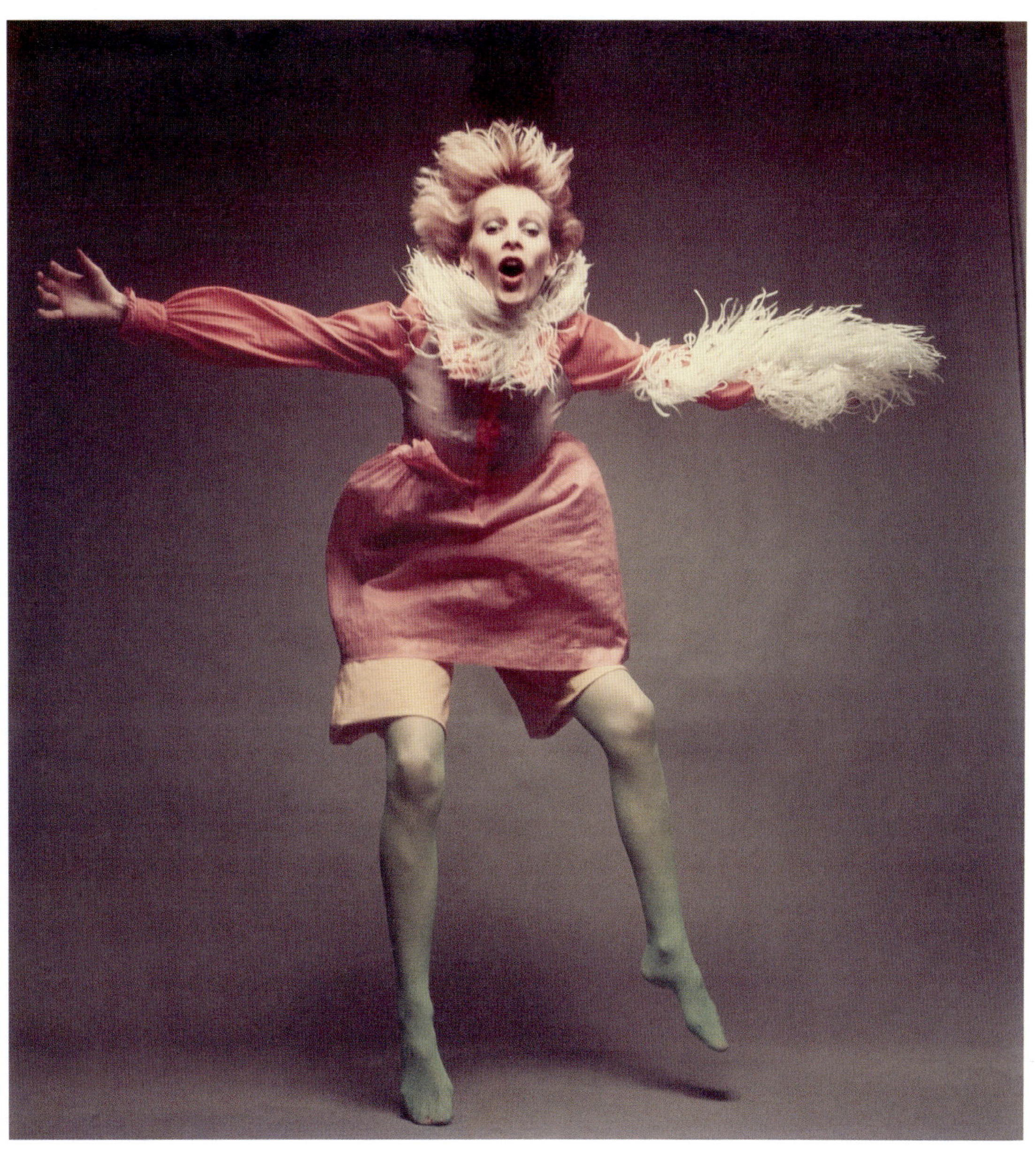

Regina Relang
Puck, 1973
C-Print, 40.4 × 38 cm
Museum für Kunst und Gewerbe Hamburg

Louise Dahl-Wolfe

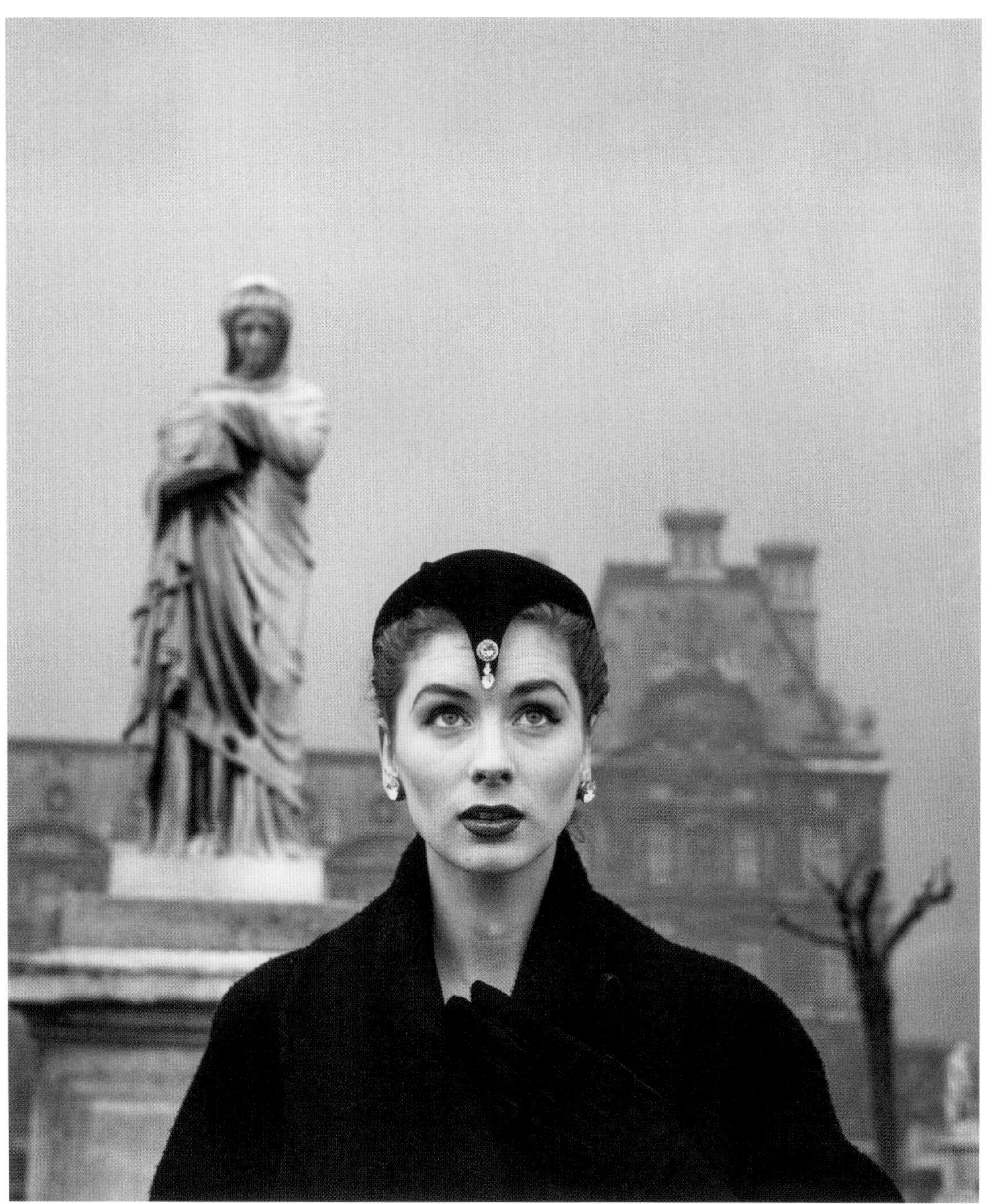

Louise Dahl-Wolfe
Suzy Parker in Dior Hat, 1960
Gelatine silver print, 30.6 × 25.9 cm
Deichtorhallen Hamburg, F.C. Gundlach Collection

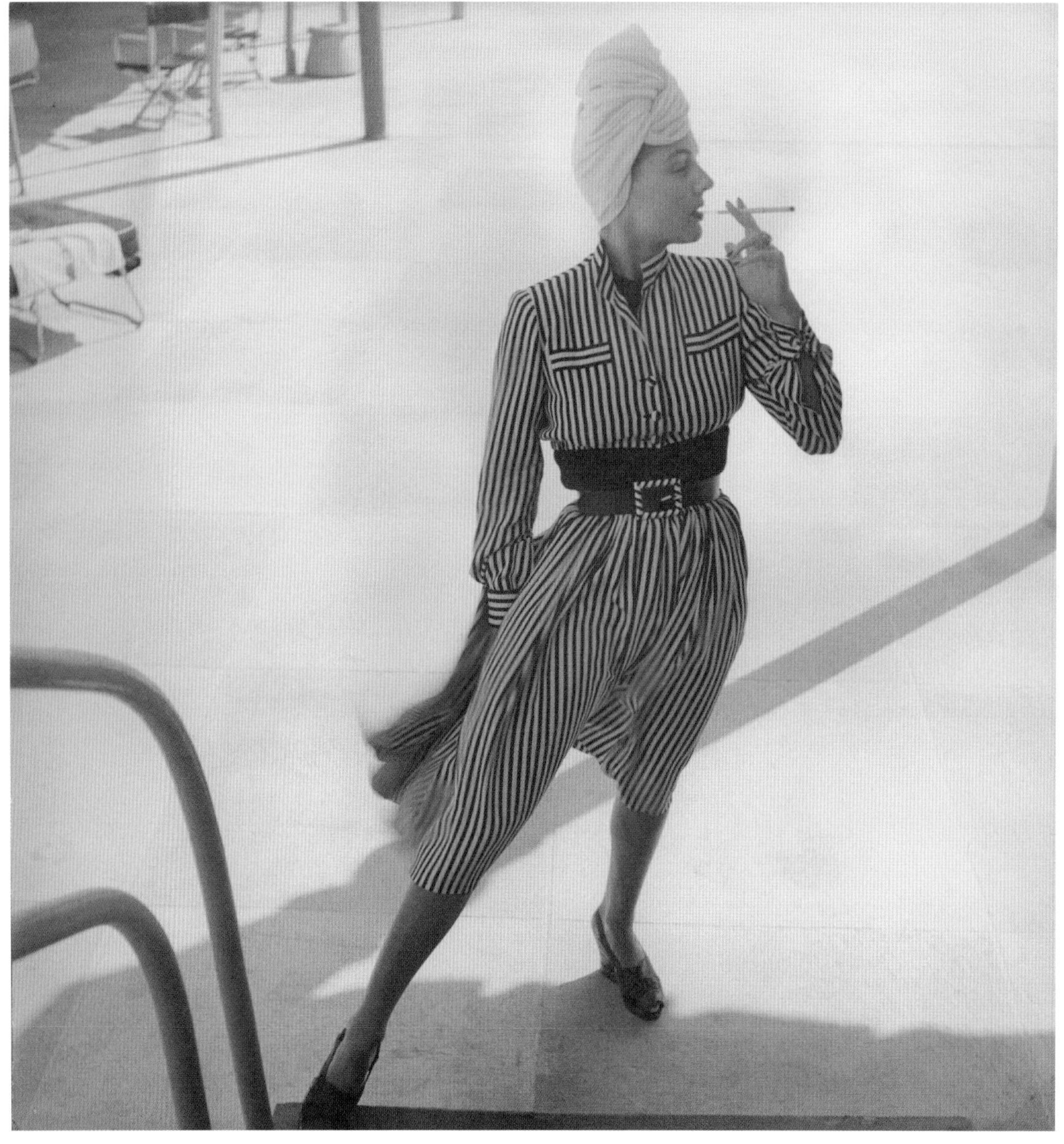

Louise Dahl-Wolfe
Lady Margaret Strickland, 1939
Gelatine silver print, 26.4 × 25.2 cm
Deichtorhallen Hamburg, F.C. Gundlach Collection

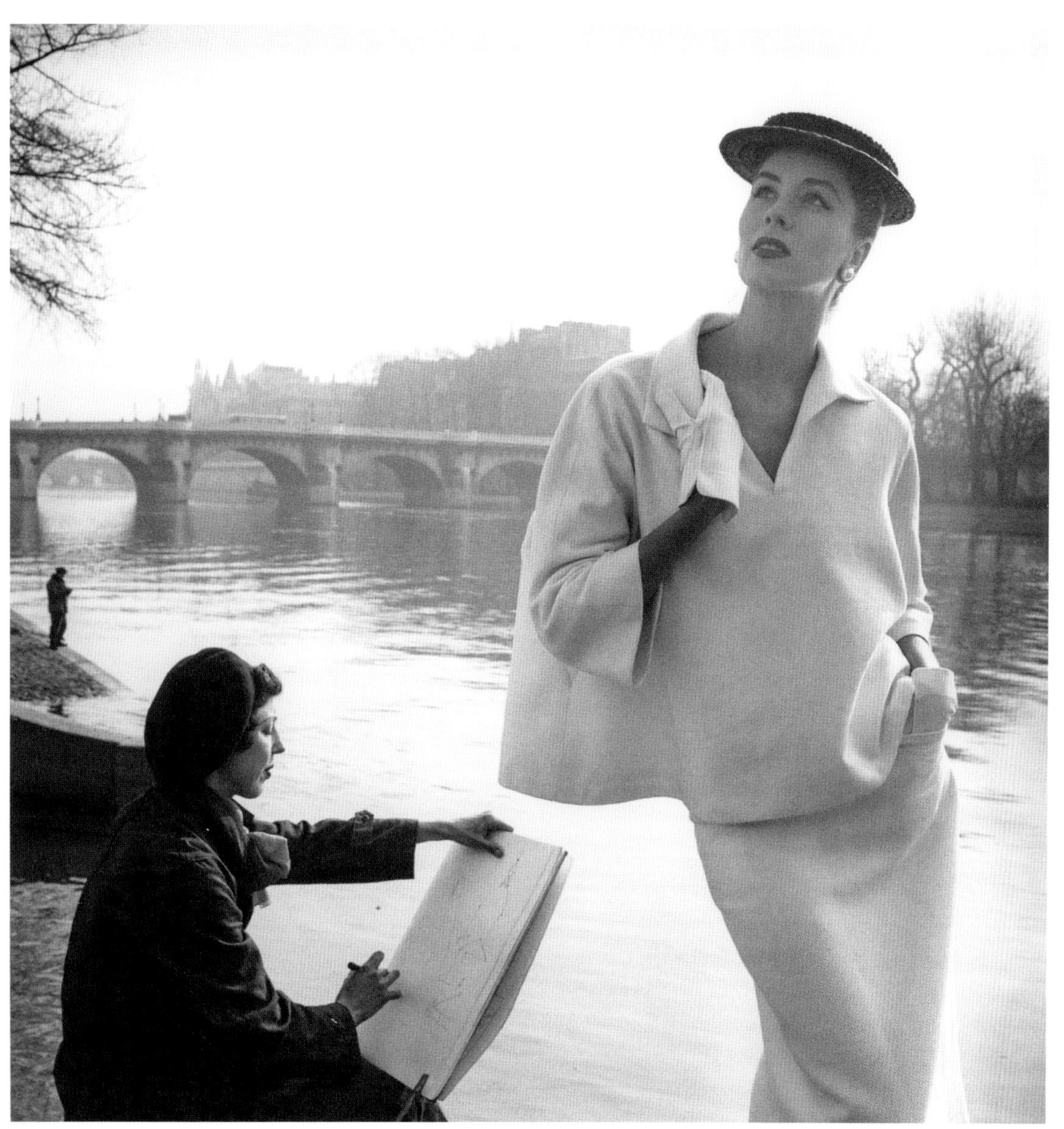

Louise Dahl-Wolfe
Suzy Parker by the Seine, Costume by Balenciaga (Betty Fenn), c. 1953
Gelatine silver print, 30.6 × 25.9 cm
Deichtorhallen Hamburg, F.C. Gundlach Collection

Lillian Bassman

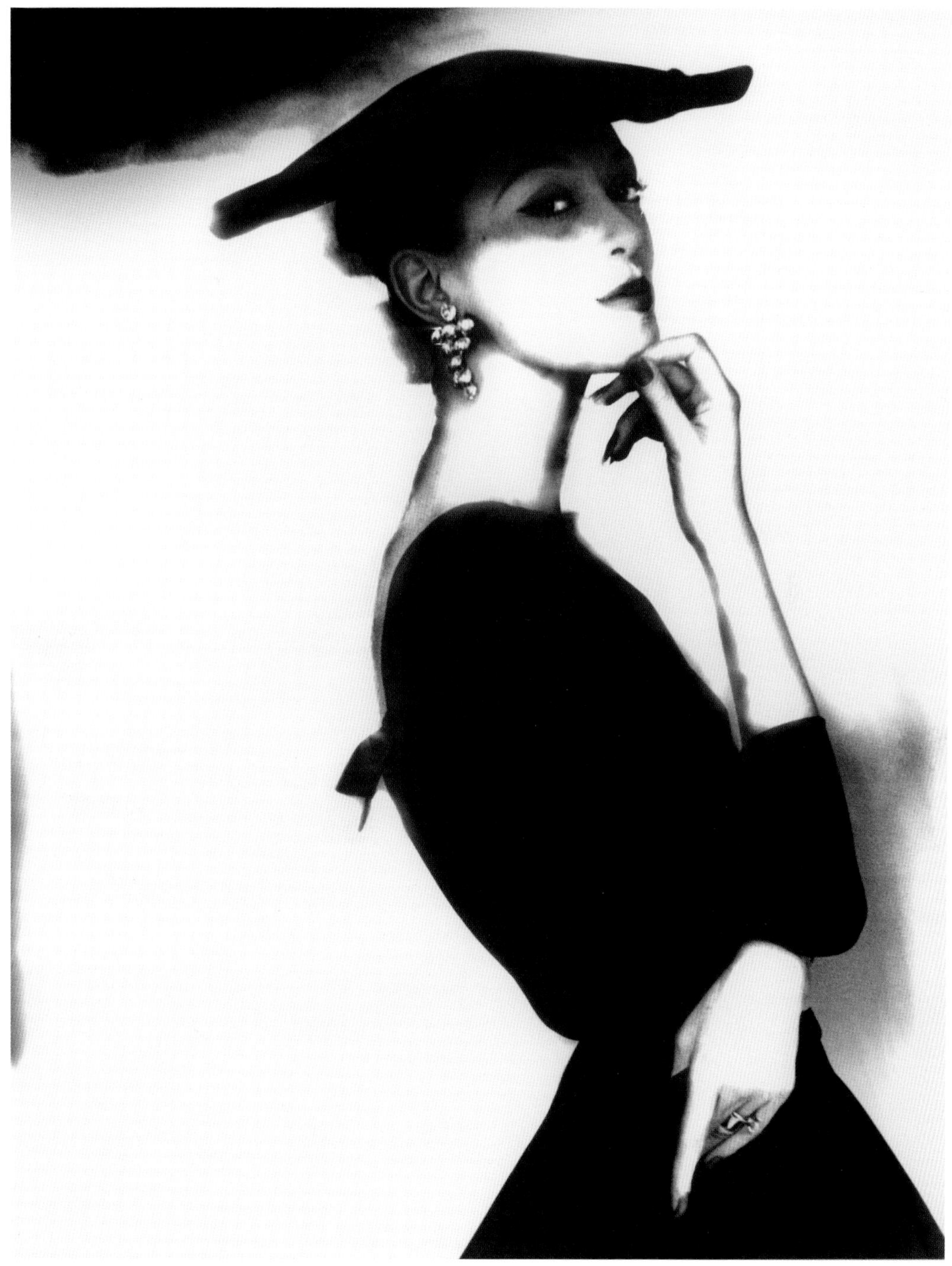

Lillian Bassman
Barbara Mullen, c. 1952/1994
Gelatine silver print, 48.7 × 37.4 cm
Deichtorhallen Hamburg, F.C. Gundlach Collection

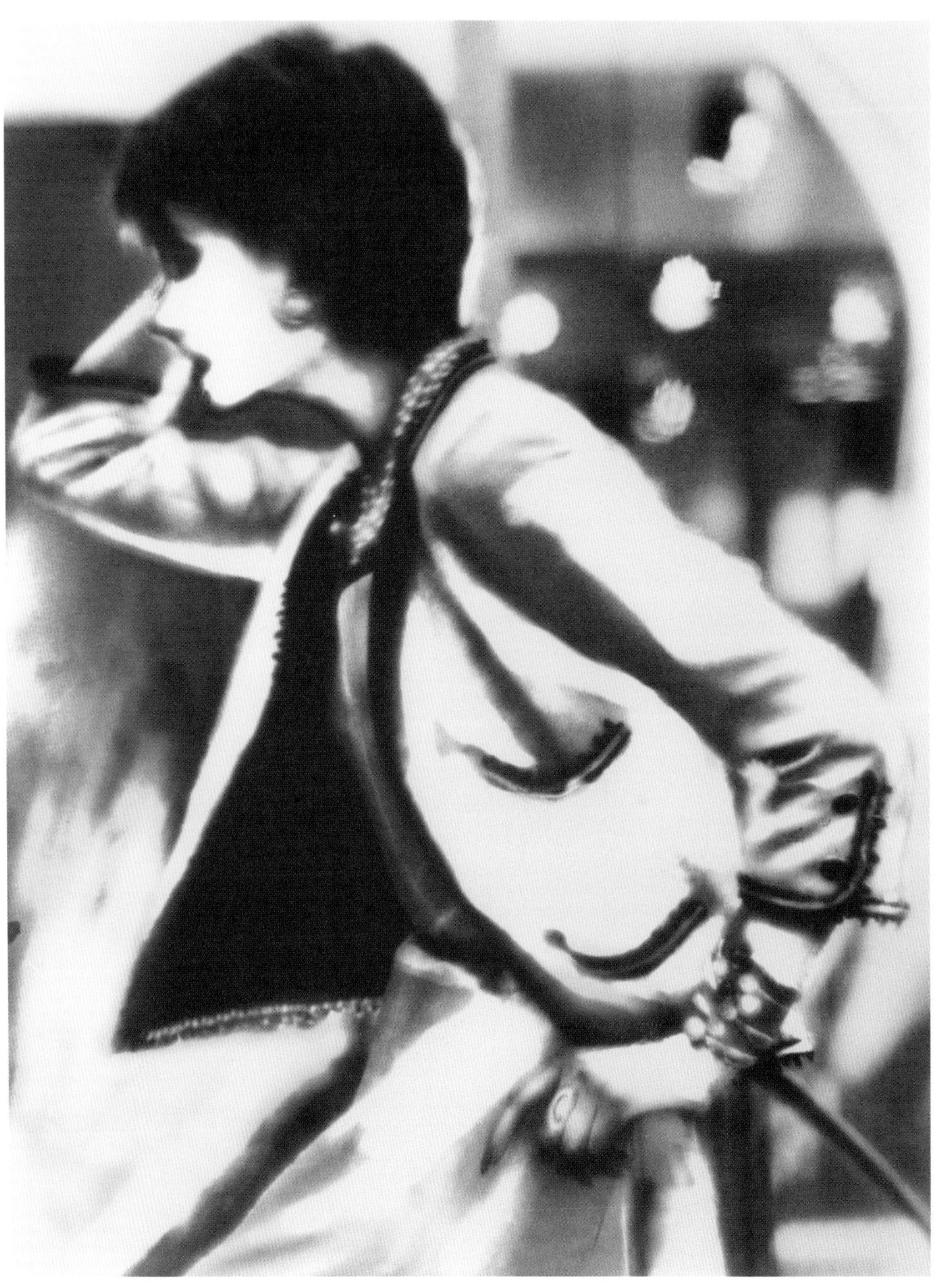

Lillian Bassman
Chanel Collection, c. 1959/1994
Gelatine silver print, 48.6 × 36.7 cm
Deichtorhallen Hamburg, F.C. Gundlach Collection

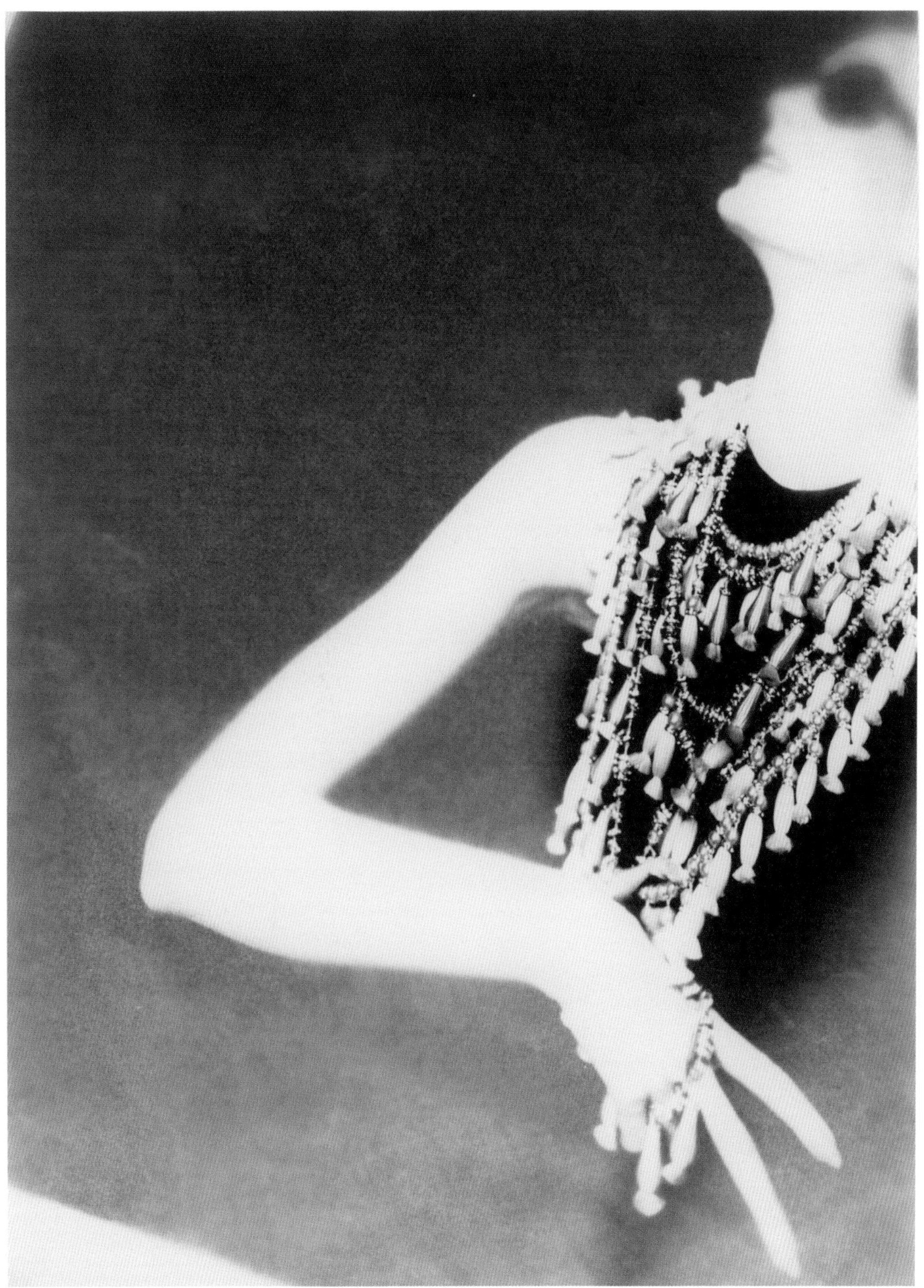

Lillian Bassman
Barbara Mullen, 1960
Gelatine silver print, 34.4 × 27.1 cm
Deichtorhallen Hamburg, F.C. Gundlach Collection

Charlotte March

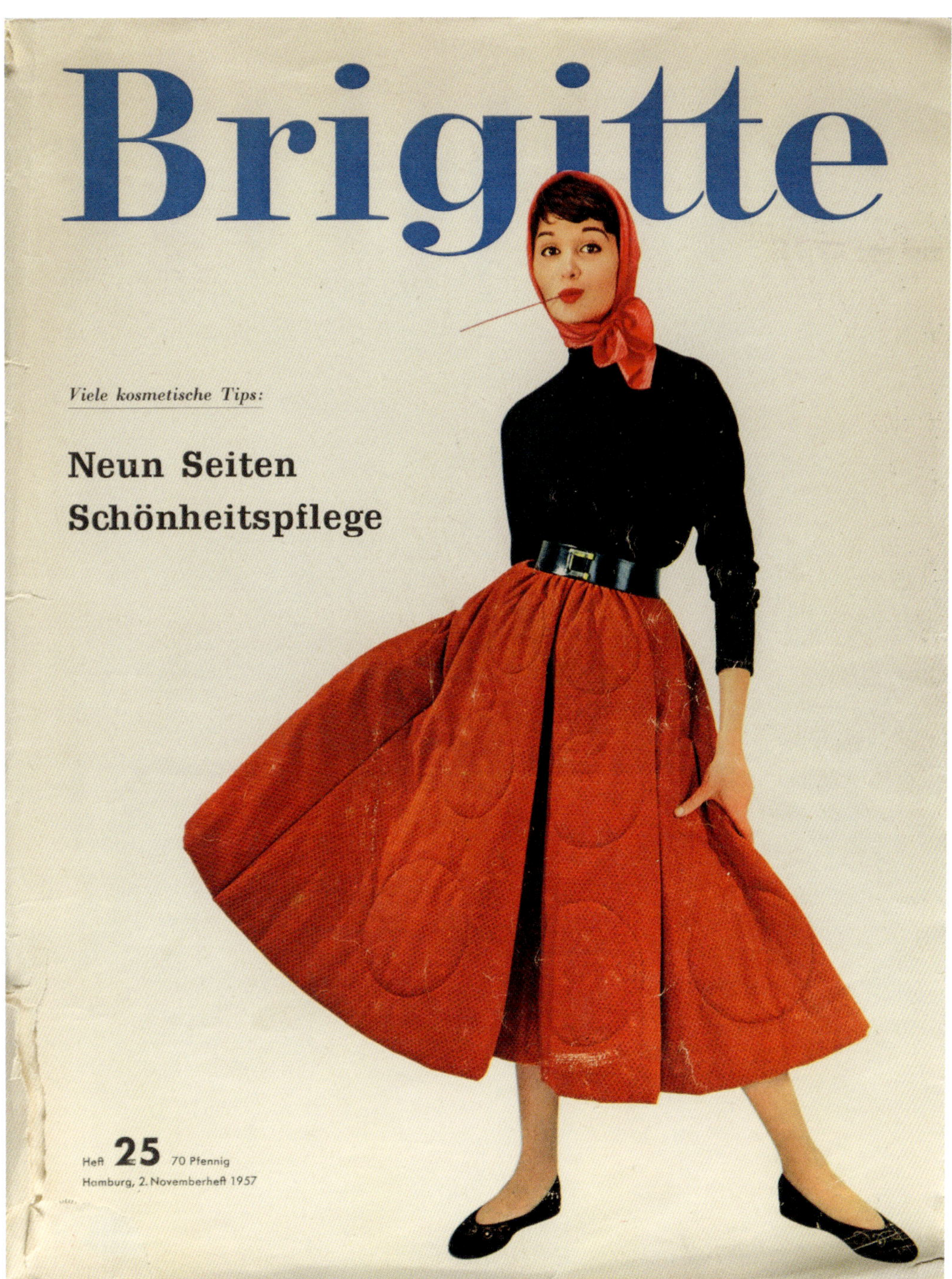

Charlotte March
Brigitte, Issue 25, 1957
Offset print, 33.1 × 25.4 cm
Museum für Kunst und Gewerbe Hamburg

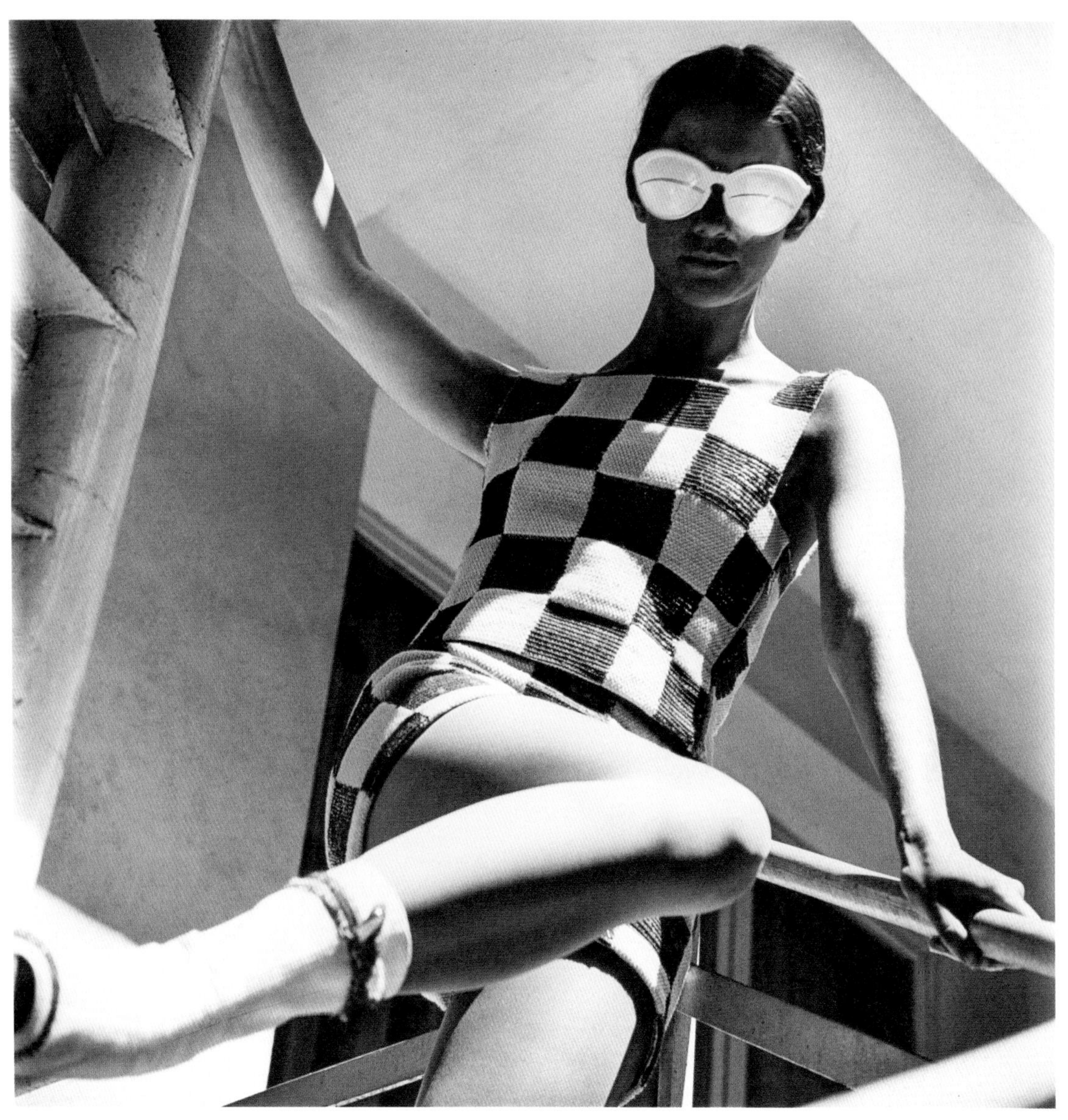

Charlotte March
Paris, Mode Courrèges, 1963
Gelatine silver print, 39.9 × 39.6 cm
Museum für Kunst und Gewerbe Hamburg

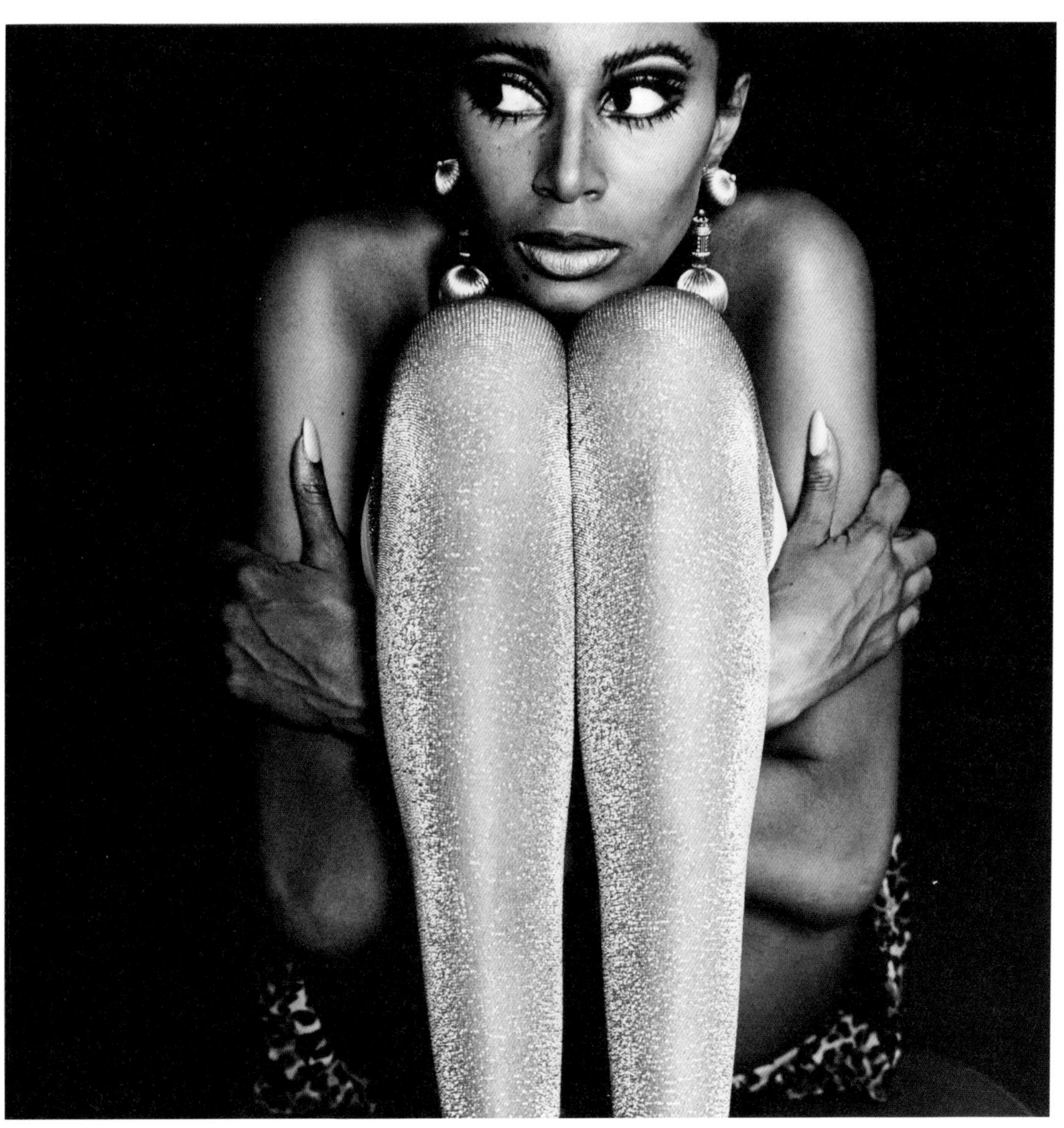

Charlotte March
Donyale-Goldstrümpfe (Donyale Gold Stockings), 1966/1997
Gelatine silver print, 28.7 × 28.4 cm
Museum für Kunst und Gewerbe Hamburg

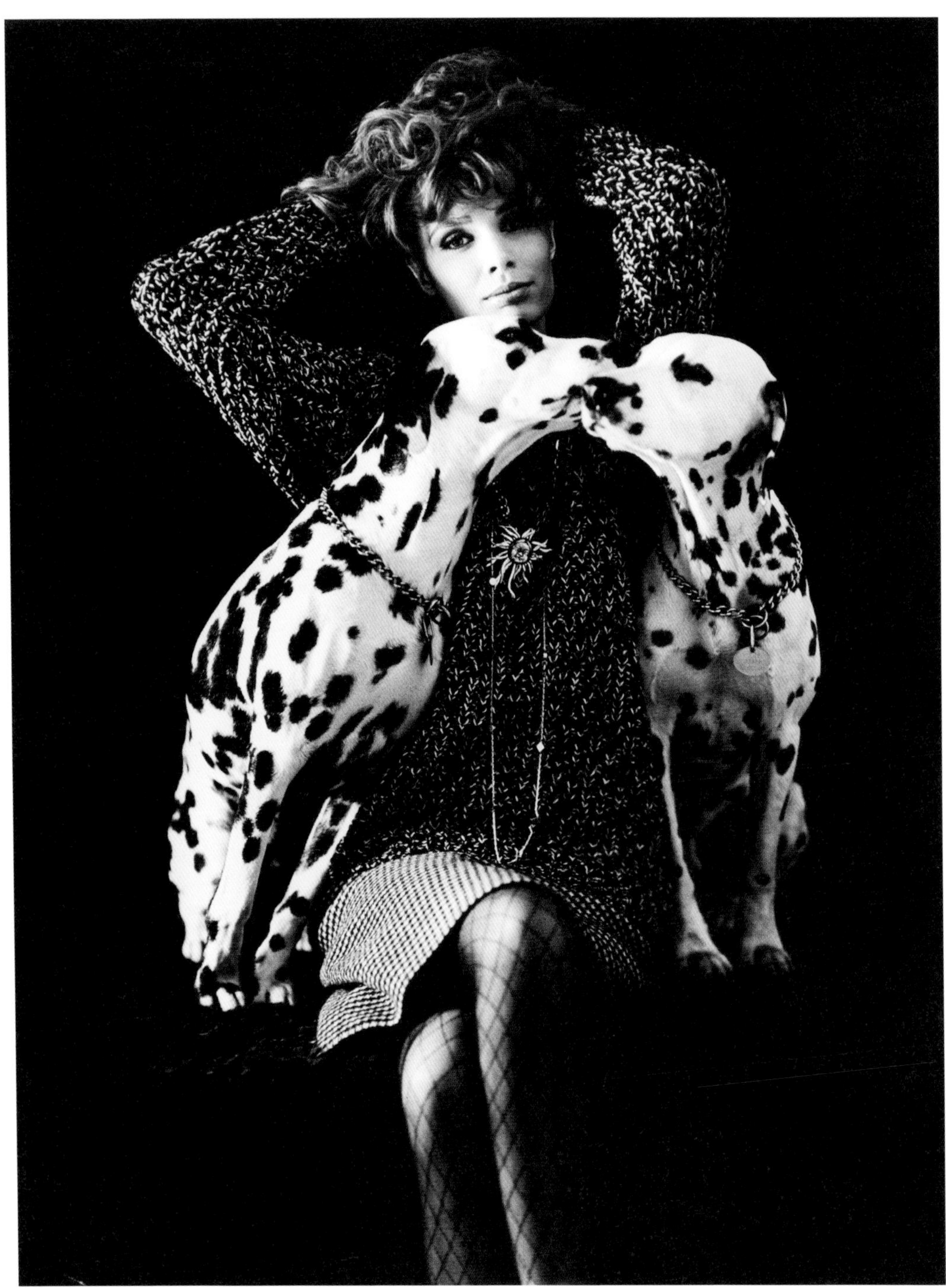

Charlotte March
Das Modell (The Model), 1960–70
Gelatine silver print, 40 × 30.3 cm
Museum für Kunst und Gewerbe Hamburg

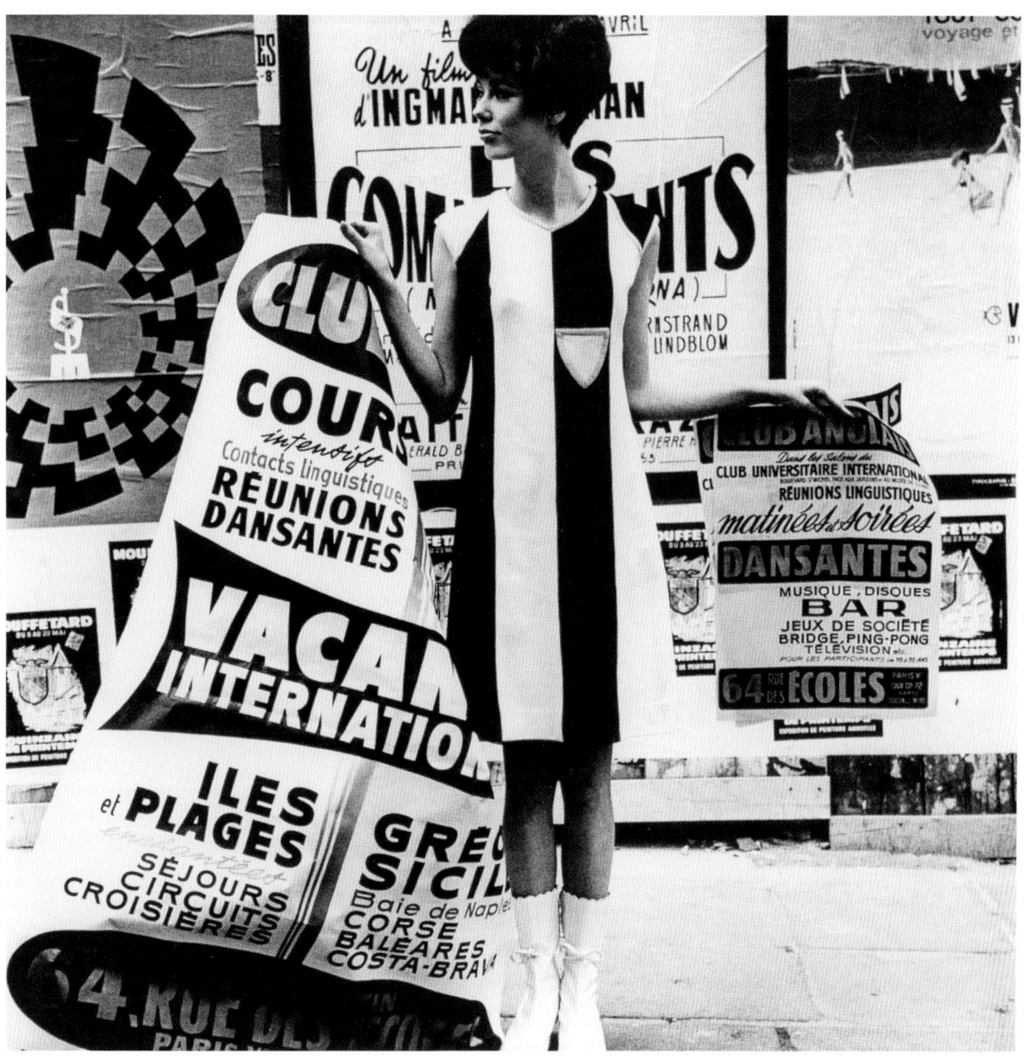

Charlotte March
Paris, Mode Paco Rabanne, 1963
Gelatine silver print, 28.5 × 28.6 cm
Museum für Kunst und Gewerbe Hamburg

Deborah Turbeville

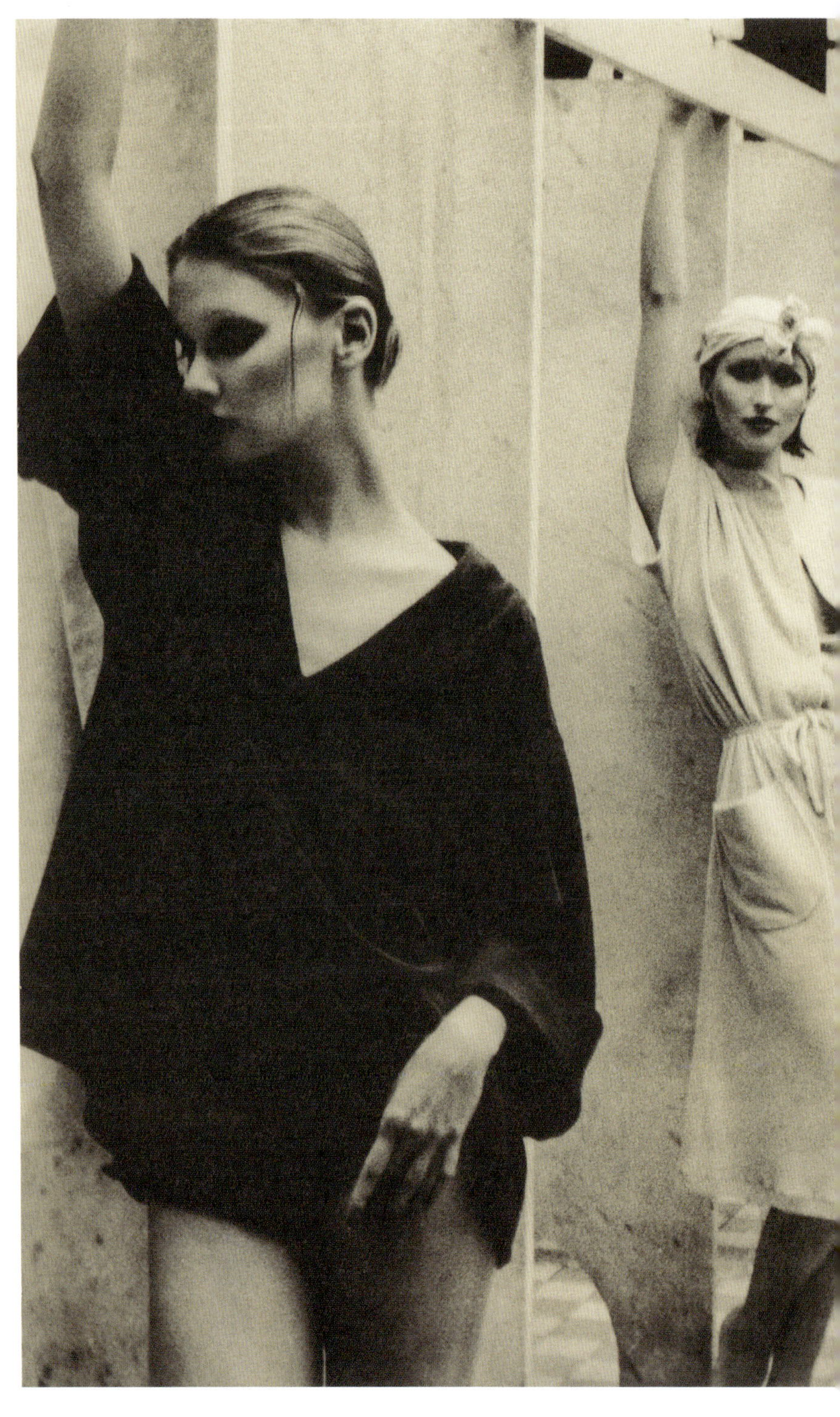

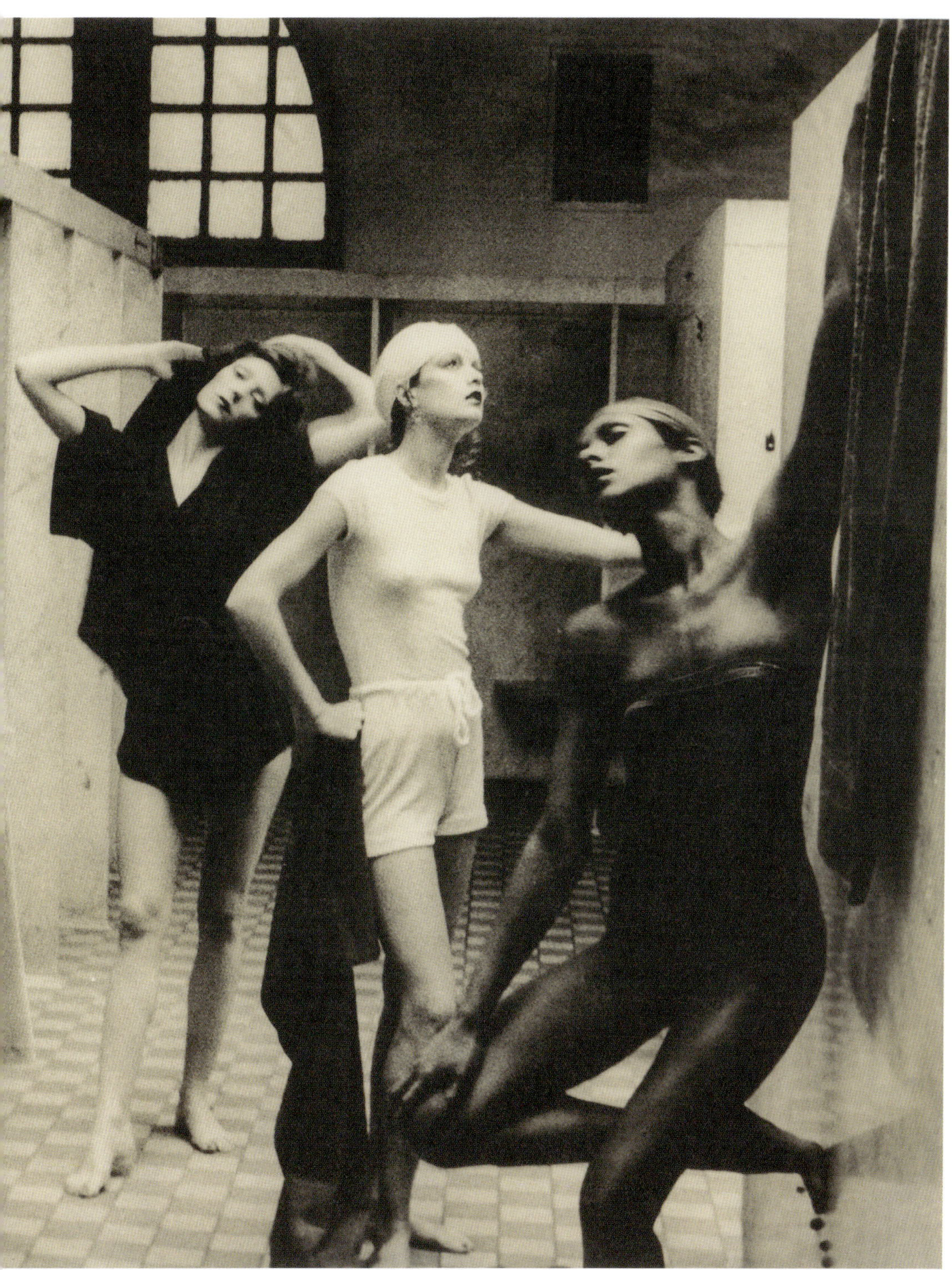

Deborah Turbeville
Untitled, 1970s
Monochrome, 33 × 48.7 cm
Deichtorhallen Hamburg, F.C. Gundlach Collection

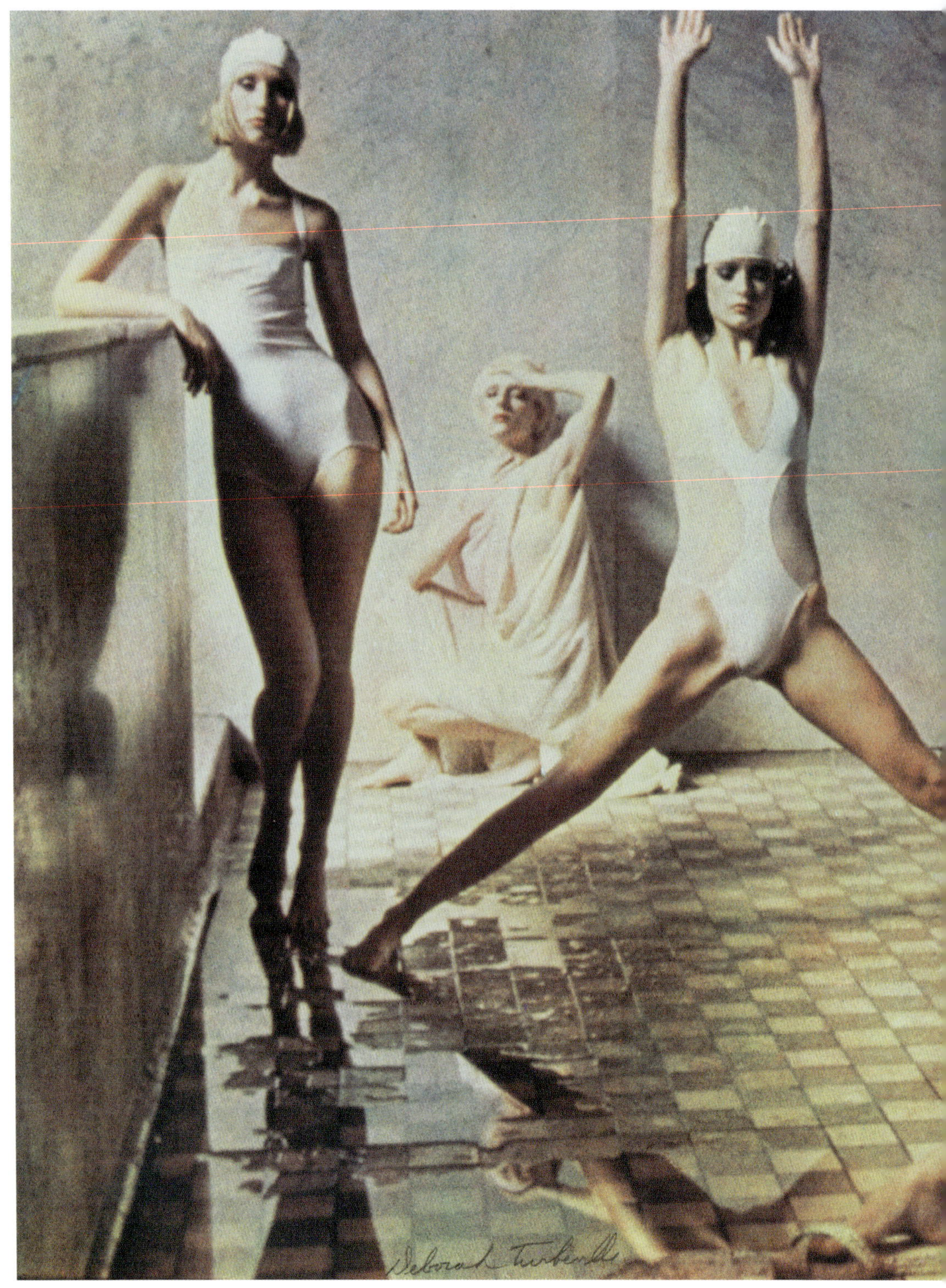

Deborah Turbeville
Bathhouse, American Vogue, 1975
C-Print, 46.7 × 64 cm
Deichtorhallen Hamburg, F.C. Gundlach Collection

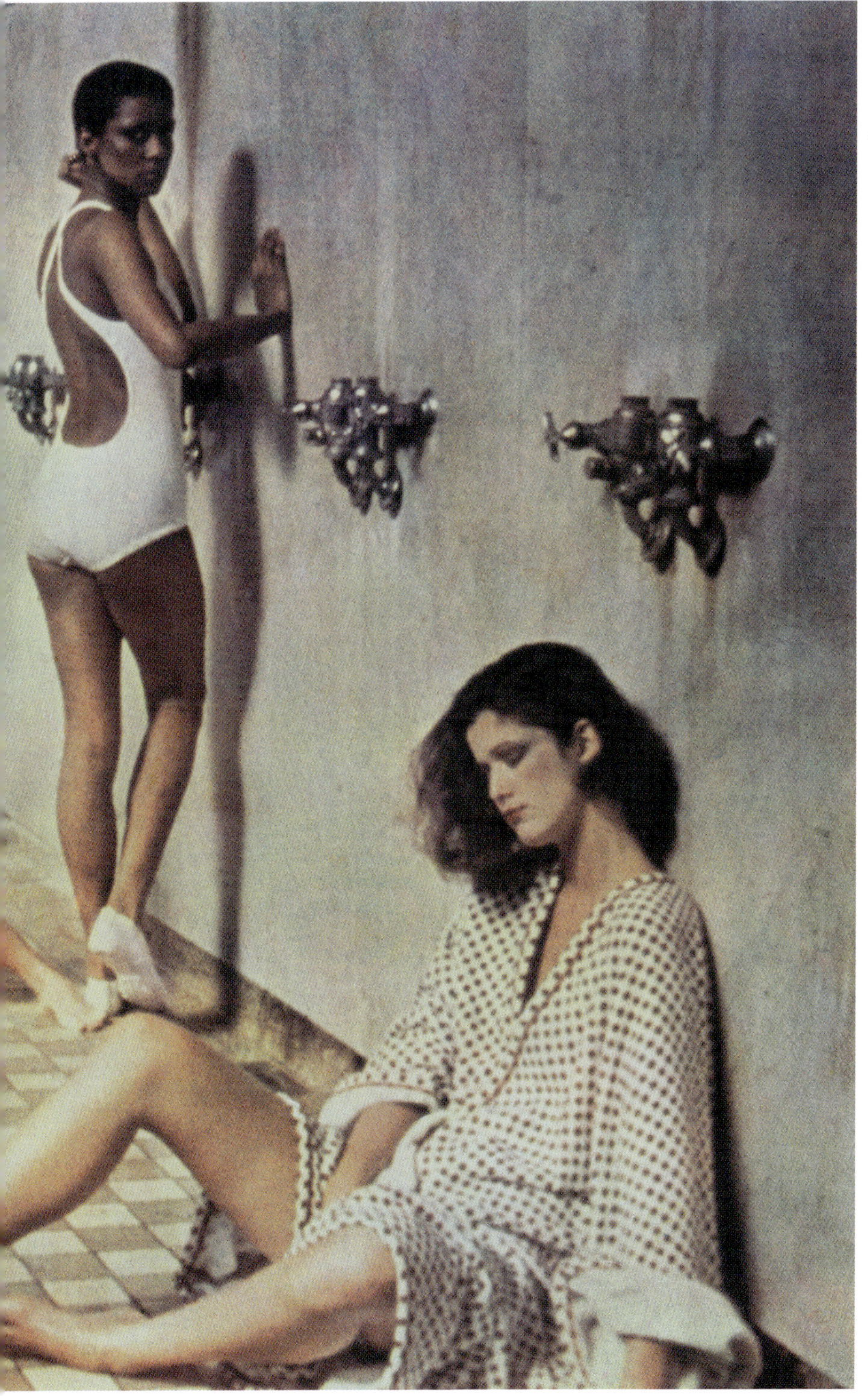

Alice Springs

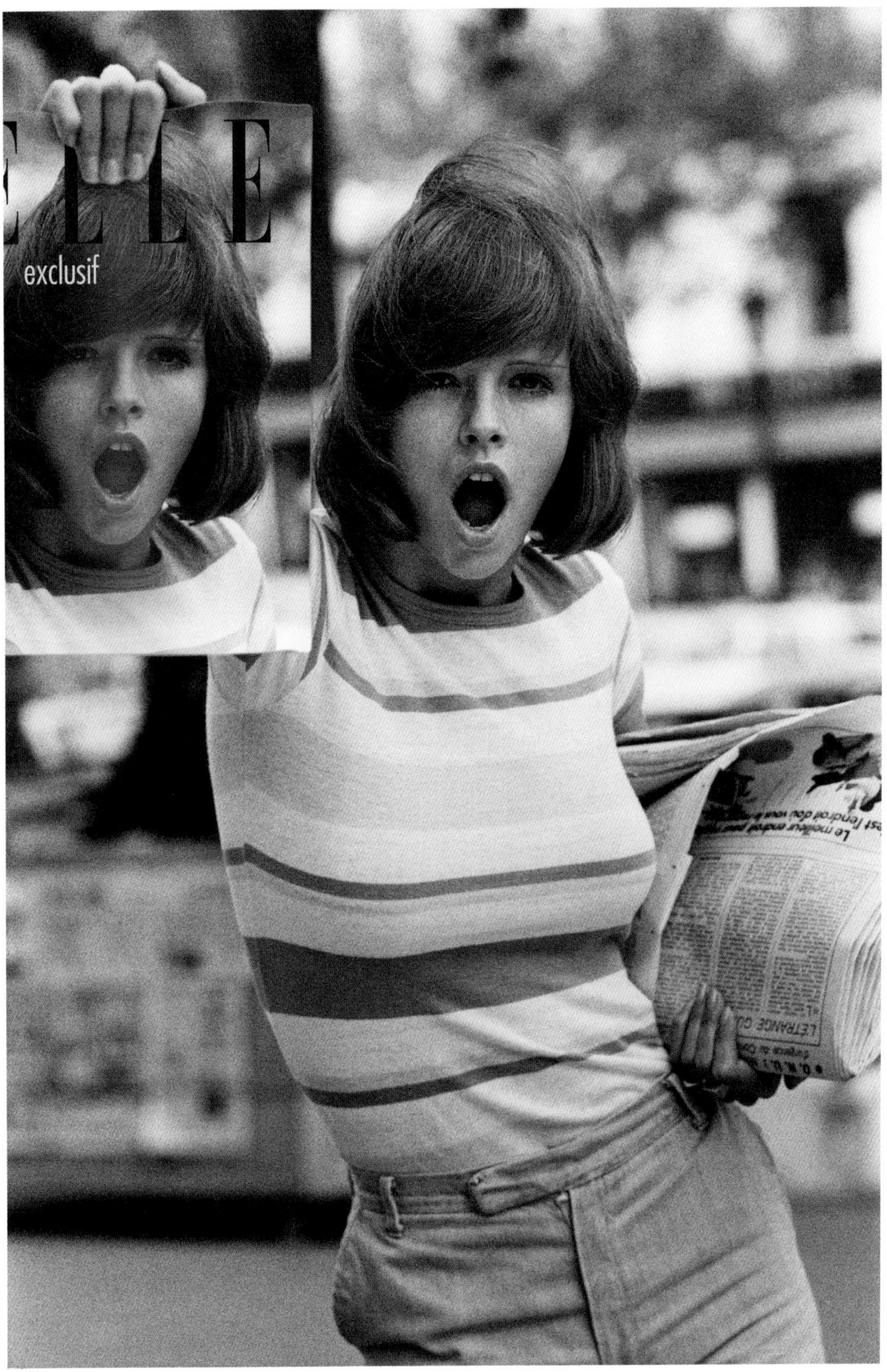

Alice Springs
Jean Louis David, 1970s/2010
Fine art baryte colour print, 80 × 53 cm
Helmut Newton Foundation

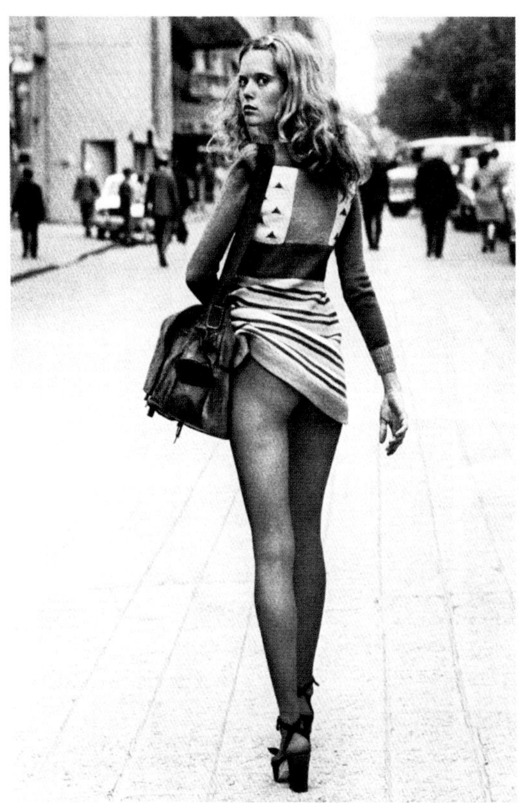

Alice Springs
Depeche Mode, 1971
Fine art baryte colour print, 80 × 53 cm
Helmut Newton Foundation

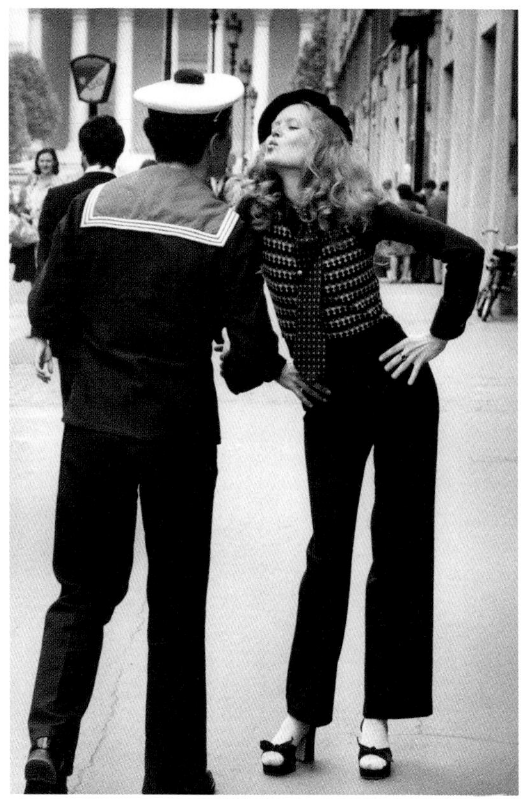

Alice Springs
Depeche Mode, 1971
Fine art baryte colour print, 80 × 53 cm
Helmut Newton Foundation

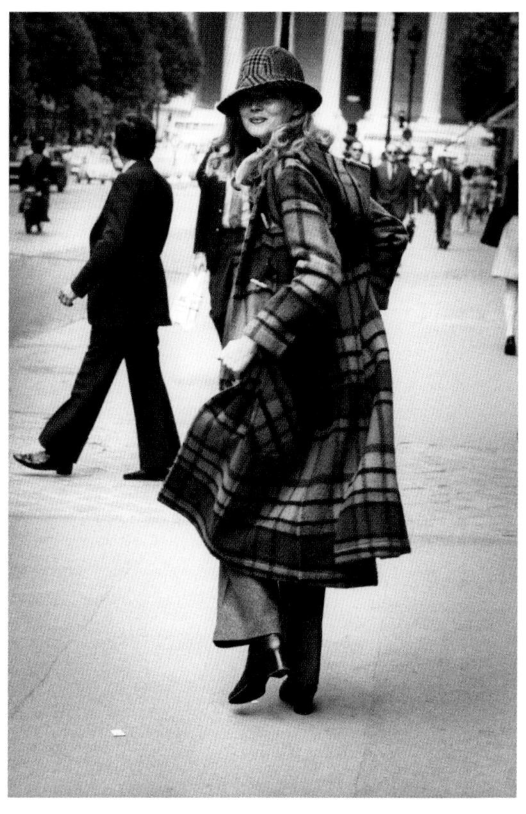

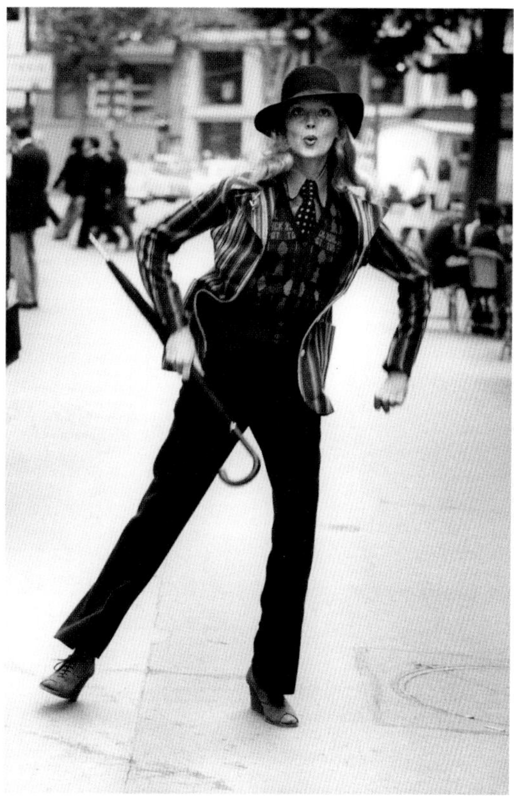

Alice Springs
Depeche Mode, 1971
Fine art baryte colour print, 80 × 53 cm
Helmut Newton Foundation

Alice Springs
Depeche Mode, 1971
Fine art baryte colour print, 80 × 53 cm
Helmut Newton Foundation

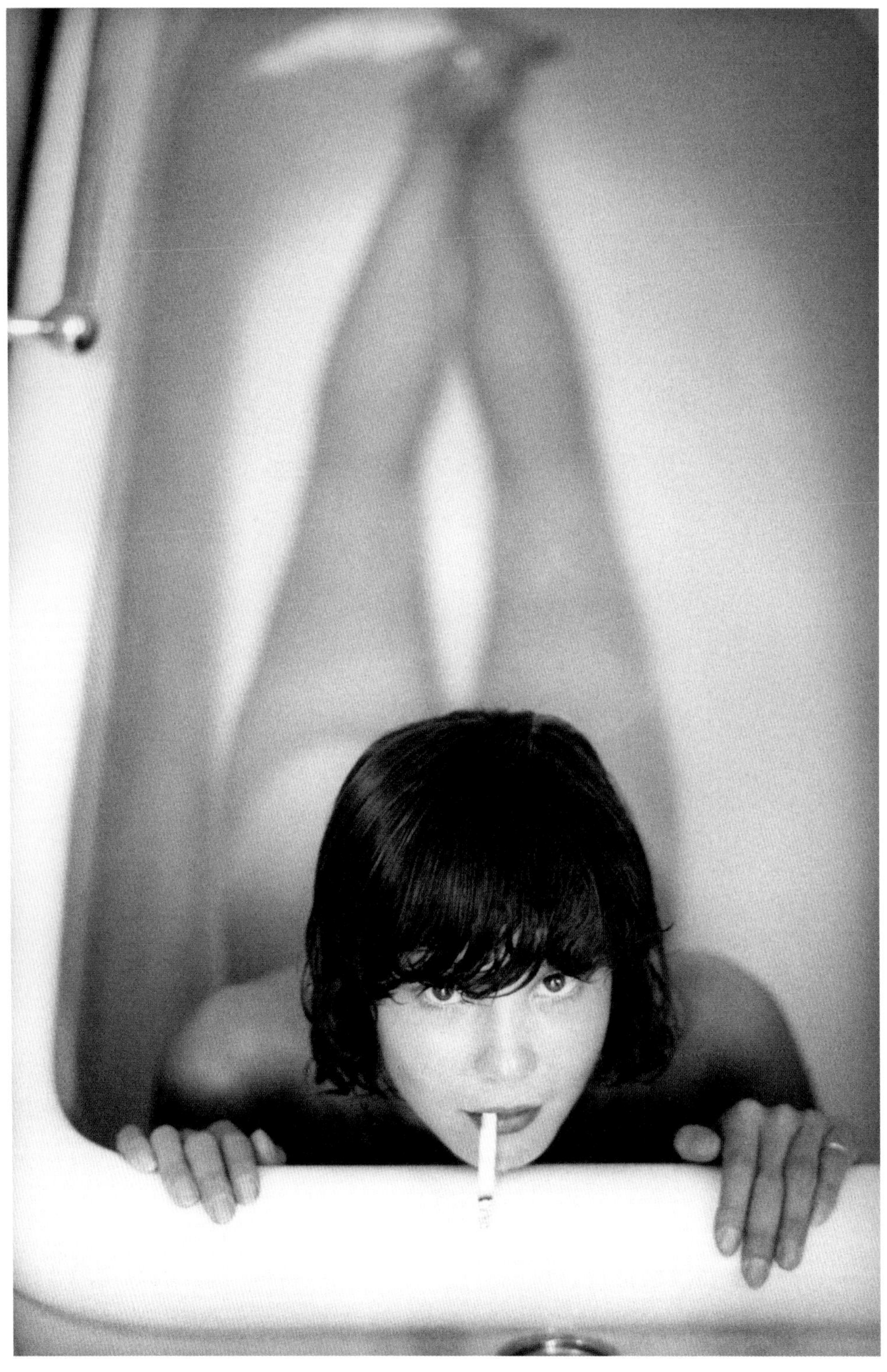

Alice Springs
Jean Louis David, 1970s/2010
Fine art baryte colour print, 80 × 53 cm
Helmut Newton Foundation

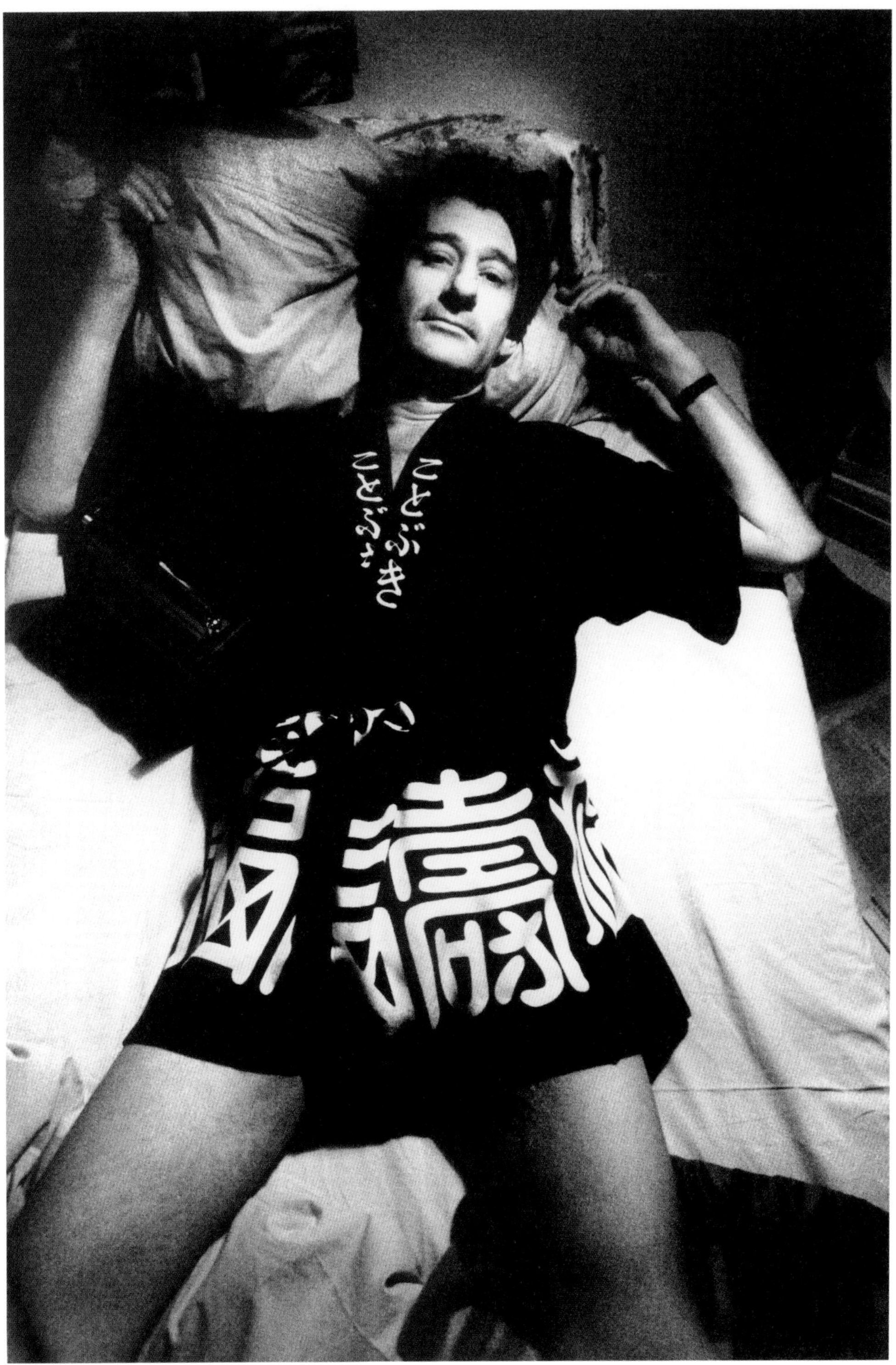

Alice Springs
Helmut Newton, 1970s/2010
Fine art baryte colour print, 120 × 80 cm
Helmut Newton Foundation

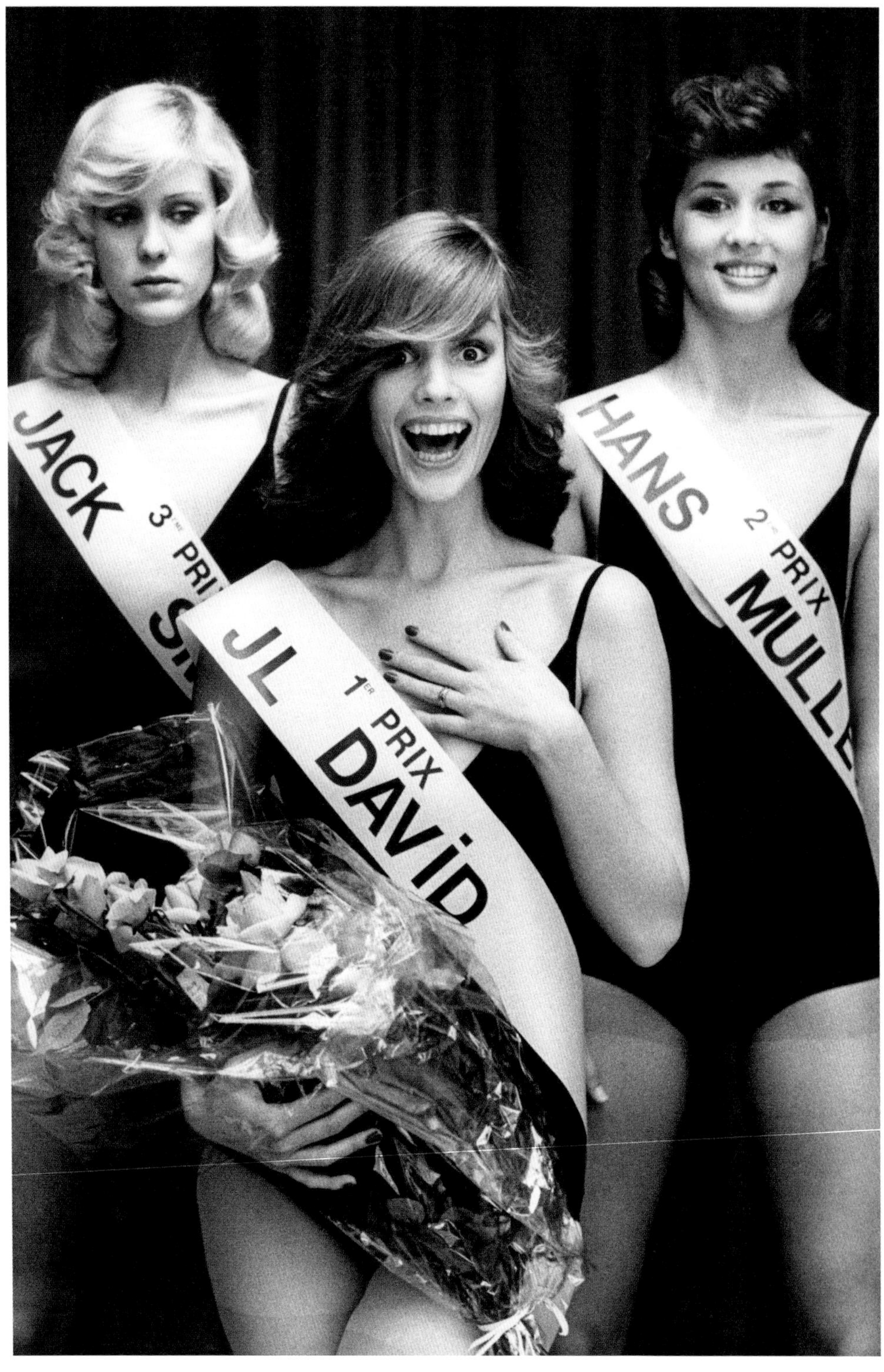

Alice Springs
Jean Louis David, 1970s/2010
Fine art baryte colour print, 80 × 53 cm
Helmut Newton Foundation

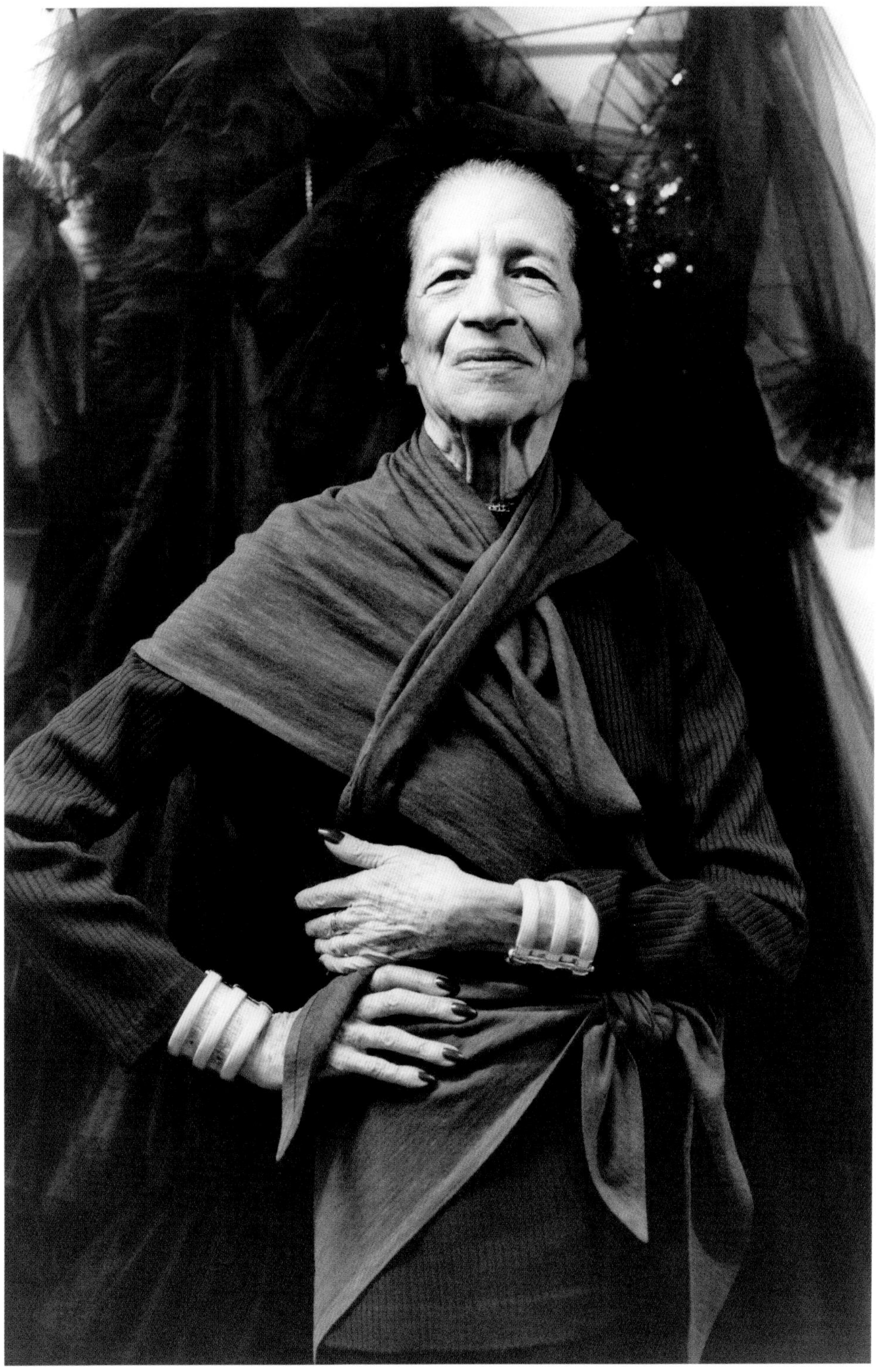

Alice Springs
Diana Vreeland, 1984
Fine art baryte colour print, 106.6 × 72.6 cm
Helmut Newton Foundation

Ute Mahler

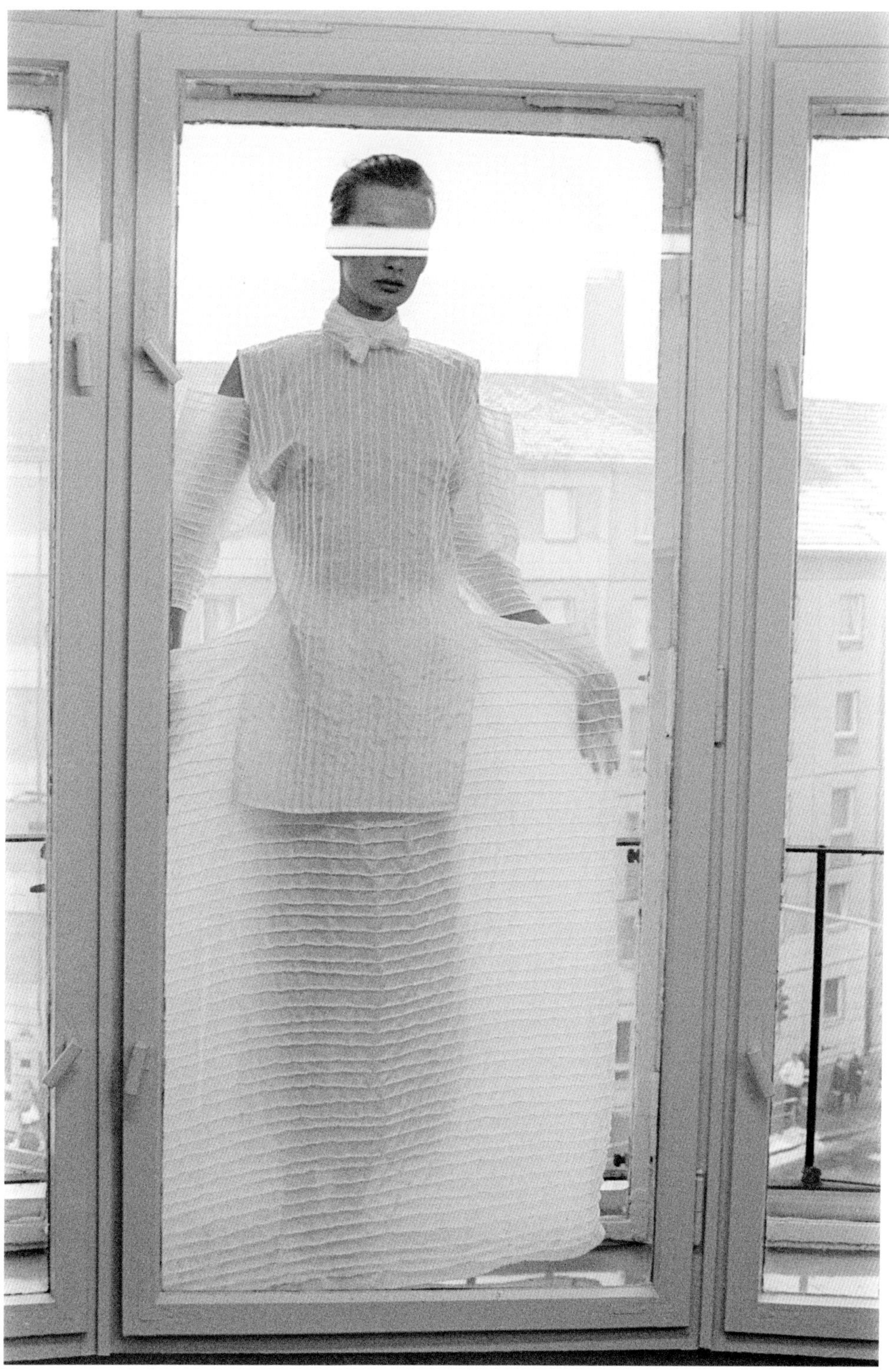

Ute Mahler
Katharina, Berlin 1990, 1990
Gelatine silver print, 45 × 30 cm
Ute Mahler

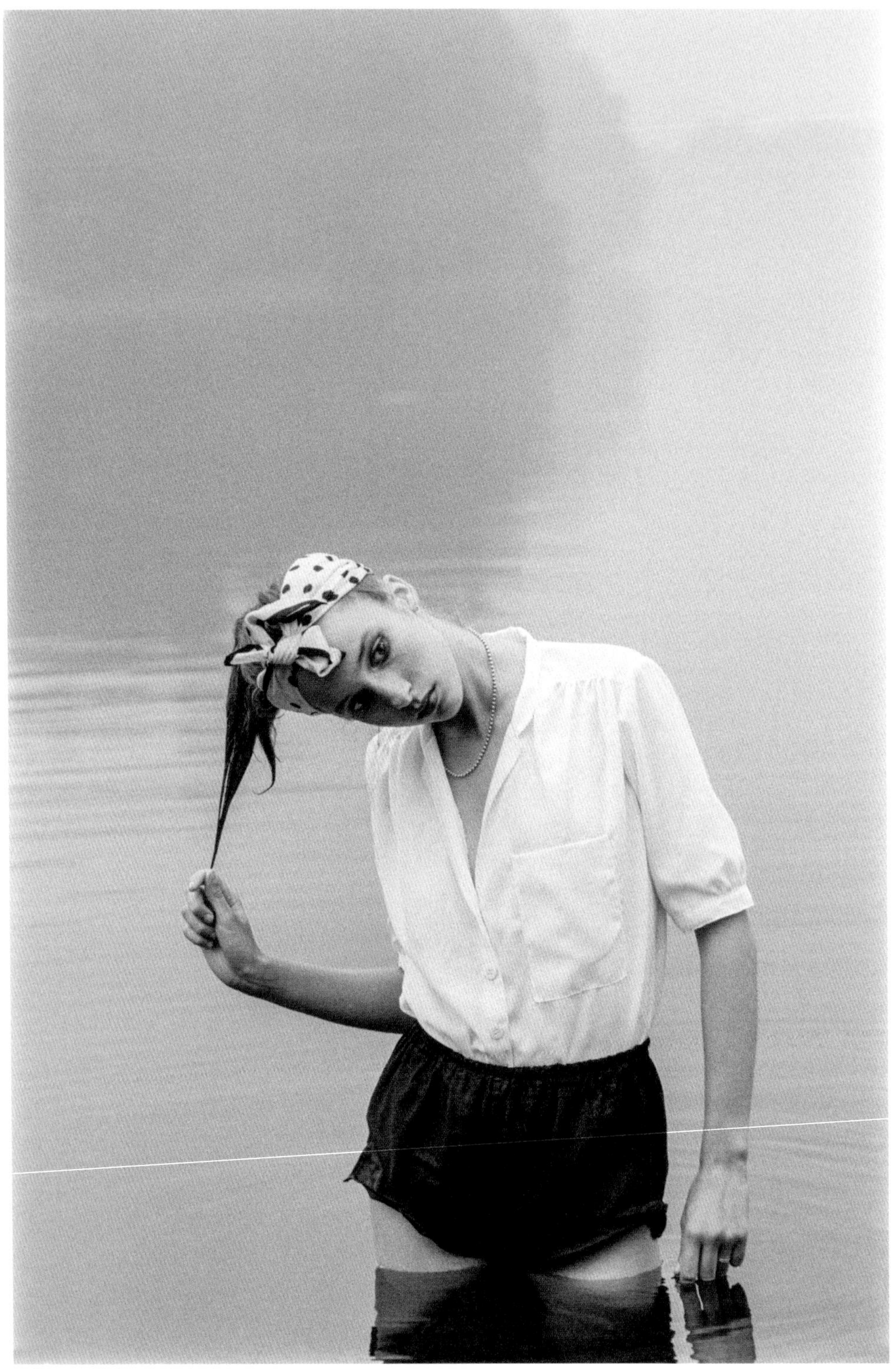

Ute Mahler
Julia, Lehnitz 1979, 1979
Gelatine silver print, 45 × 30 cm
Ute Mahler

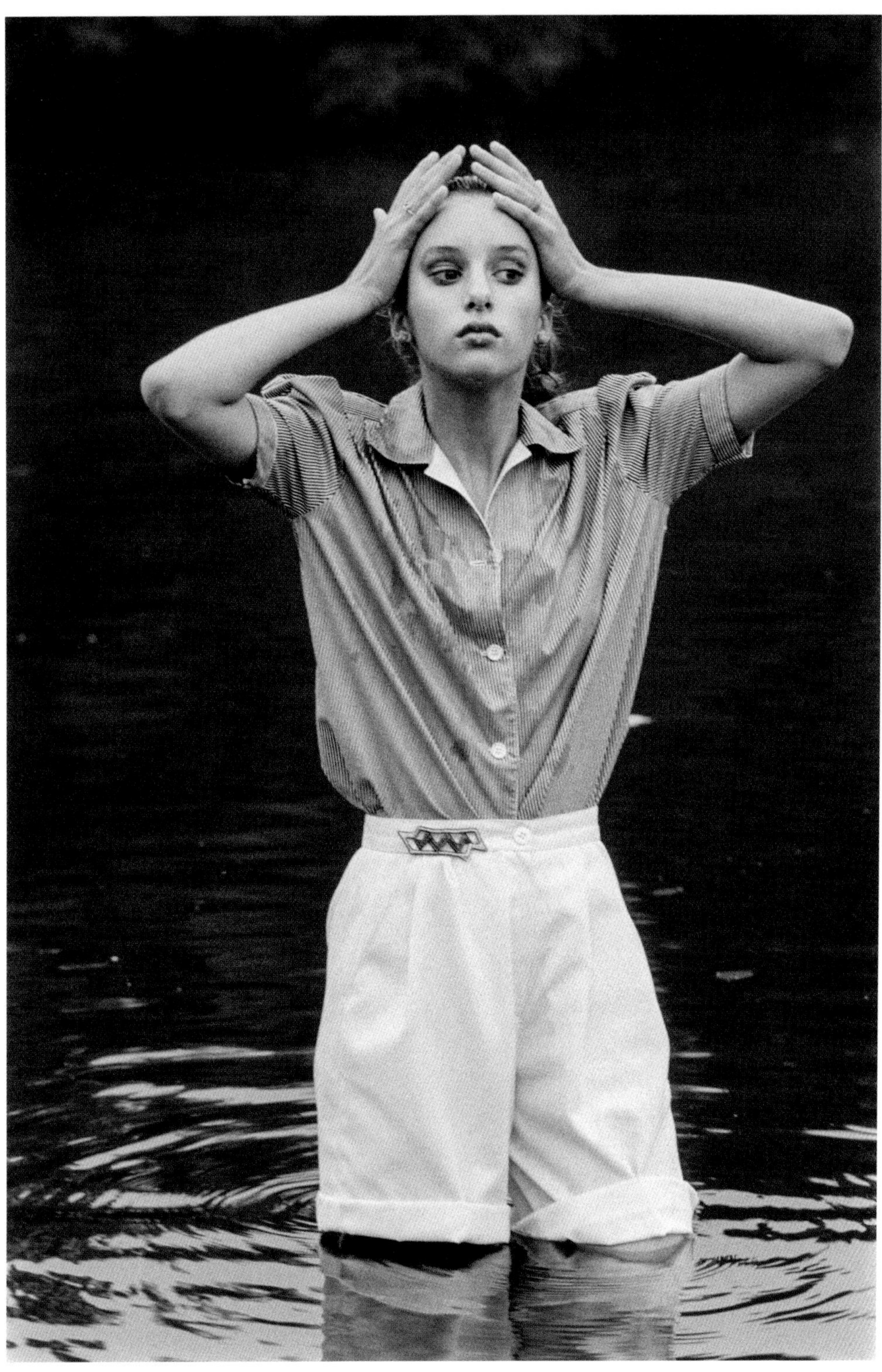

Ute Mahler
Julia, Lehnitz 1979, 1979
Gelatine silver print, 45 × 30 cm
Ute Mahler

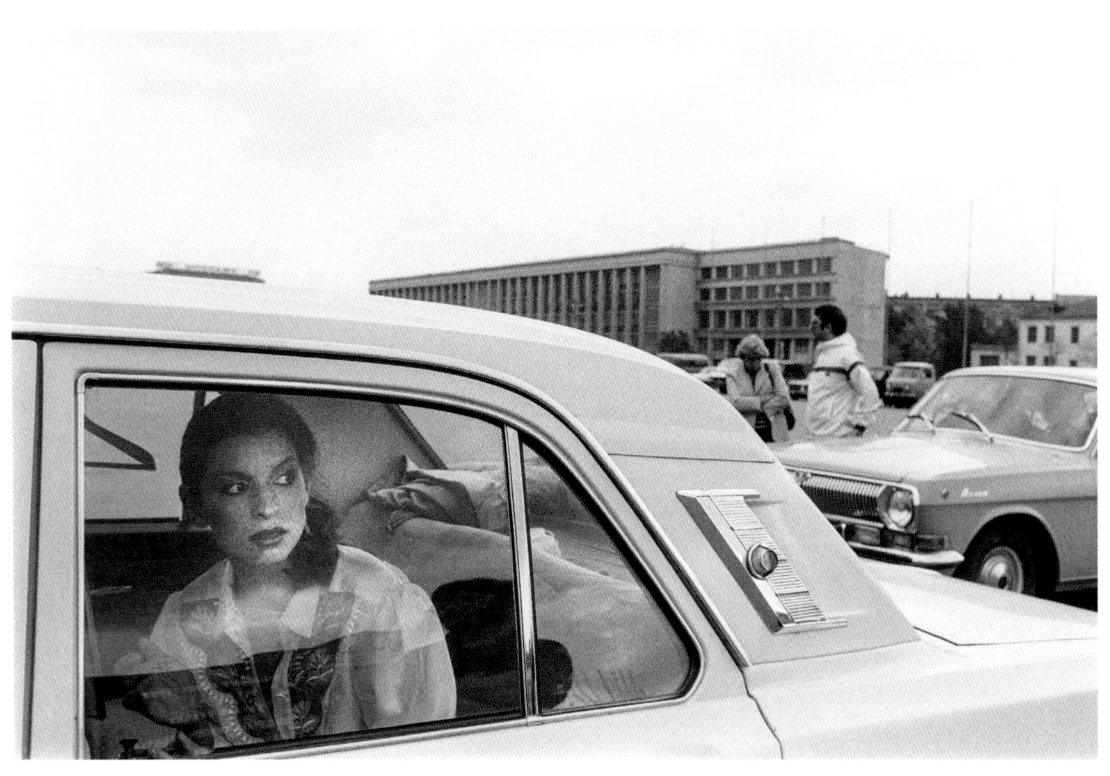

Ute Mahler
Elke, Minsk 1981, 1981
Gelatine silver print, 30 × 45 cm
Ute Mahler

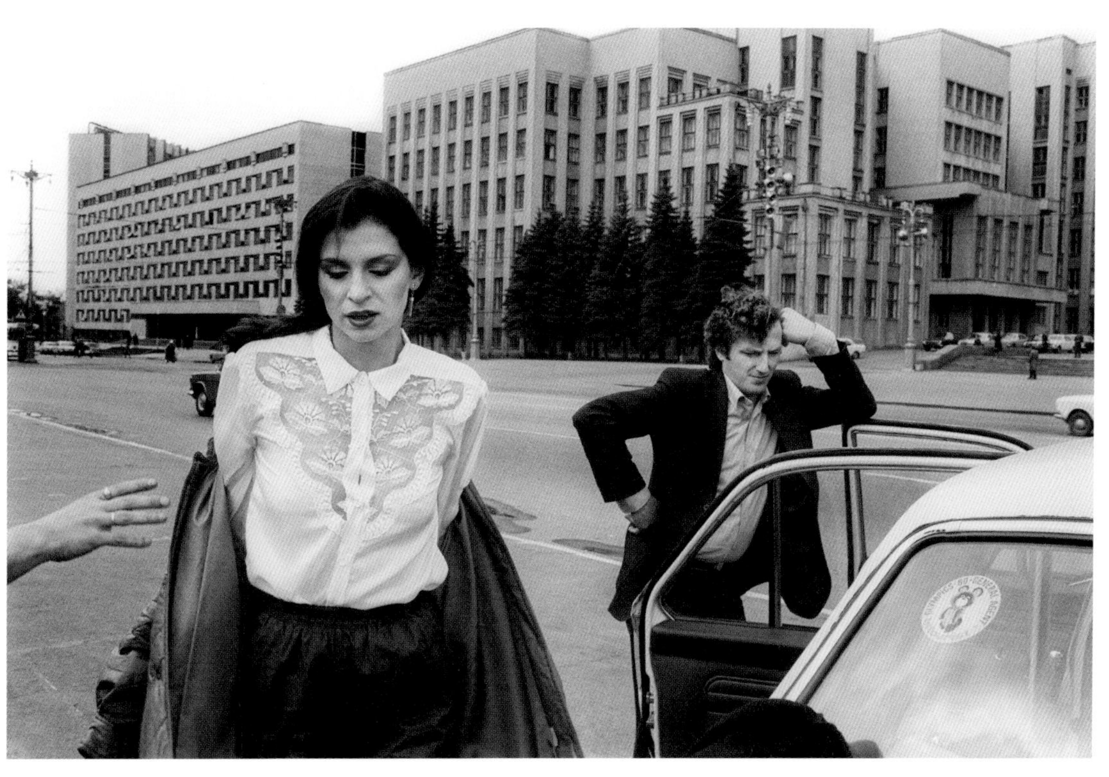

Ute Mahler
Elke, Minsk 1981, 1981
Gelatine silver print, 30 × 45 cm
Ute Mahler

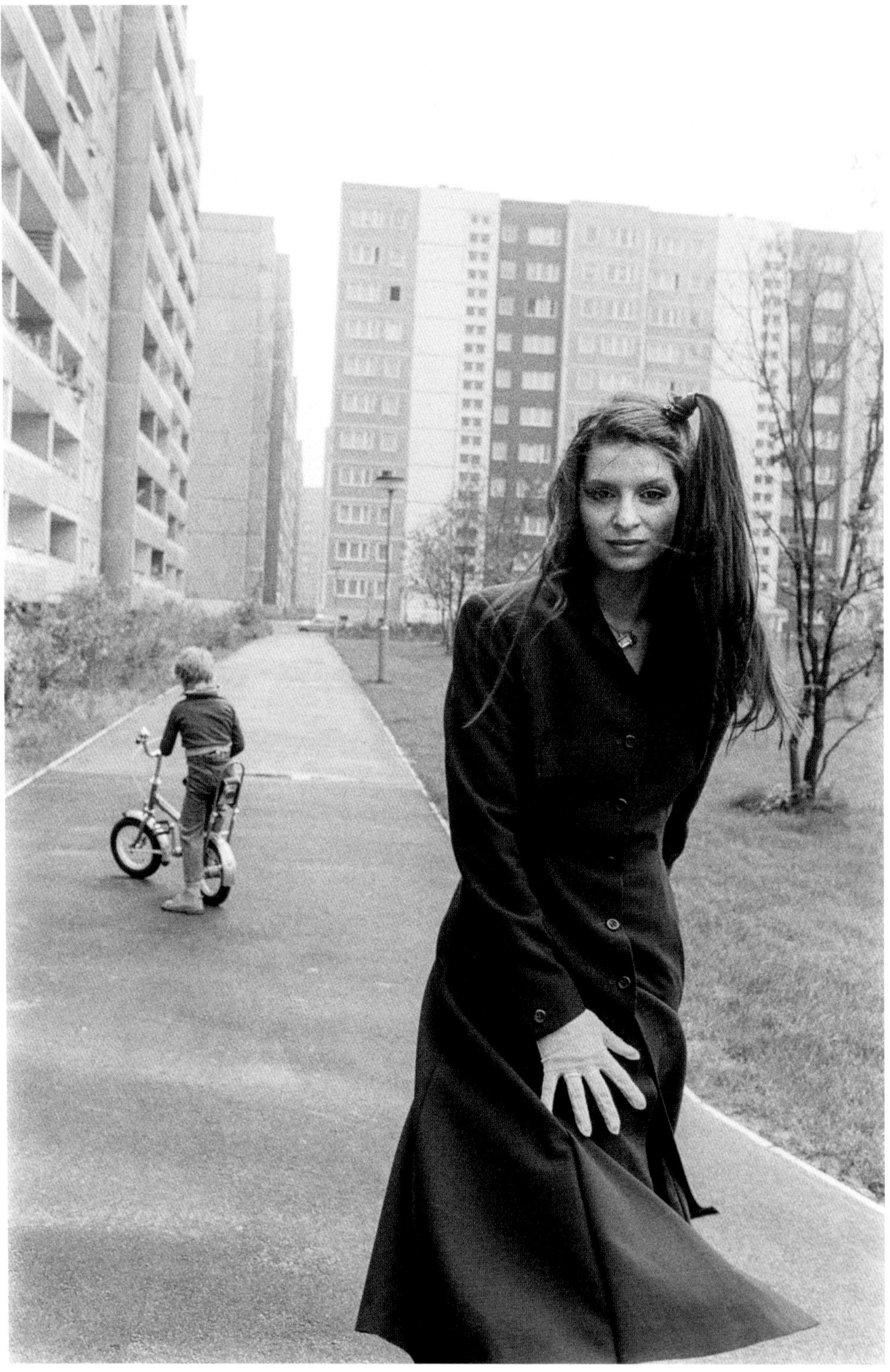

Ute Mahler
Elke, Berlin-Marzahn 1980, 1980
Gelatine silver print, 45 × 30 cm
Ute Mahler

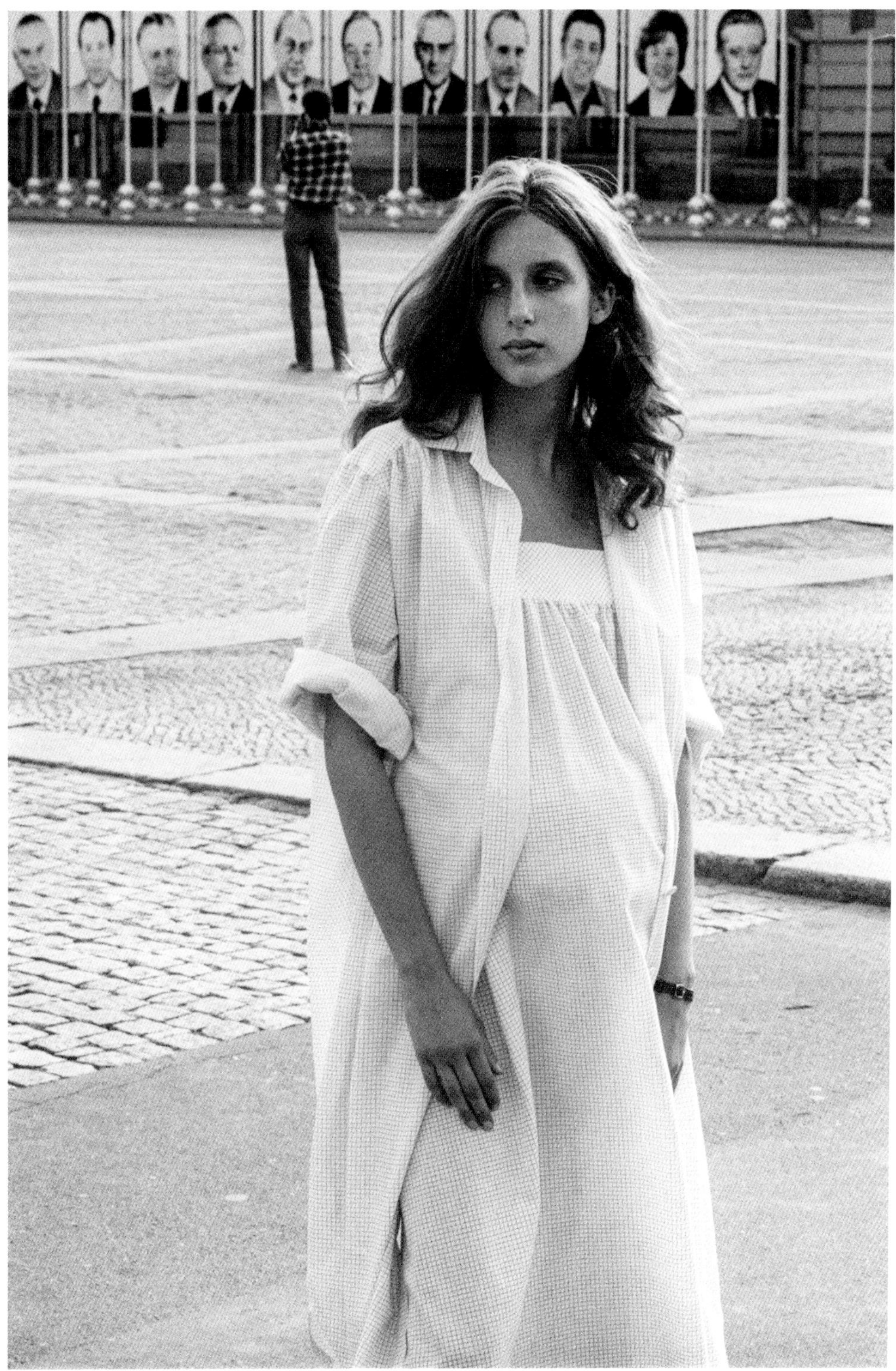

Ute Mahler
Julia, Berlin Bebelplatz 1981, 1981
Gelatine silver print, 45 × 30 cm
Ute Mahler

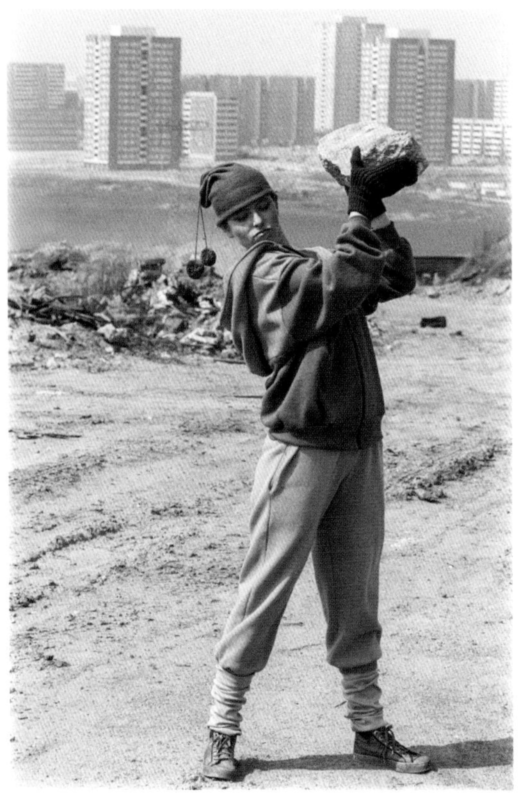

Ute Mahler
Marisa, Berlin-Marzahn 1983, 1983
Gelatine silver print, 18 × 12 cm
Ute Mahler

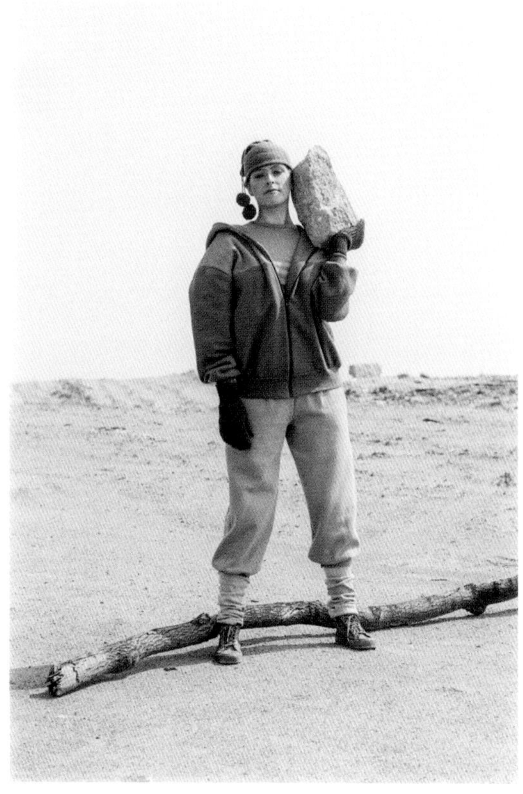

Ute Mahler
Marisa, Berlin-Marzahn 1983, 1983
Gelatine silver print, 18 × 12 cm
Ute Mahler

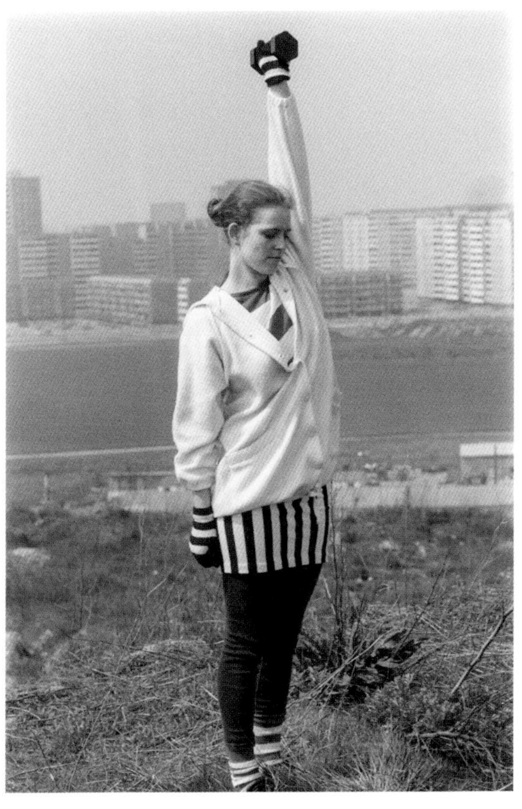

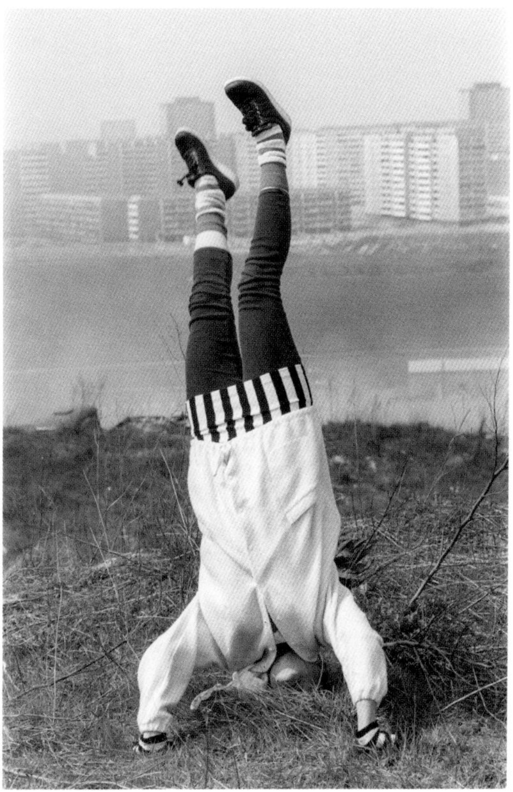

Ute Mahler
Marisa, Berlin-Marzahn 1983, 1983
Gelatine silver print, 18 × 12 cm
Ute Mahler

Ute Mahler
Marisa, Berlin-Marzahn 1983, 1983
Gelatine silver print, 18 × 12 cm
Ute Mahler

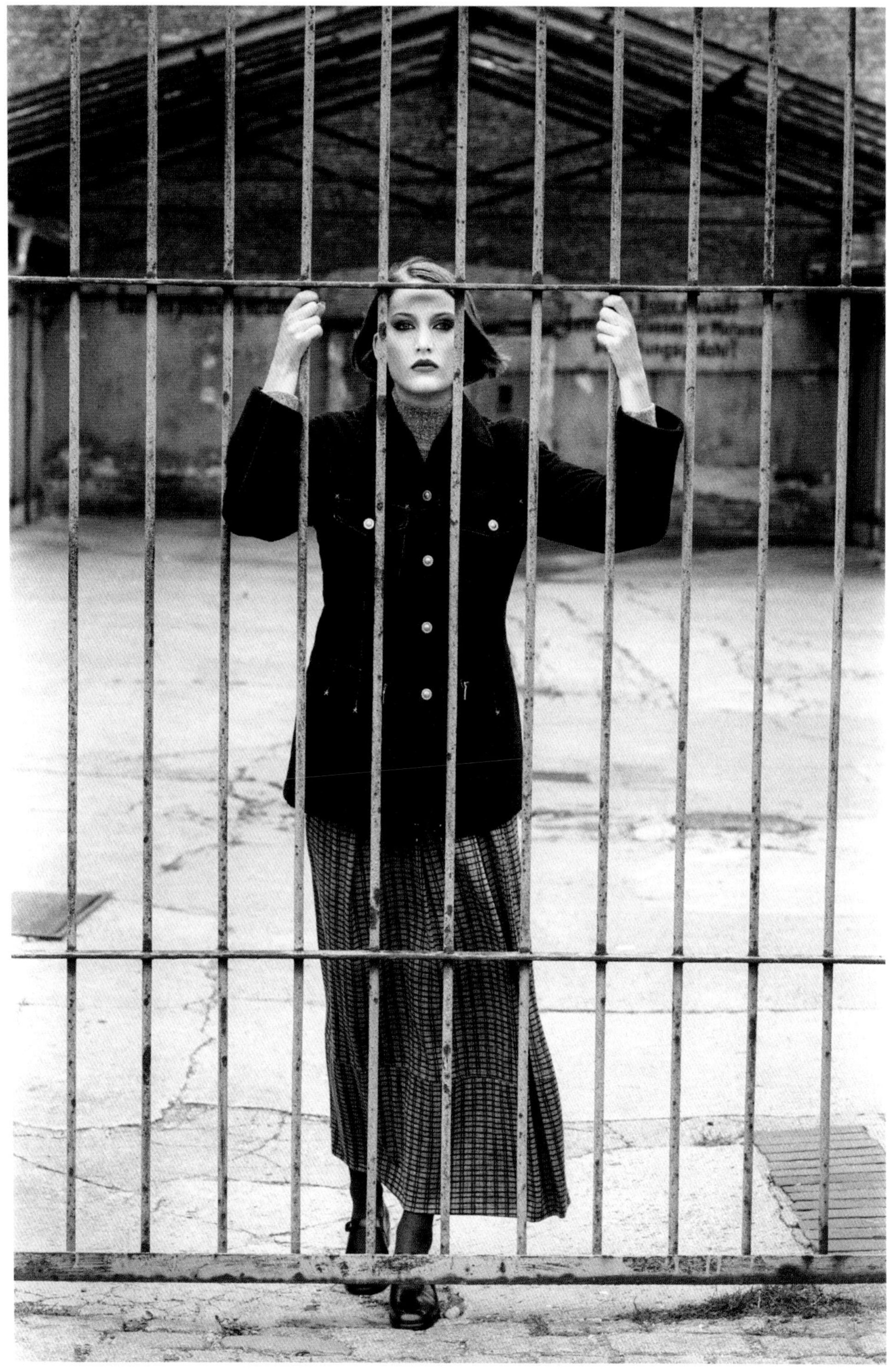

Ute Mahler
Stephanie, Prenzlauer Berg 1994, 1994
Gelatine silver print, 45 × 30 cm
Ute Mahler

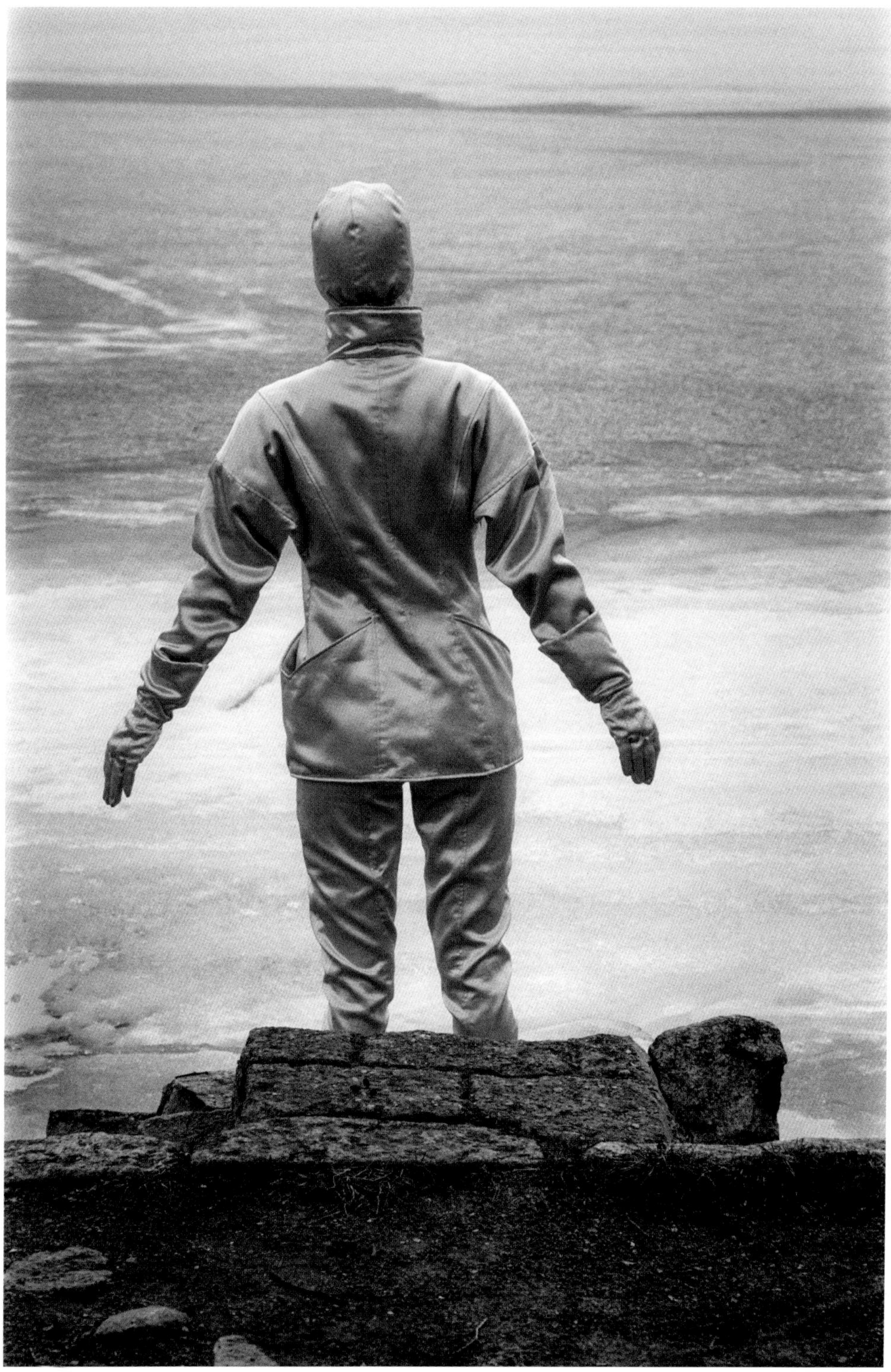

Ute Mahler
Jeanette, Lehnitz 1986, 1986
Gelatine silver print, 45 × 30 cm
Ute Mahler

Sibylle Bergemann

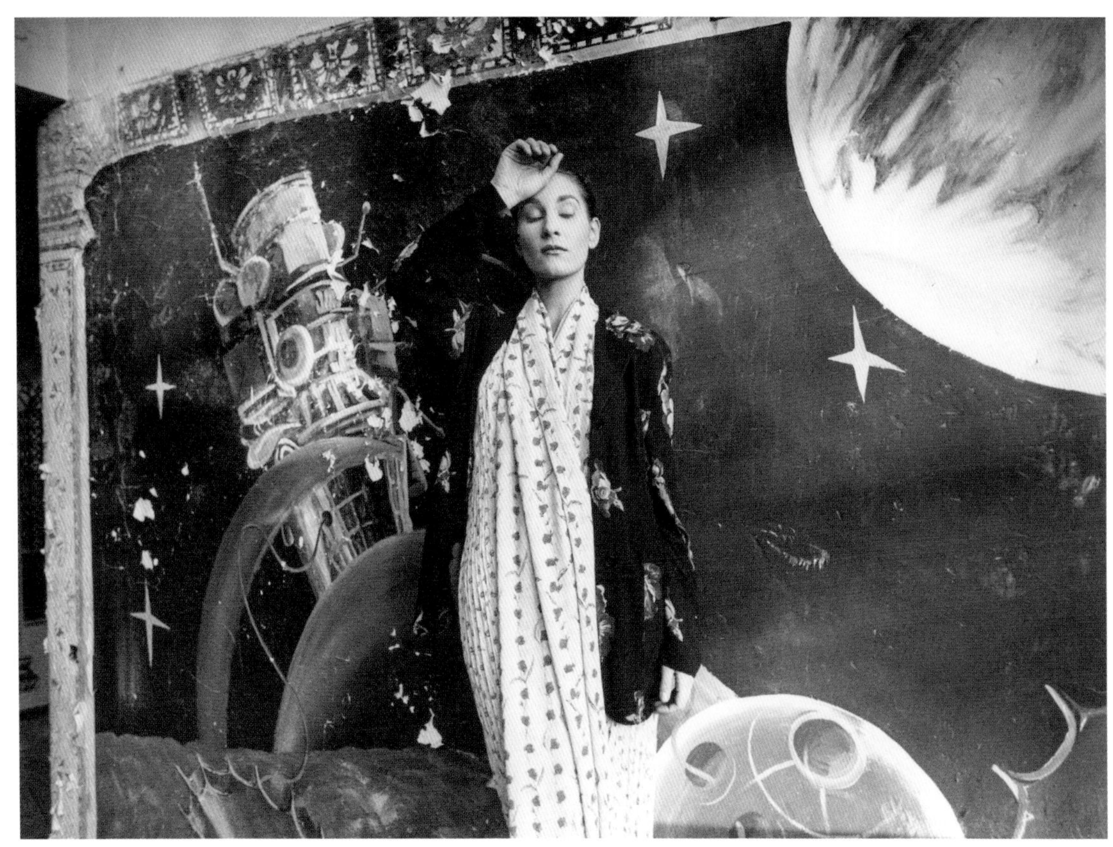

Sibylle Bergemann
Jüterbog 1984, 1984
Gelatine silver print, 28.6 × 38.8 cm
Deichtorhallen Hamburg, F.C. Gundlach Collection

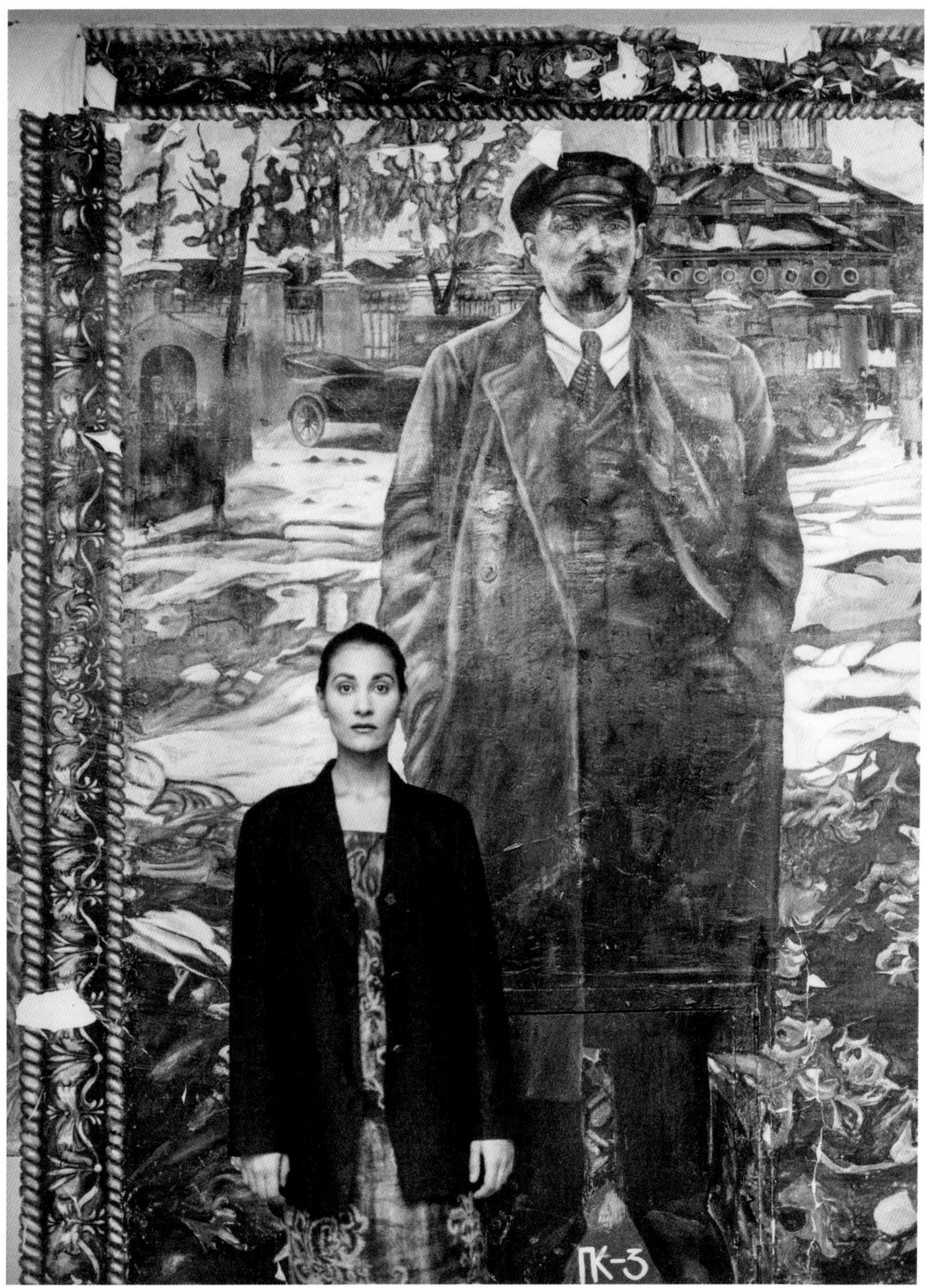

Sibylle Bergemann
Jüterbog 1994, 1994
Gelatine silver print, 39 × 28.9 cm
Deichtorhallen Hamburg, F.C. Gundlach Collection

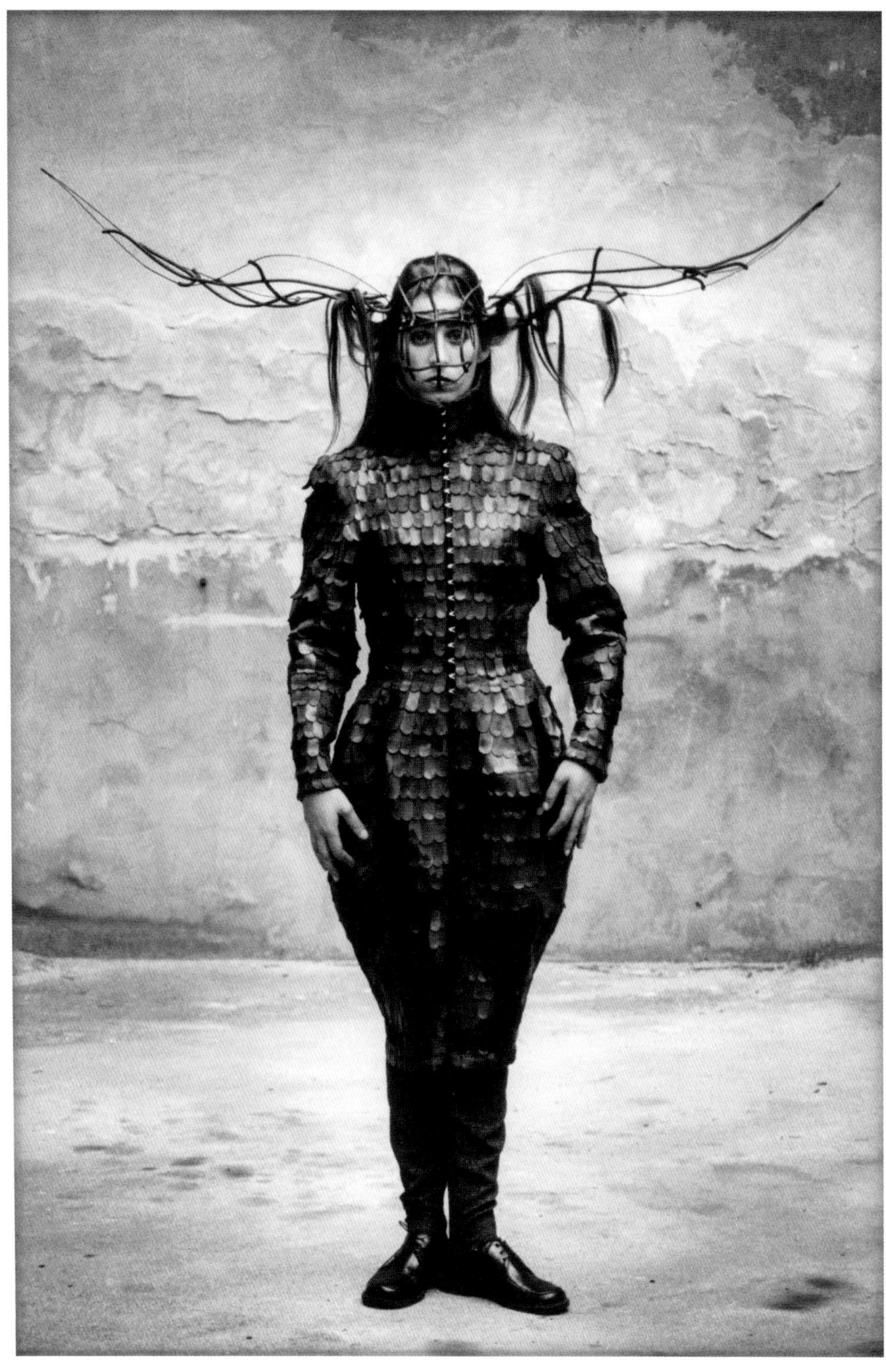

Sibylle Bergemann
Katharina Reinwald, 1989
Gelatine silver print, 38 × 25.4 cm
Deichtorhallen Hamburg, F.C. Gundlach Collection

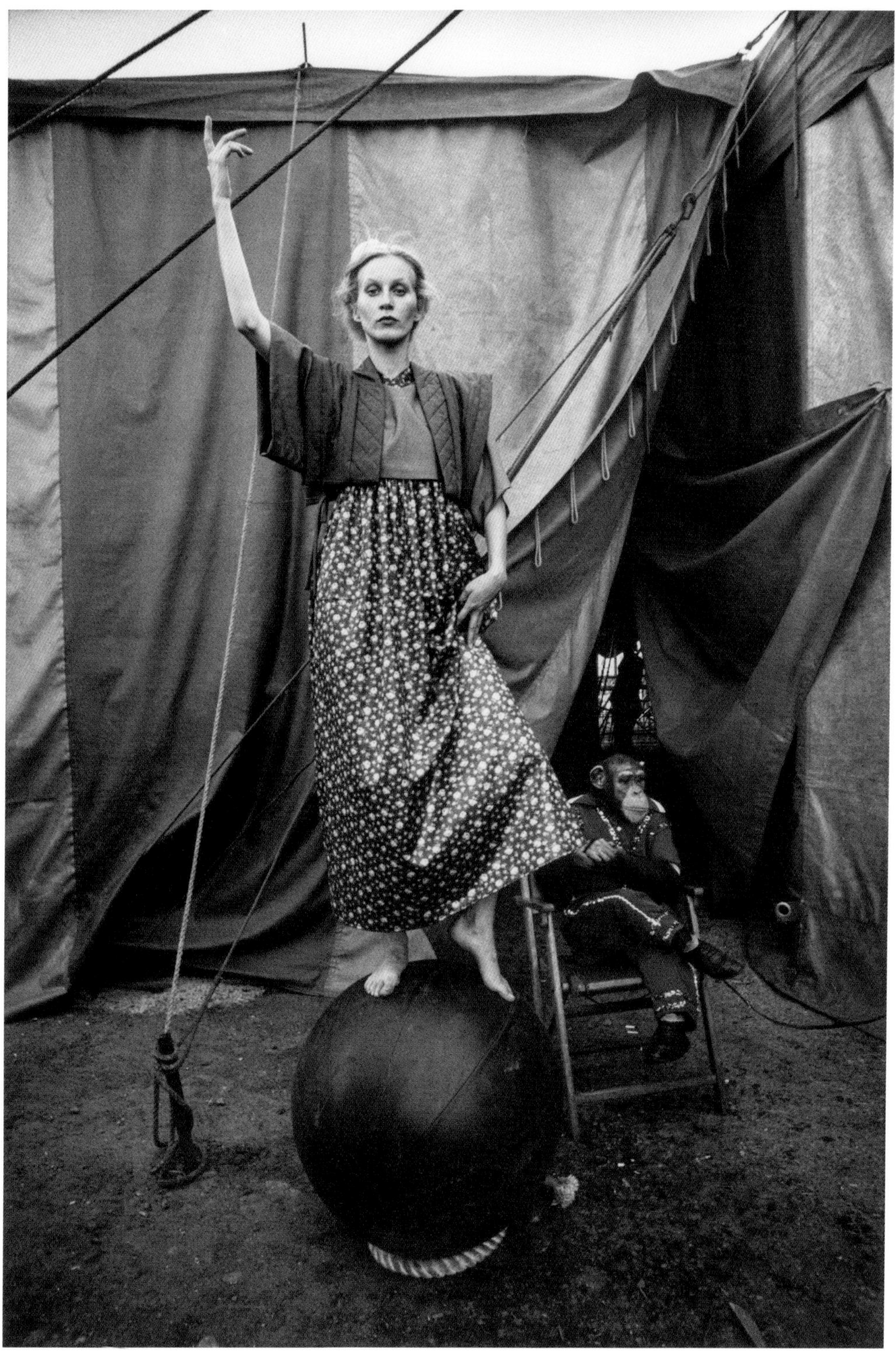

Sibylle Bergemann
Untitled, 1976
Gelatine silver print, 37.5 × 25.5 cm
Deichtorhallen Hamburg, F.C. Gundlach Collection

Sarah Moon

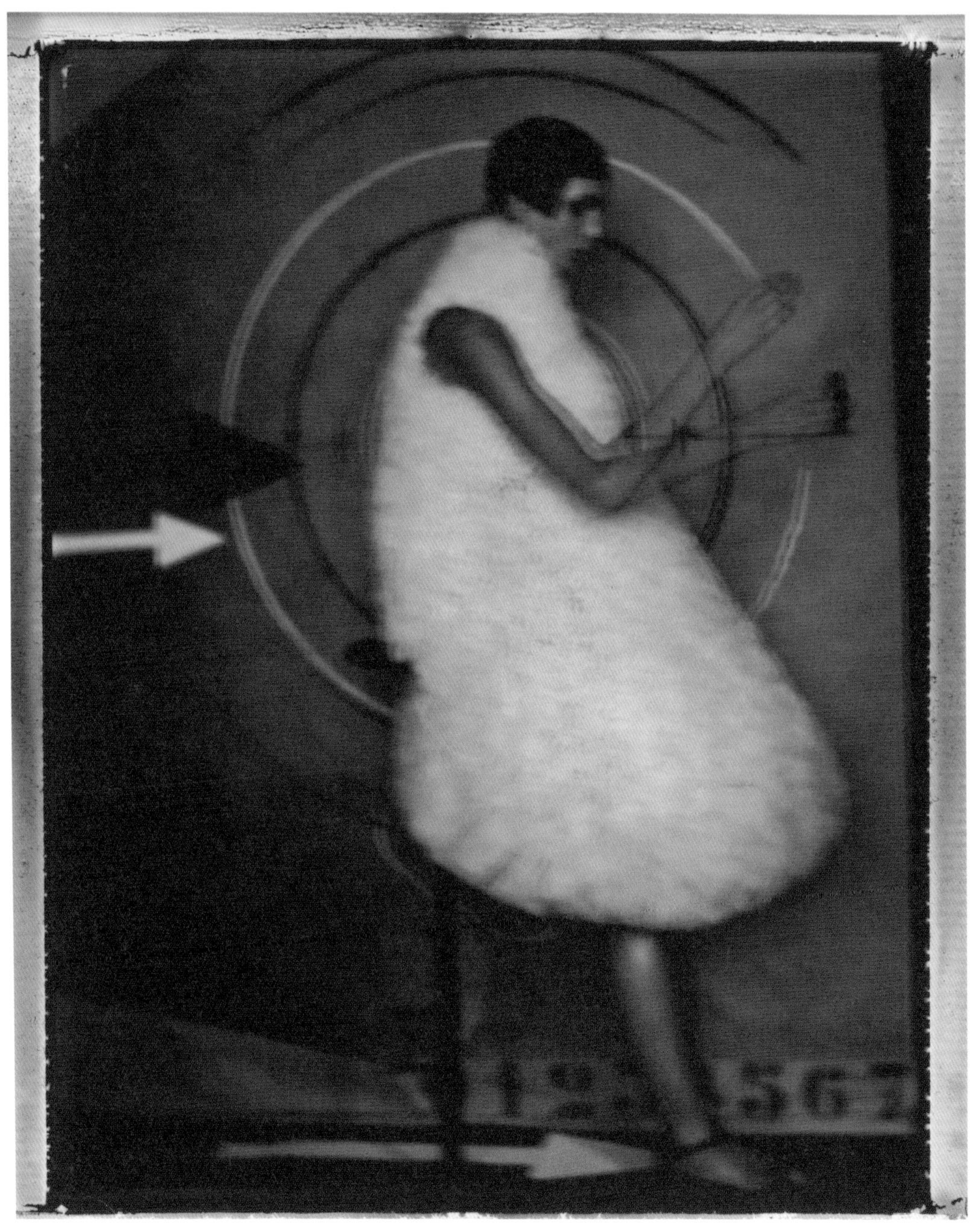

Sarah Moon
The Clock, 1998
Polaroid, 32.6 × 26.8 cm
Deichtorhallen Hamburg, F.C. Gundlach Collection

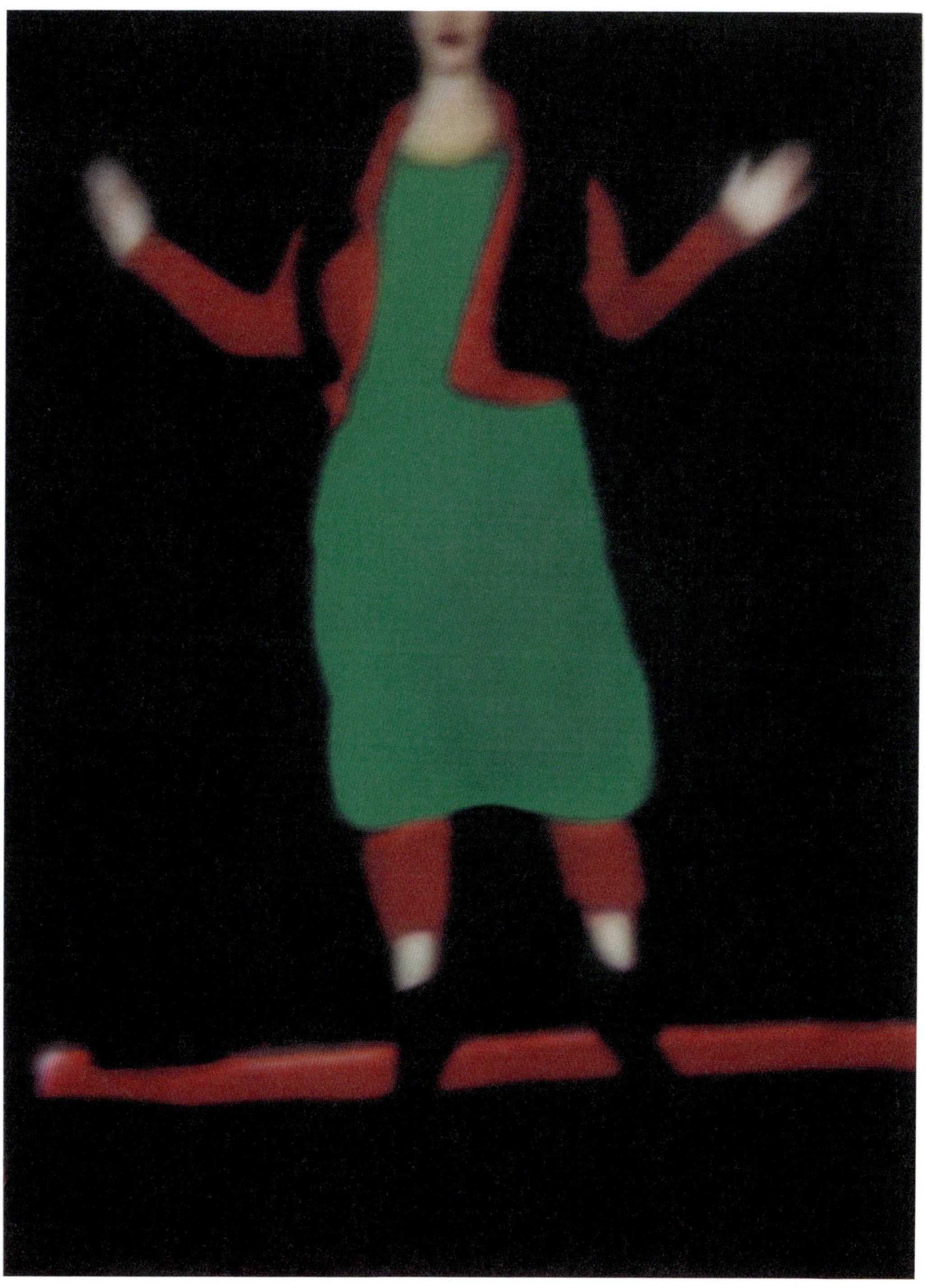

Sarah Moon
Fashion I, Issey Miyake, 1995
Colour pigment transfer print, c. 59.5 × 44.2 cm
Deichtorhallen Hamburg, F.C. Gundlach Collection

GABO

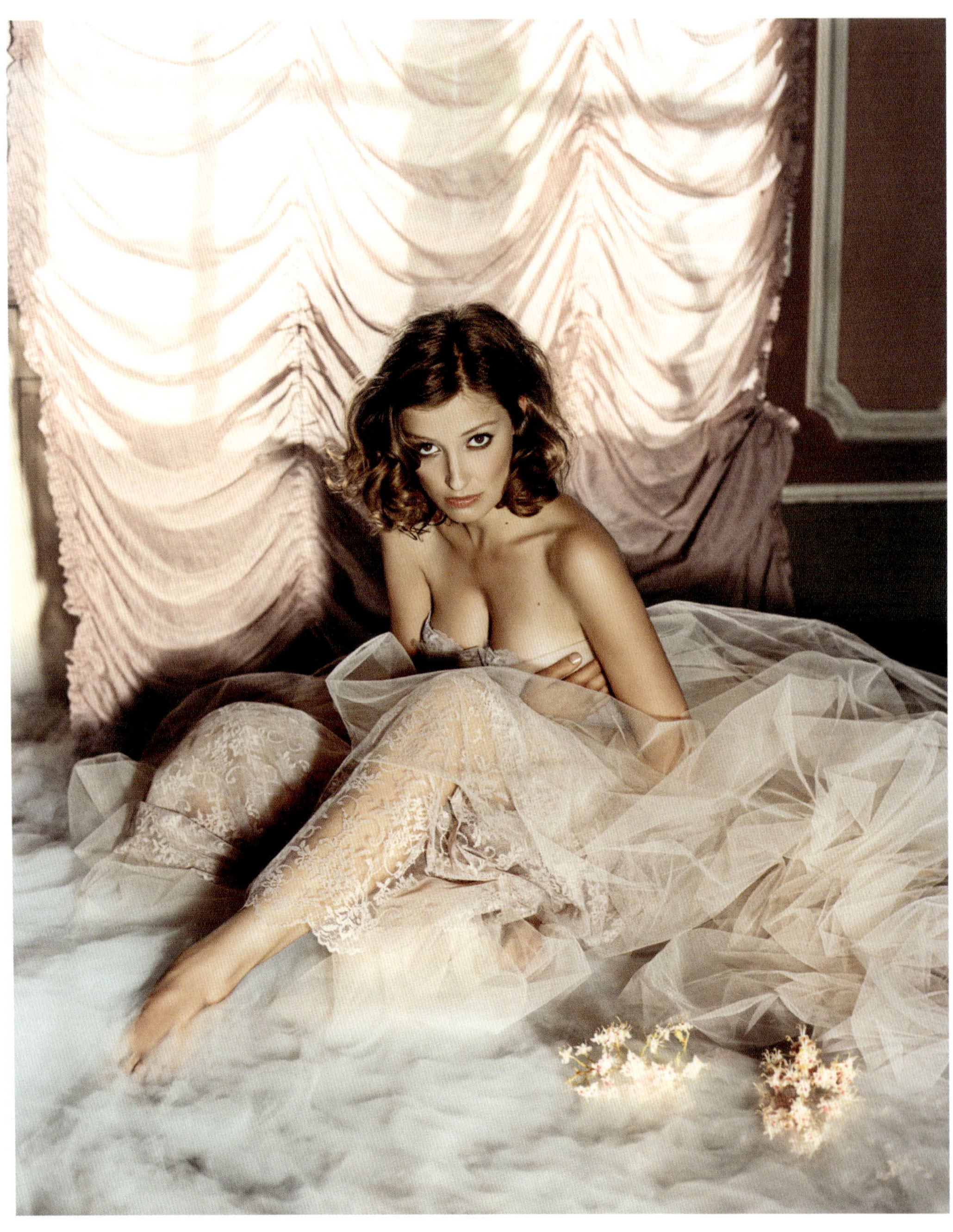

GABO
Alexandra Maria Lara, 2007
Fine art print on Hahnemühle handmade paper, 60 × 48.5 cm
GABO

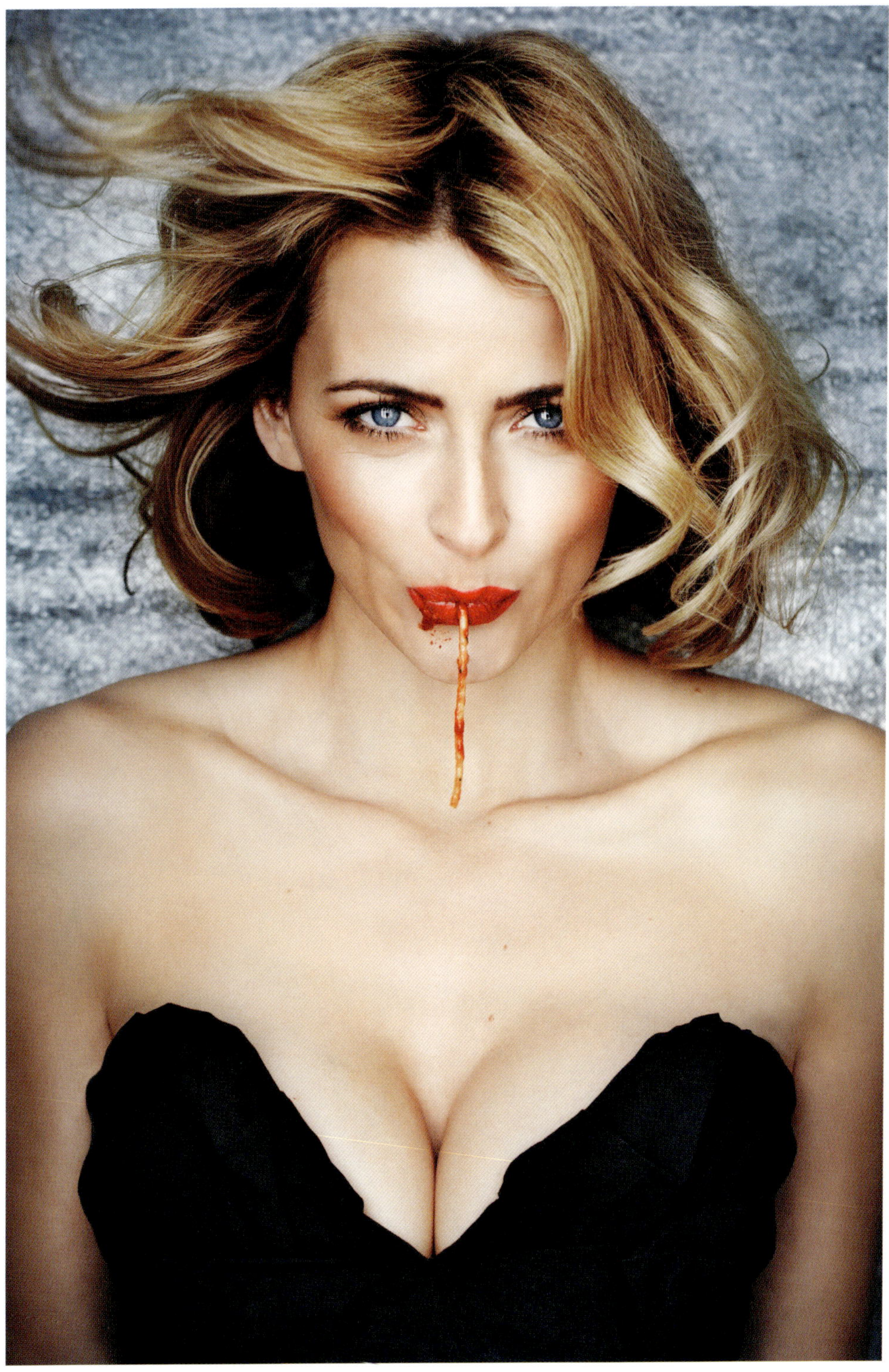

GABO
Eva Padberg, 2012
Fine art print on Hahnemühle handmade paper, 60 × 40 cm
GABO

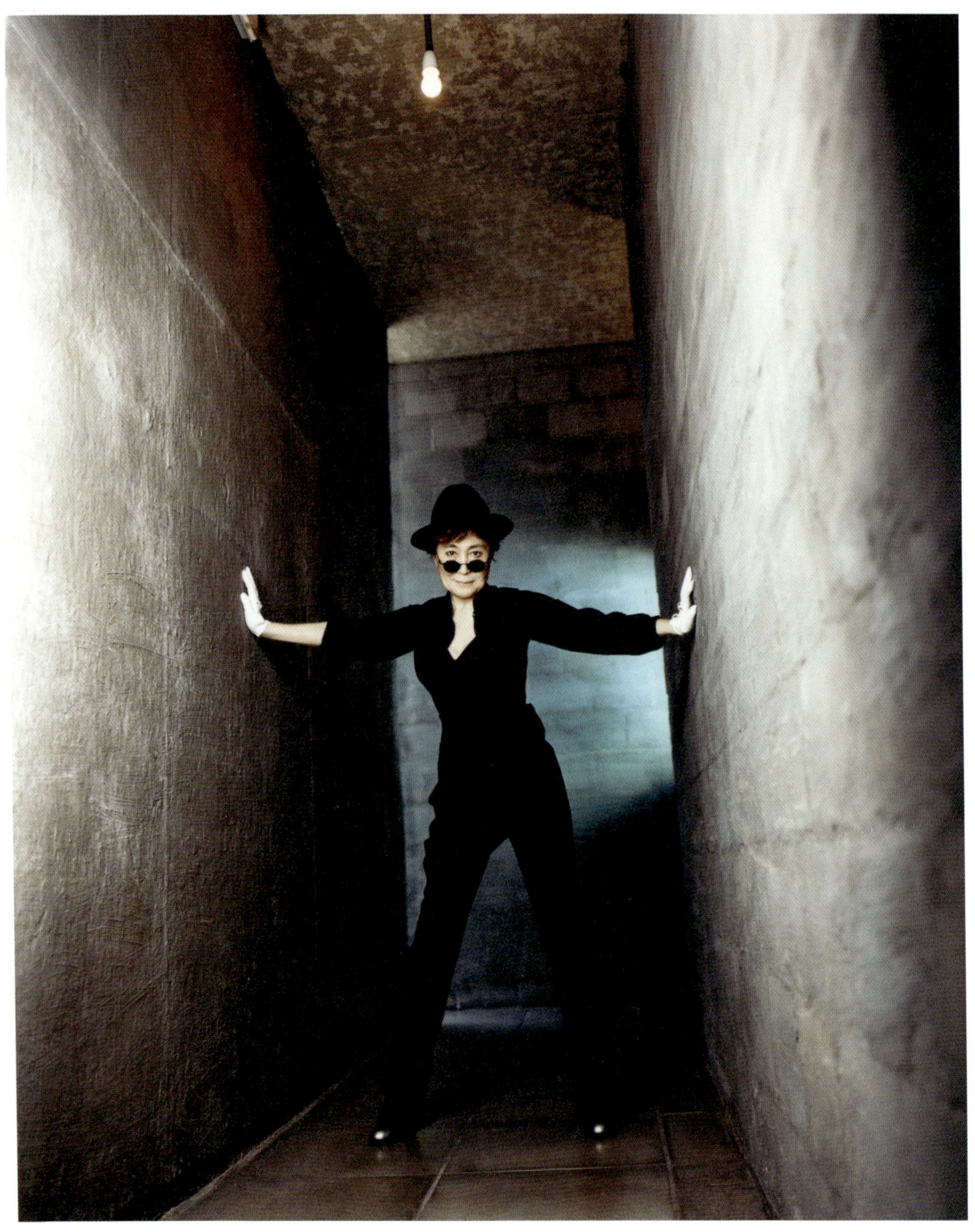

GABO
Analog Yoko Ono, 2015
Fine art print on Hahnemühle handmade paper, 60 × 48.5 cm
GABO

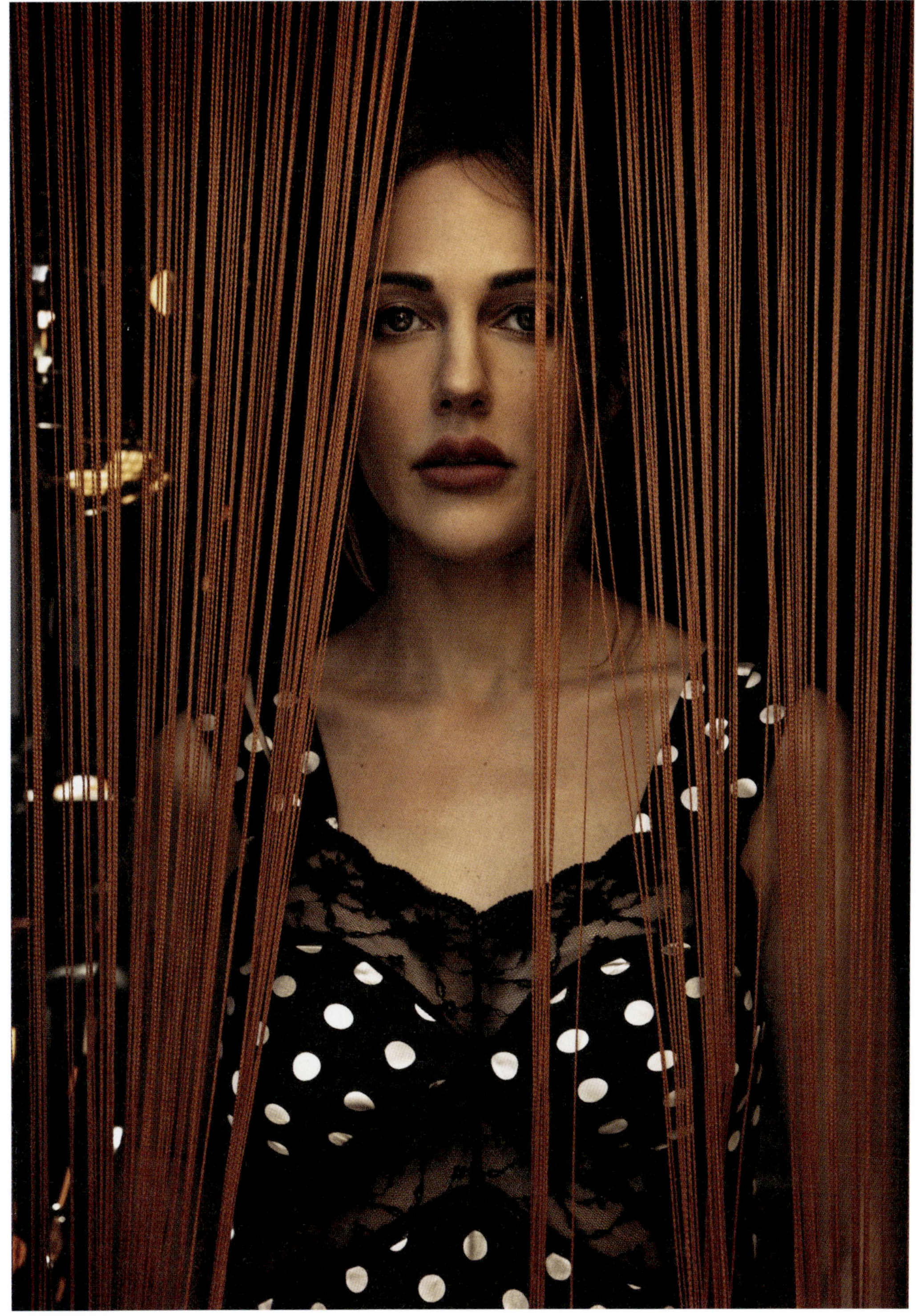

GABO
Meryem Uzerli, 2020
Fine art print on Hahnemühle handmade paper, 60 × 41.5 cm
GABO

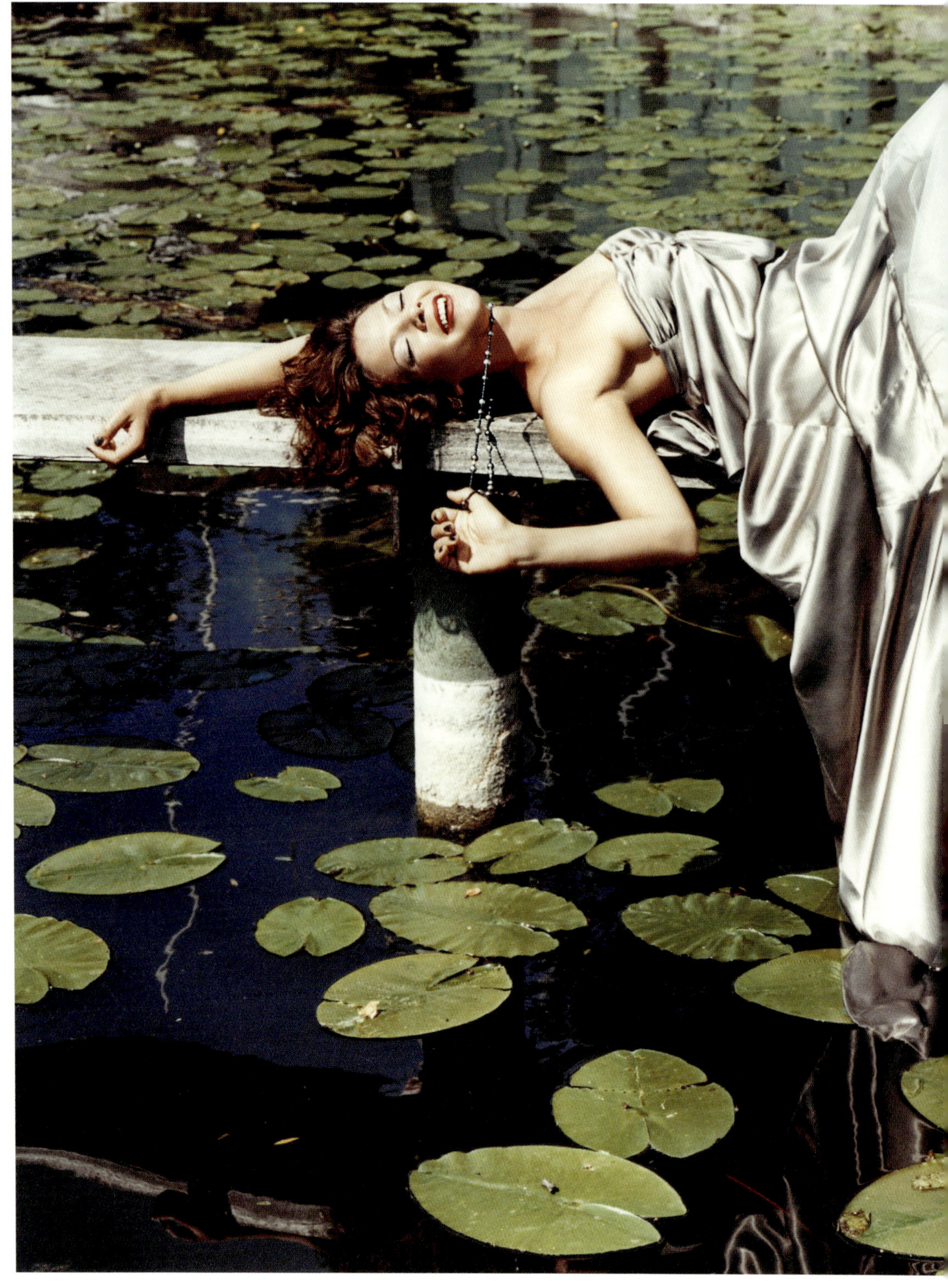

GABO
Jessica Schwarz, 2017
Fine art print on Hahnemühle handmade paper, 48.5 × 60 cm
GABO

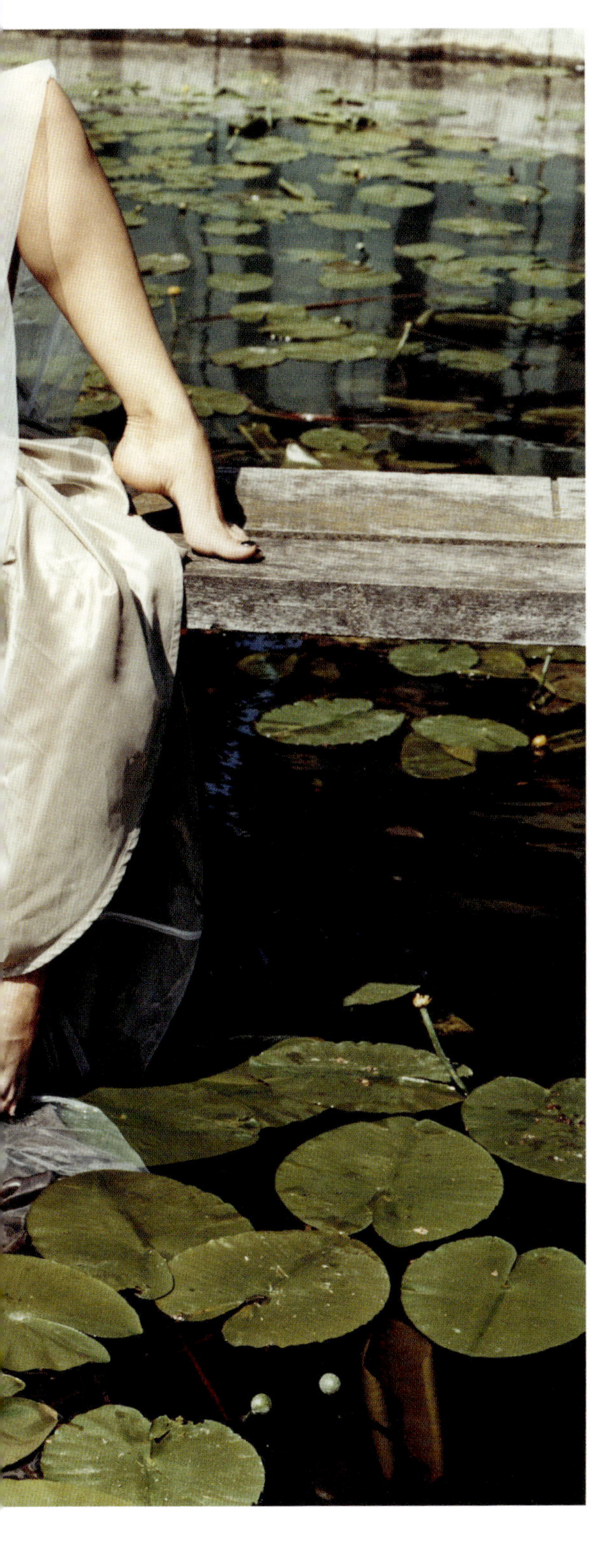

Bettina Rheims

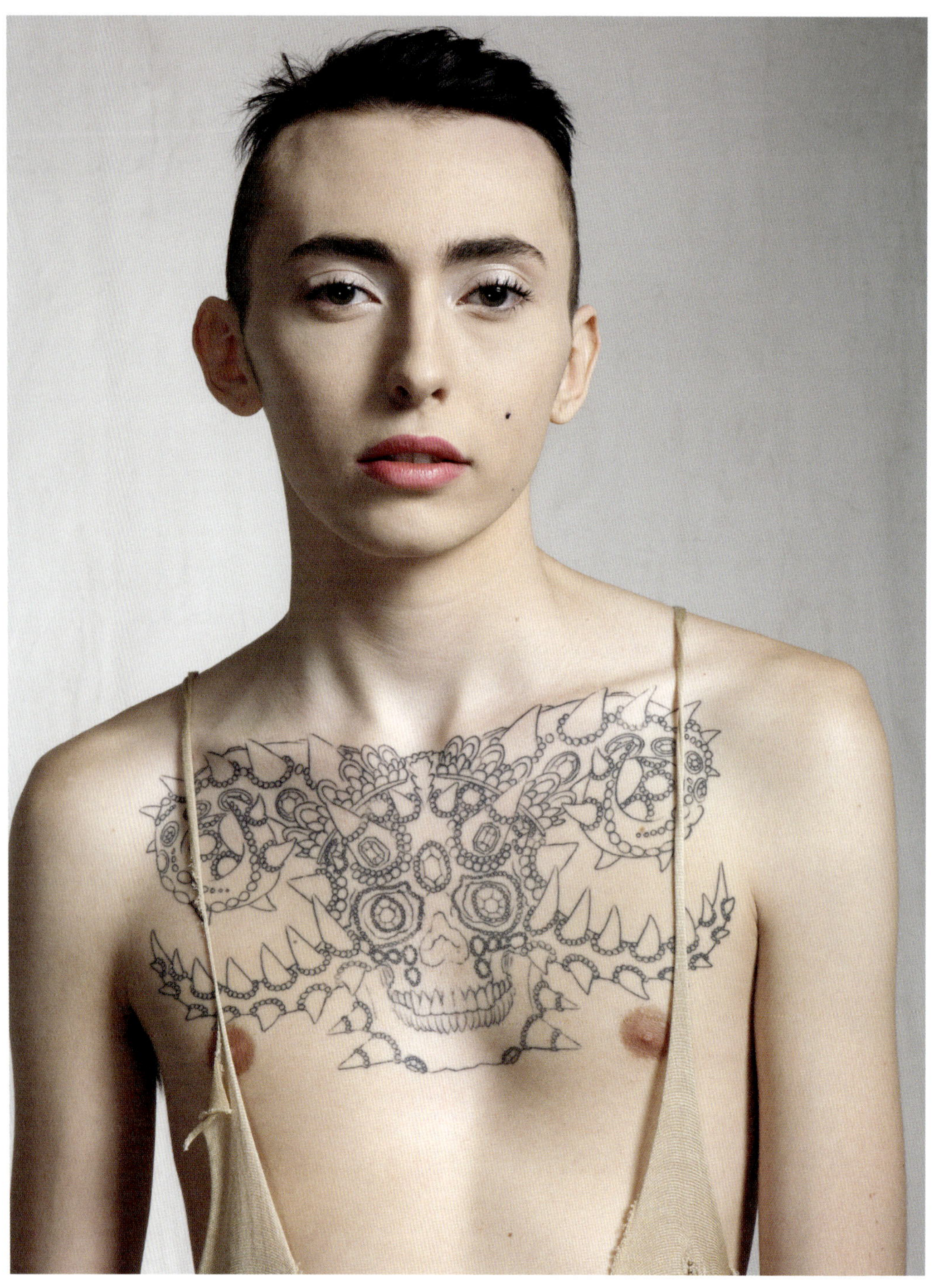

Bettina Rheims
Edward V. III [from the series *Gender Studies*], 2011
C-print, 95 × 71 cm
CAMERA WORK, Berlin

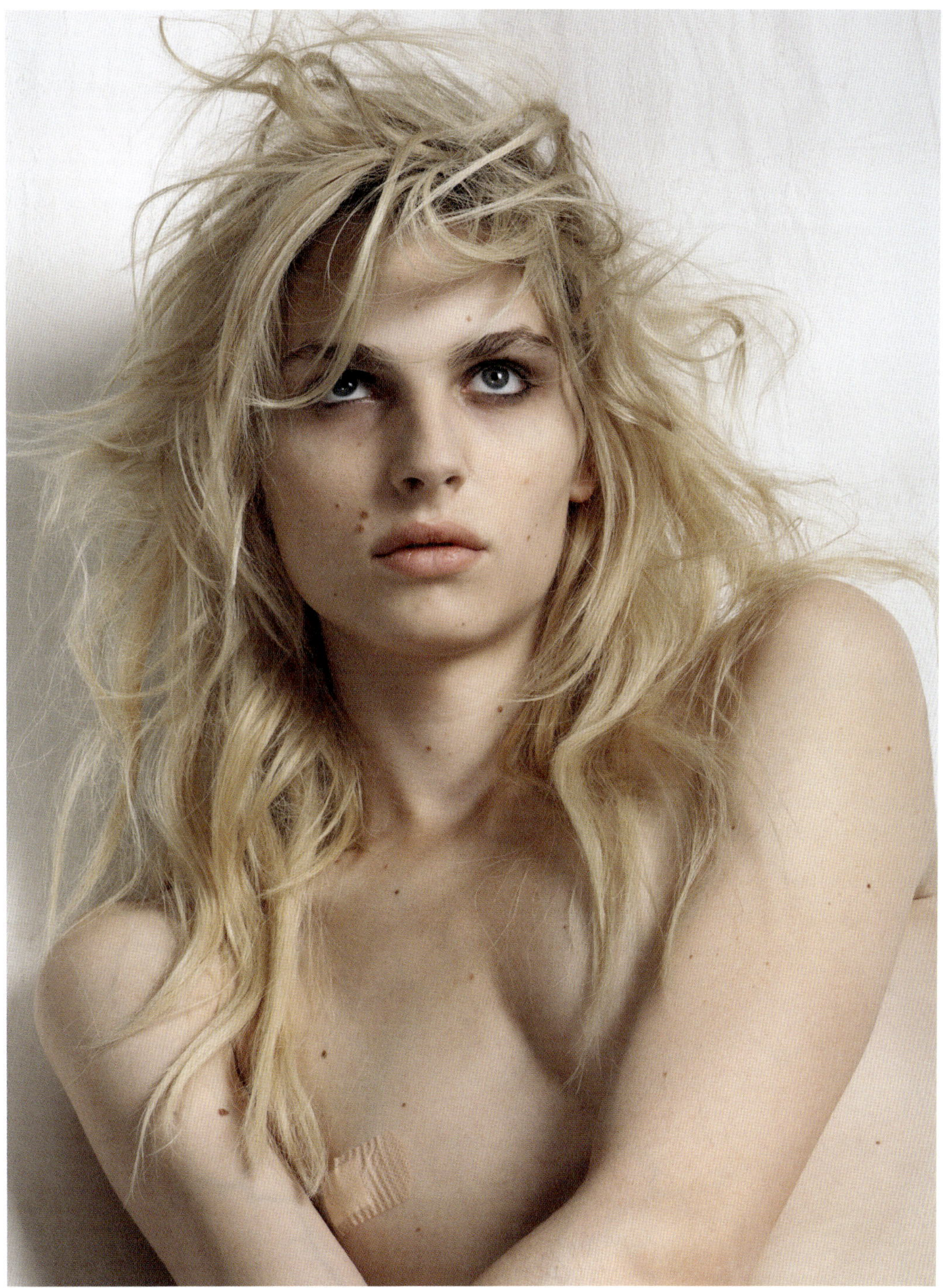

Bettina Rheims
Andrej P. III [from the series *Gender Studies*], 2011
C-print, 95 × 71 cm
CAMERA WORK, Berlin

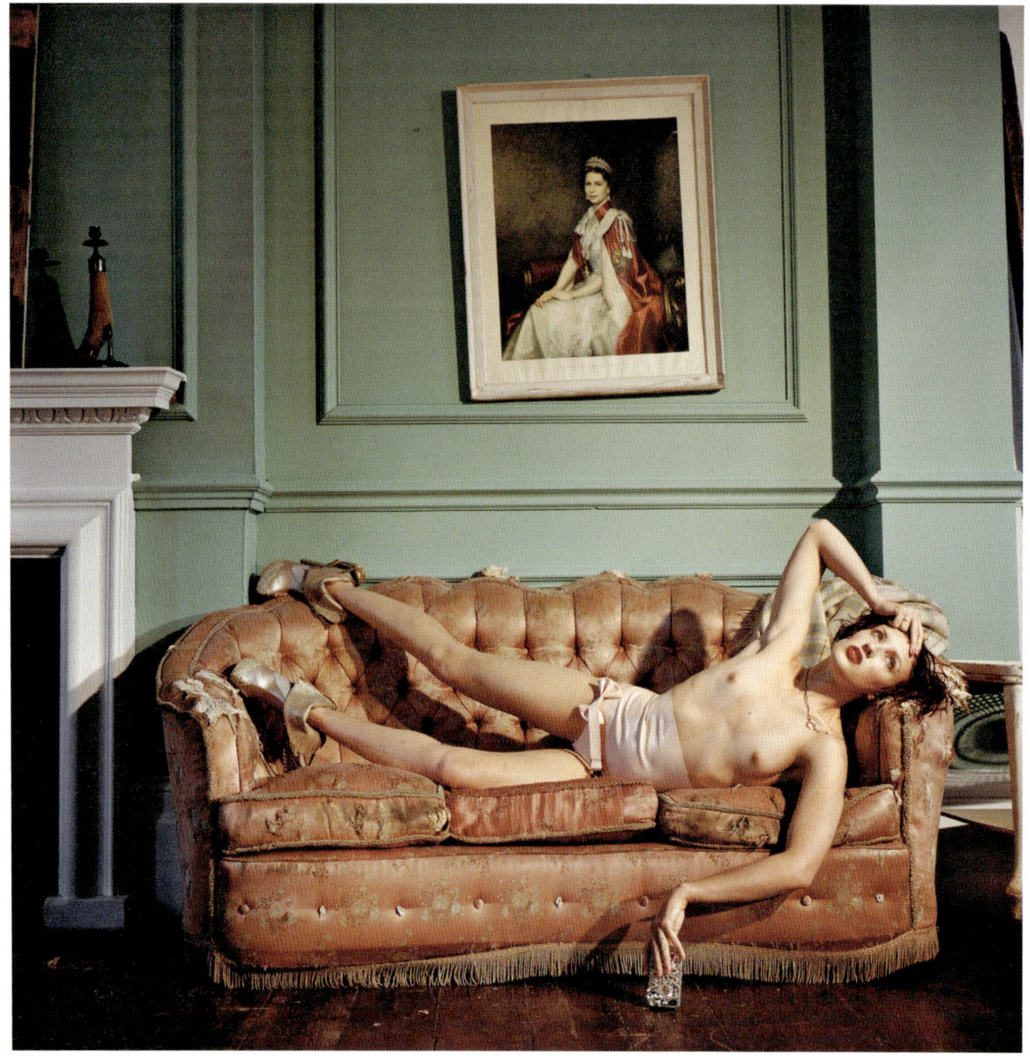

Bettina Rheims
Georgie Bee Wearing Her Own Amazing Shoes [from the series *Bonkers! A Fortnight in London*], 2014
C-print, 100 × 100 cm
CAMERA WORK, Berlin

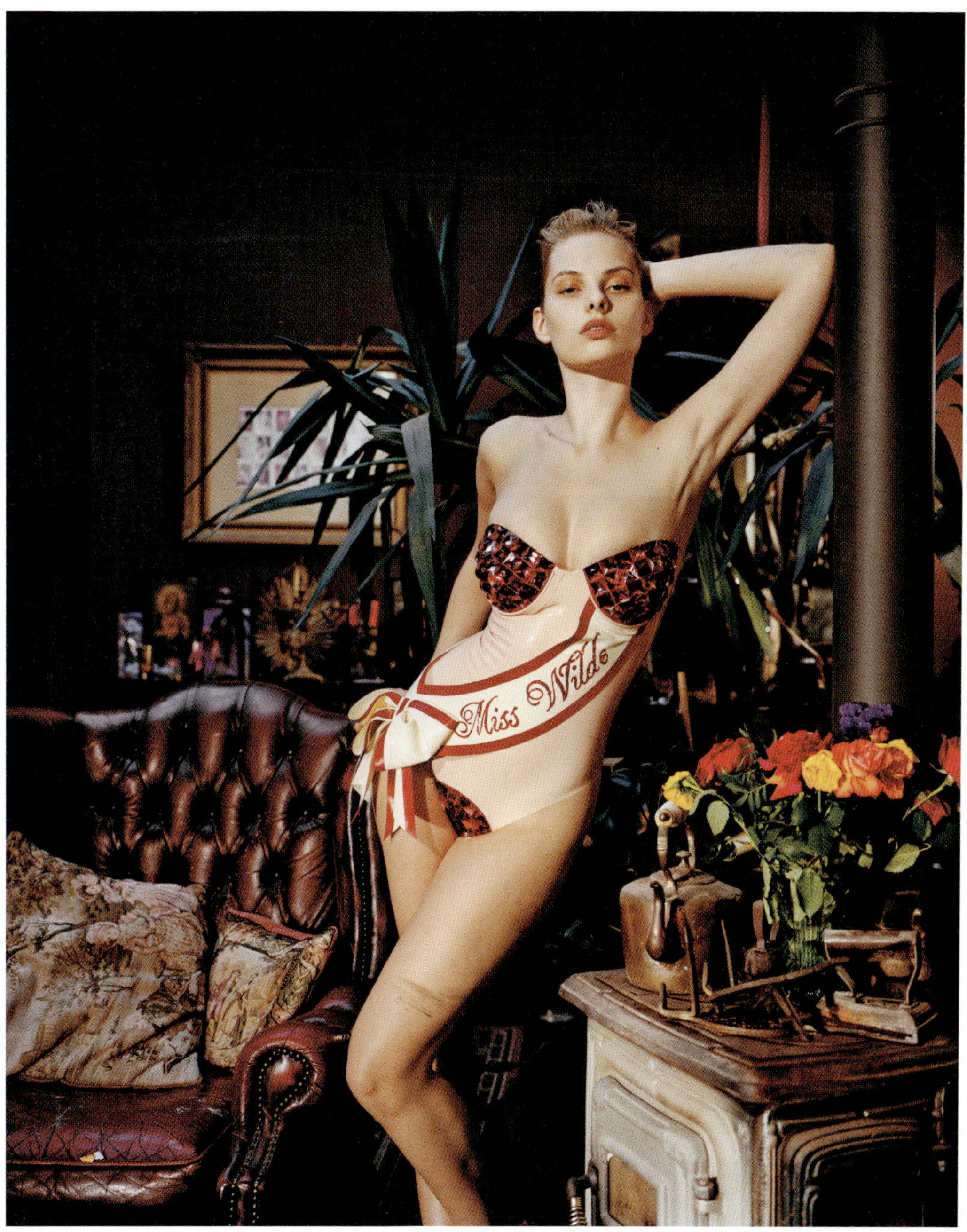

Bettina Rheims
Dioni Tabbers, Miss Wilde [from the series *Bonkers! A Fortnight in London*], 2014
C-print, 122 × 100 cm
CAMERA WORK, Berlin

Ellen von Unwerth

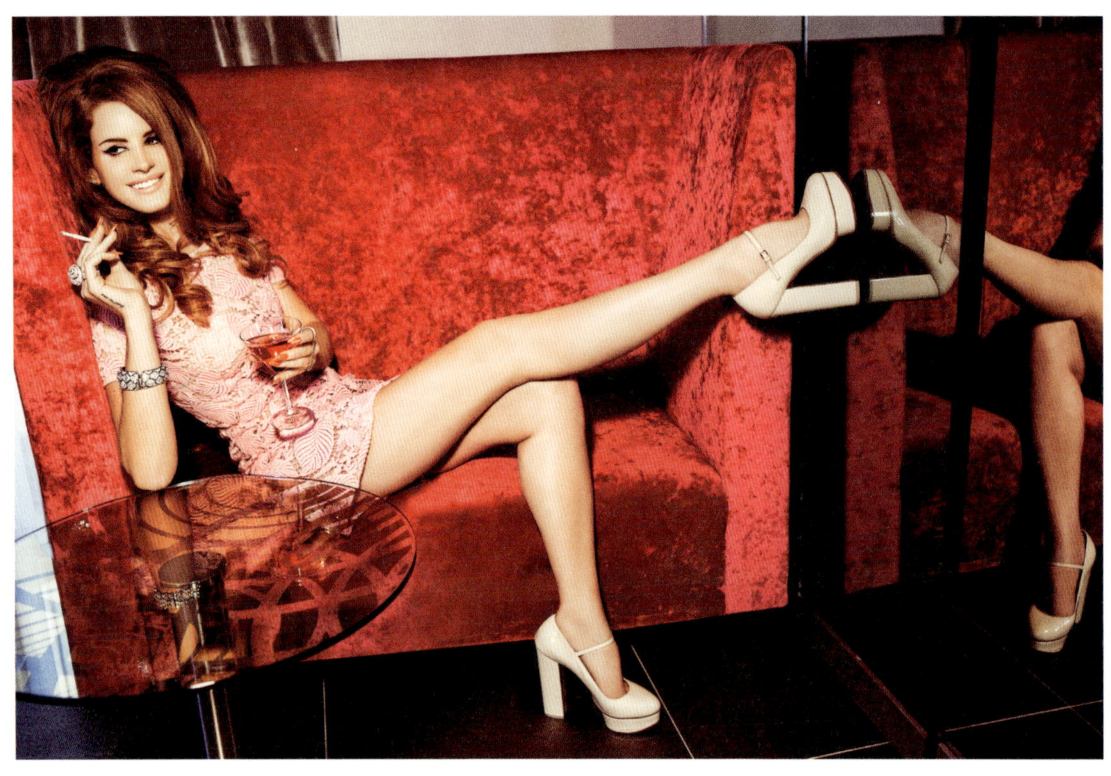

Ellen von Unwerth
Lana del Rey, 2012
C-print, 75.5 × 109 cm
Ellen von Unwerth Studios

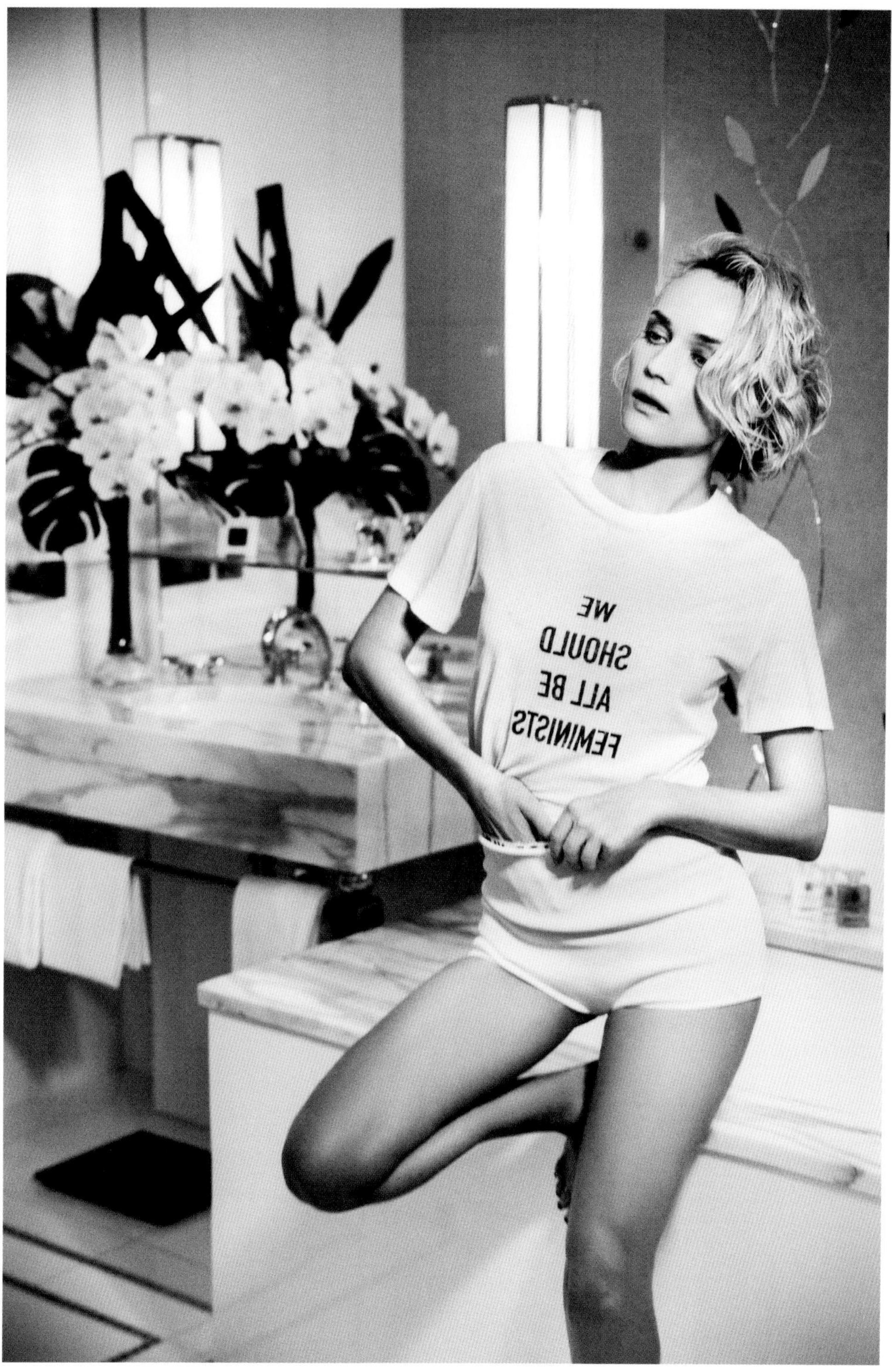

Ellen von Unwerth
Diane Kruger, 2017
C-print, 110 × 75.5 cm
Ellen von Unwerth Studios

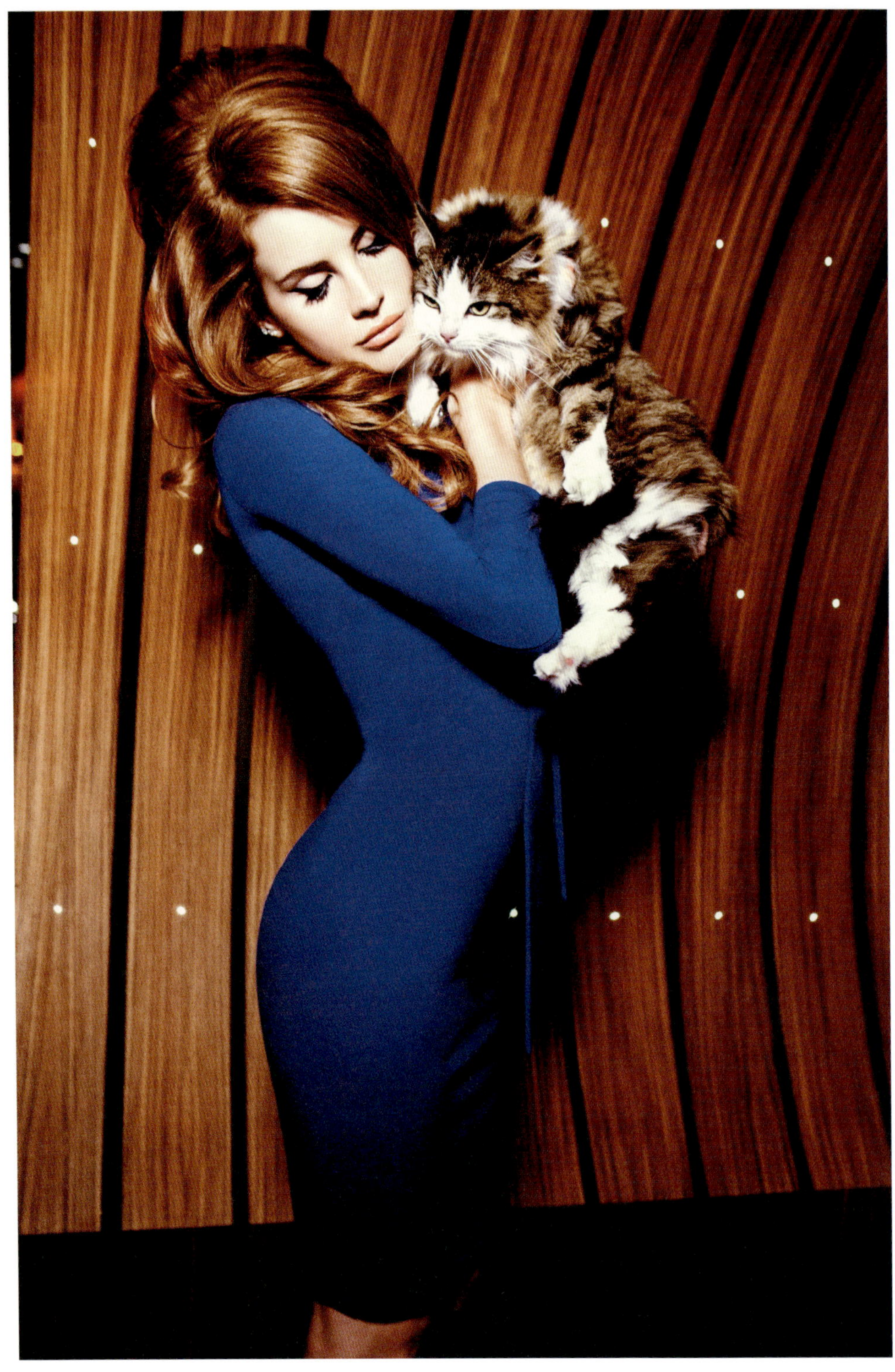

Ellen von Unwerth
Lana del Rey, 2012
C-print, 109 × 75.5 cm
Ellen von Unwerth Studios

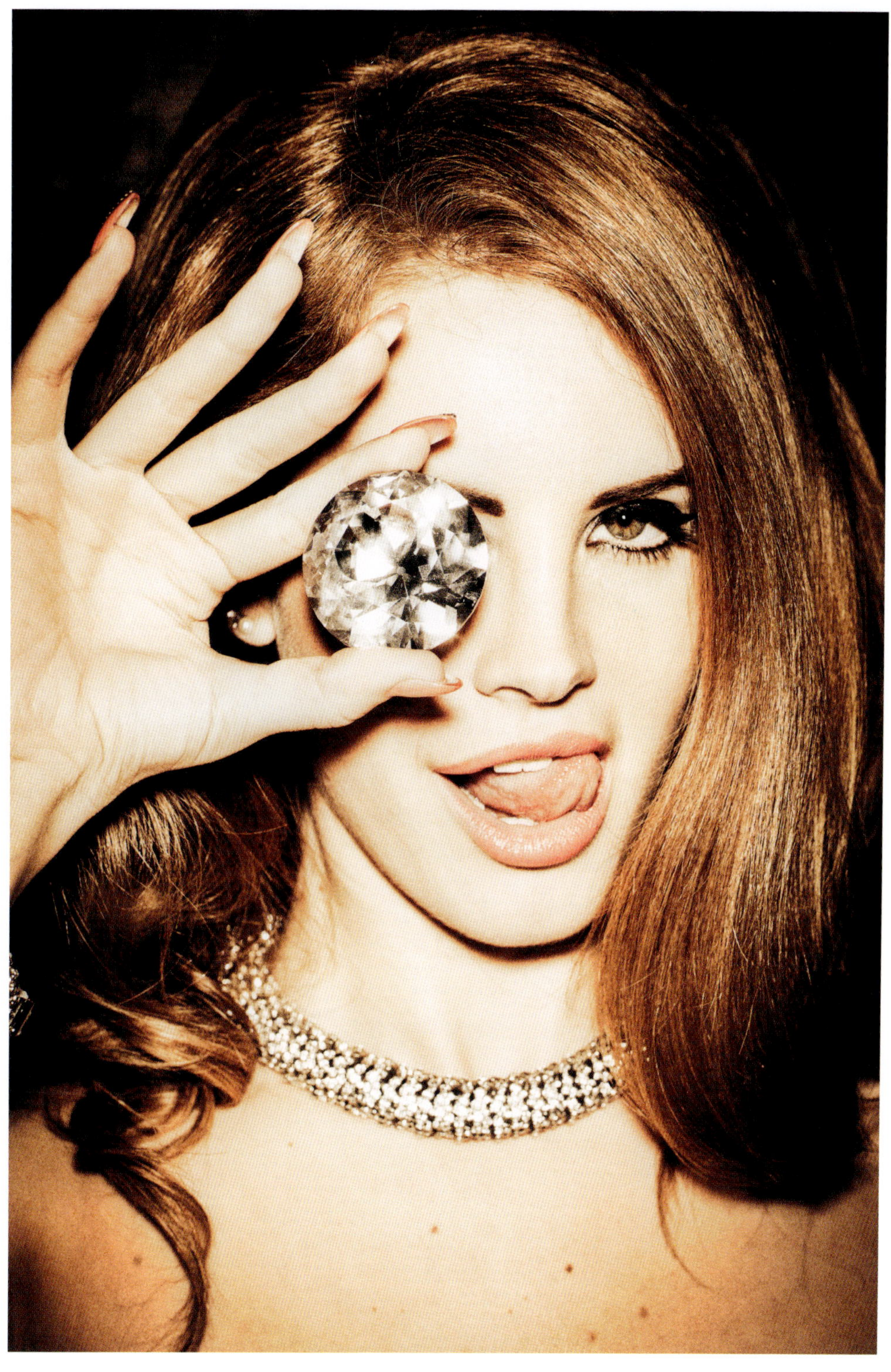

Ellen von Unwerth
Lana del Rey, 2012
C-print, 109 × 75.5 cm
Ellen von Unwerth Studios

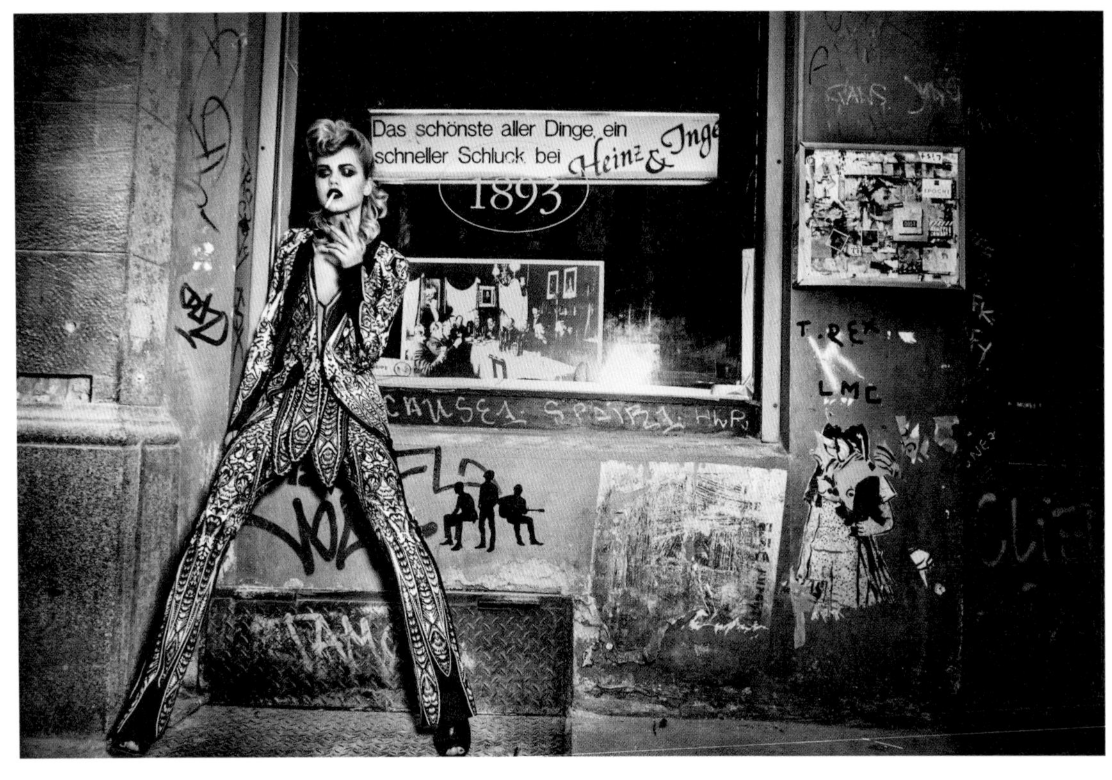

Ellen von Unwerth
Alt-Berlin (Old Town Berlin), 2014
Archival pigment print, 40 × 50 cm
CAMERA WORK, Berlin

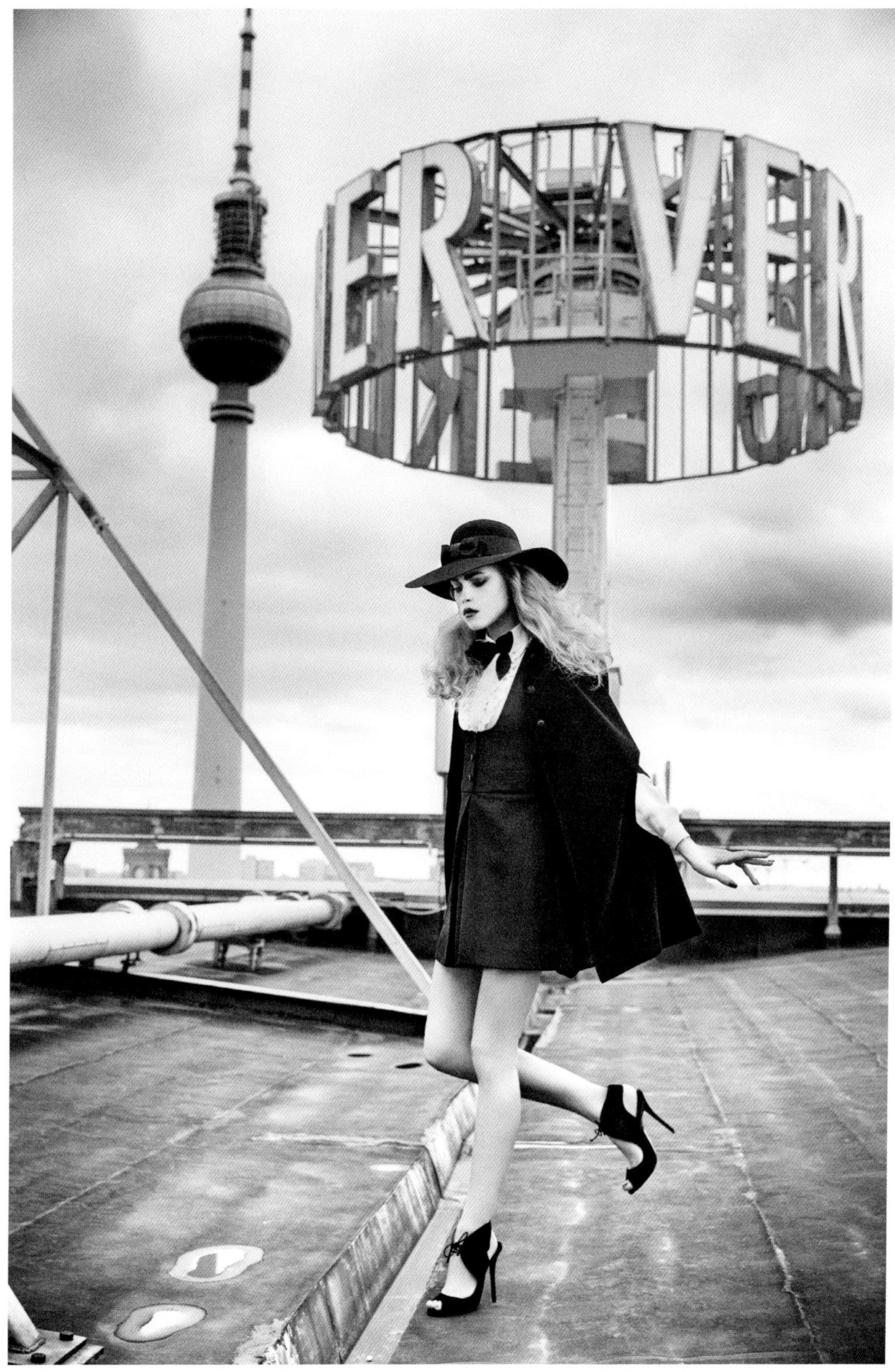

Ellen von Unwerth
Berliner Verlag (Publisher Berliner Verlag), 2014
Archival pigment print, 50 × 40 cm
CAMERA WORK, Berlin

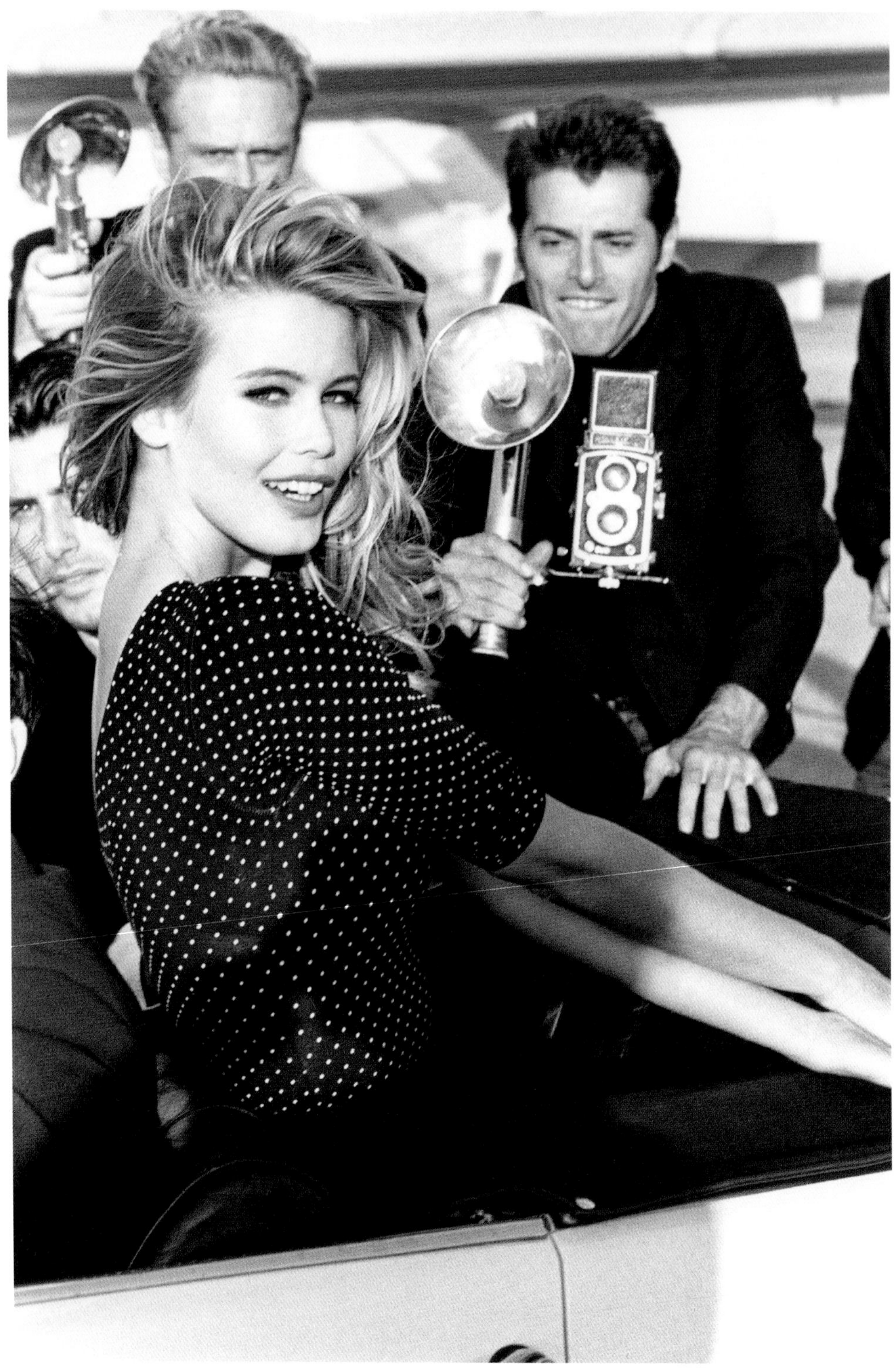

Ellen von Unwerth
Claudia Schiffer Paparazzi, Morocco, 1989
Archival pigment print, 62.5 × 50 cm
CAMERA WORK, Berlin

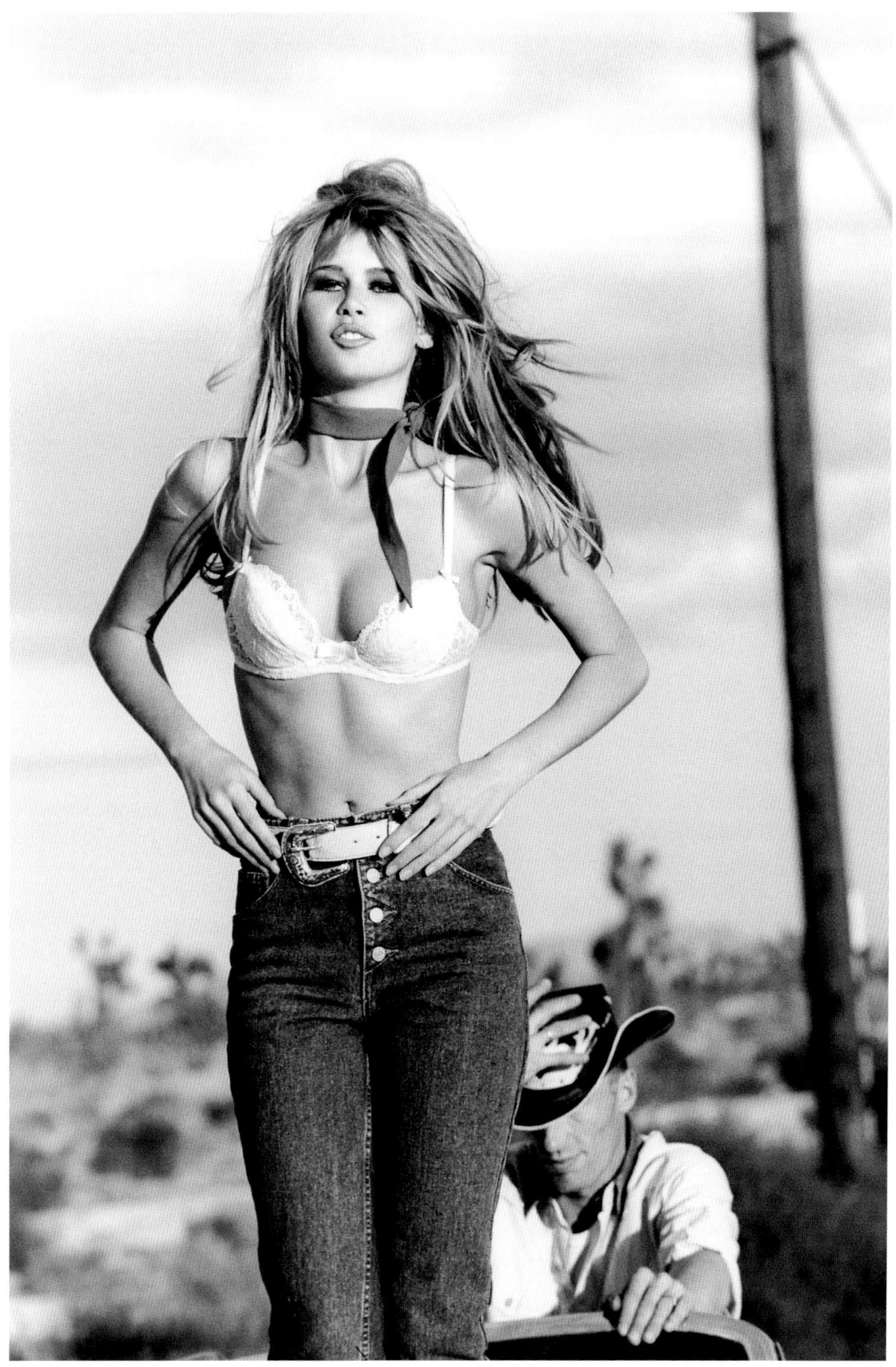

Ellen von Unwerth
Claudia Schiffer Guess Who?, 1989
Archival pigment print, 60 × 41.6 cm
CAMERA WORK, Berlin

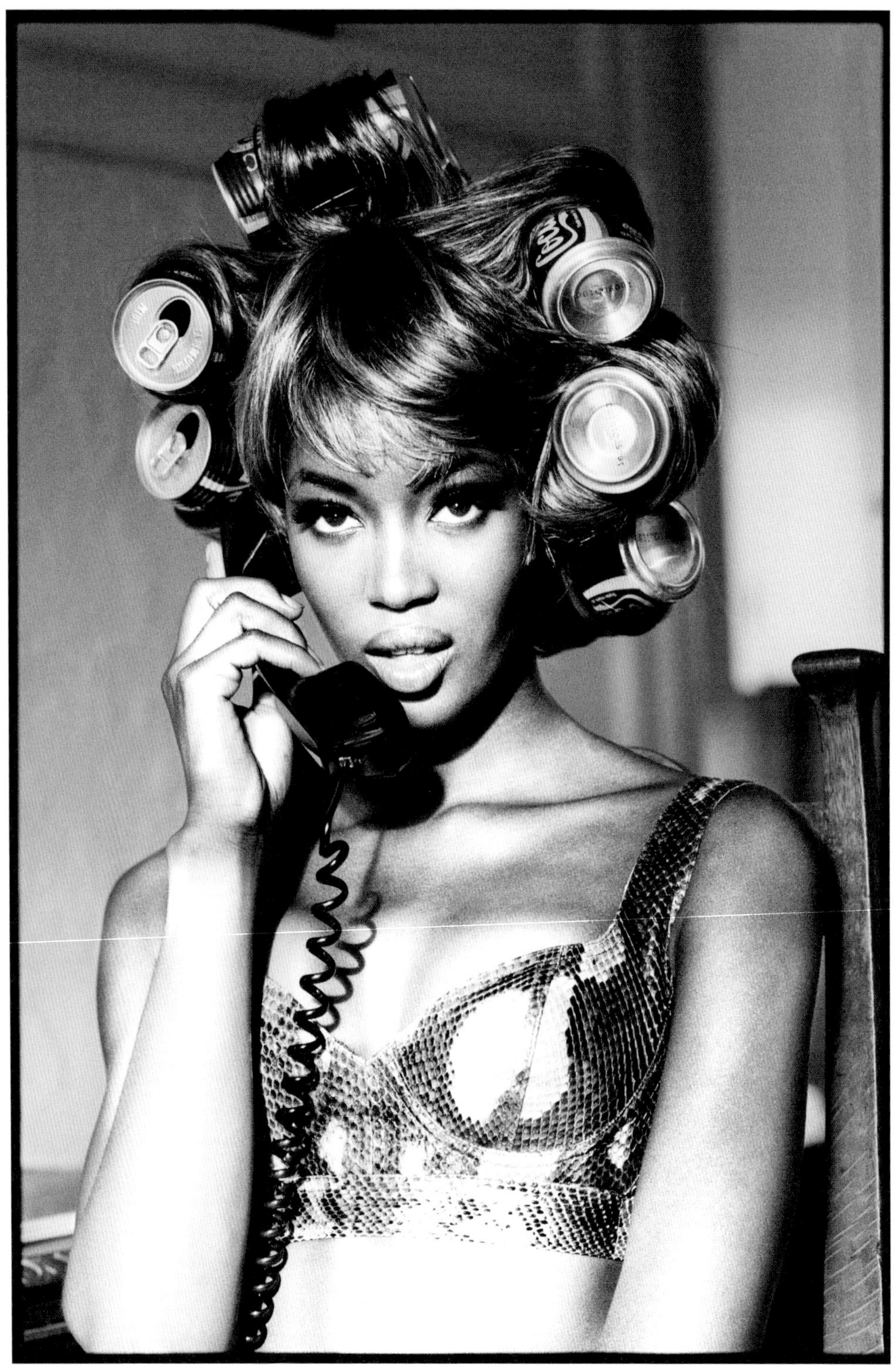

Ellen von Unwerth
Naomi's Rollers, 2004
Archival pigment print, 60 × 50 cm
CAMERA WORK, Berlin

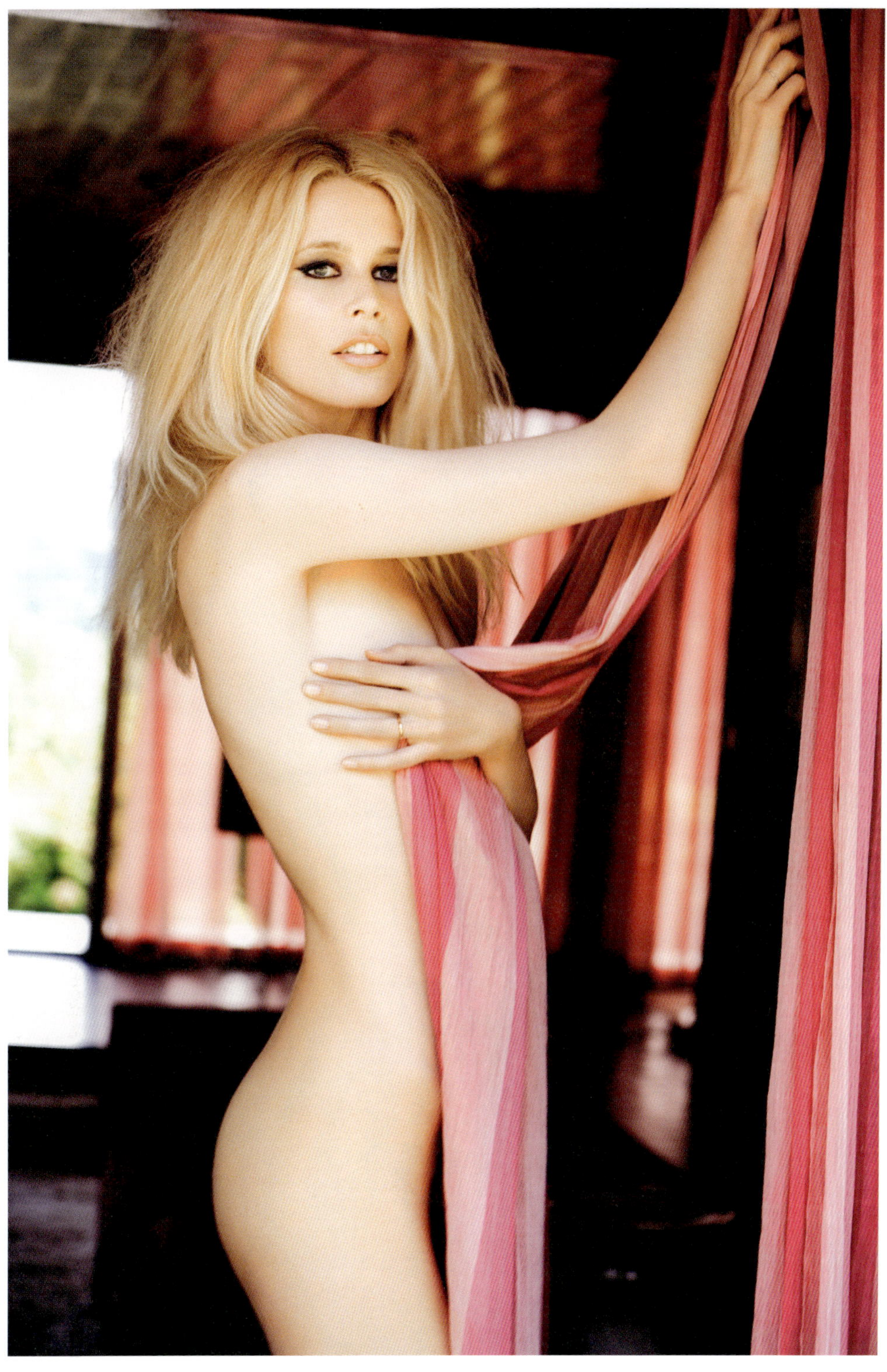

Ellen von Unwerth
Claudia Schiffer for Purple Magazine, 2007
Colour cibachrome print, 180 × 120 cm
CAMERA WORK, Berlin

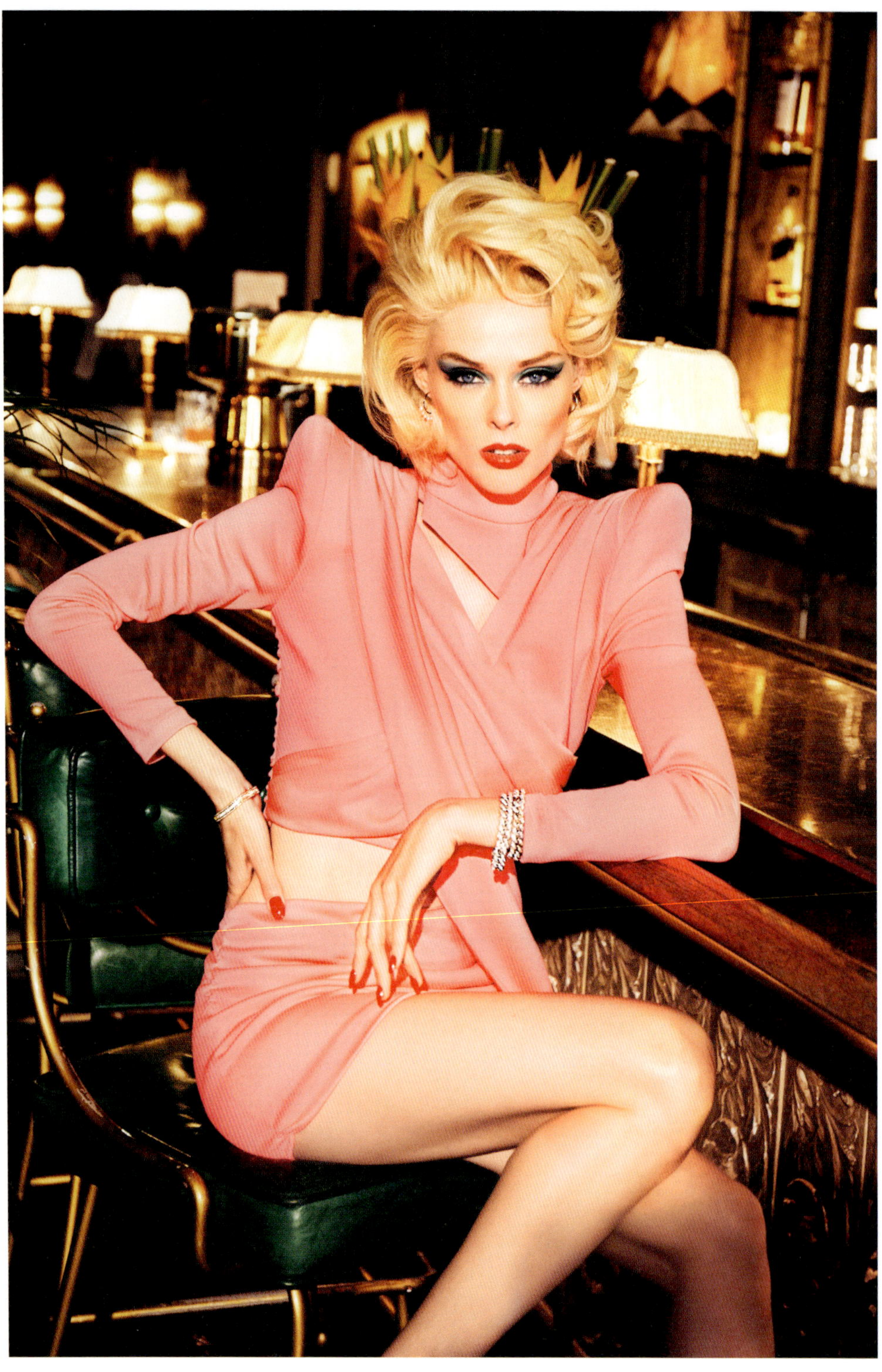

Ellen von Unwerth
Coco Rocha, 2021
C-print, 109 × 75.5 cm
Ellen von Unwerth Studios

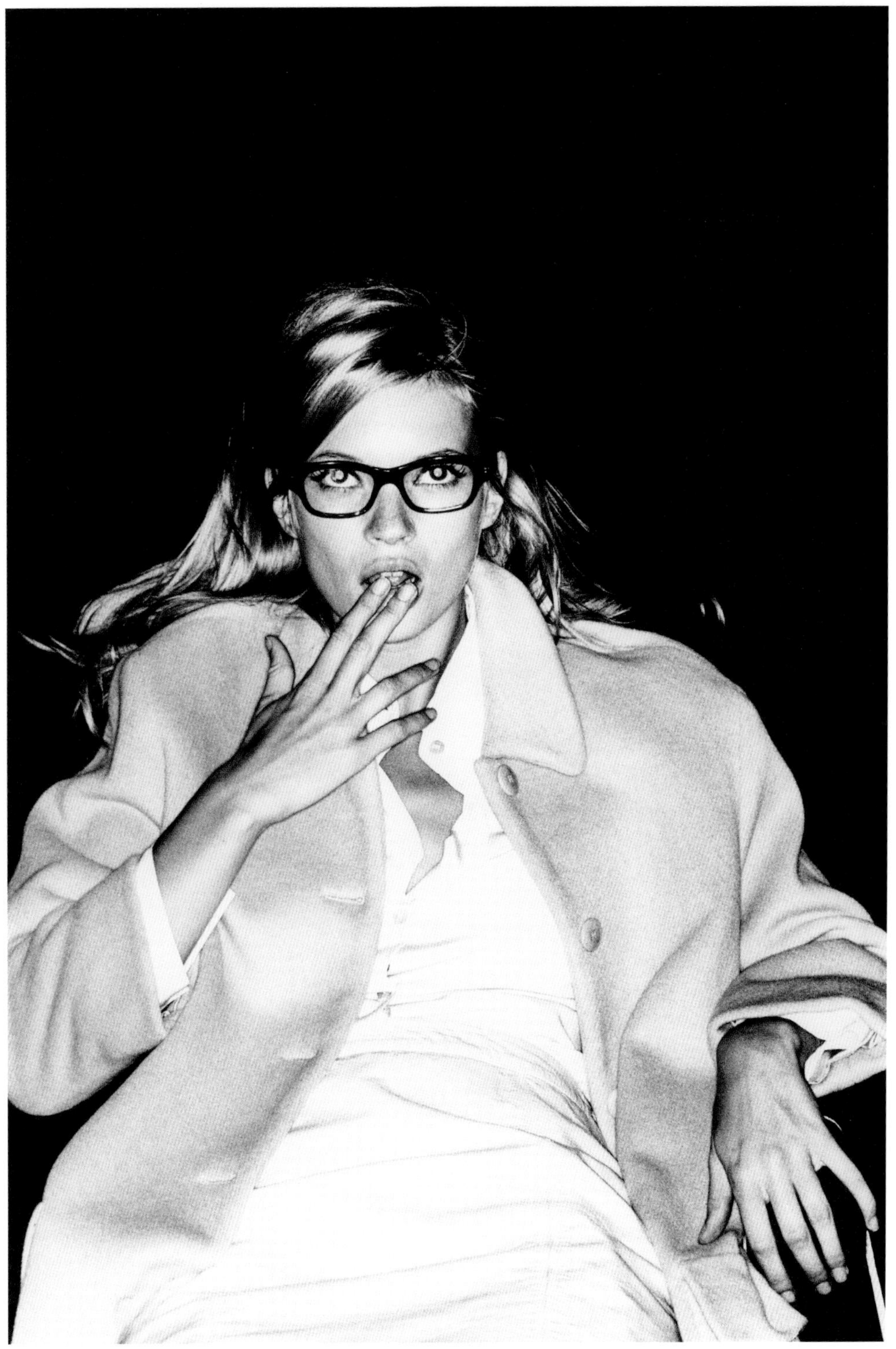

Ellen von Unwerth
Kino (Cinema), 1998
Archival pigment print, 62.5 × 50 cm
CAMERA WORK, Berlin

Liv Liberg

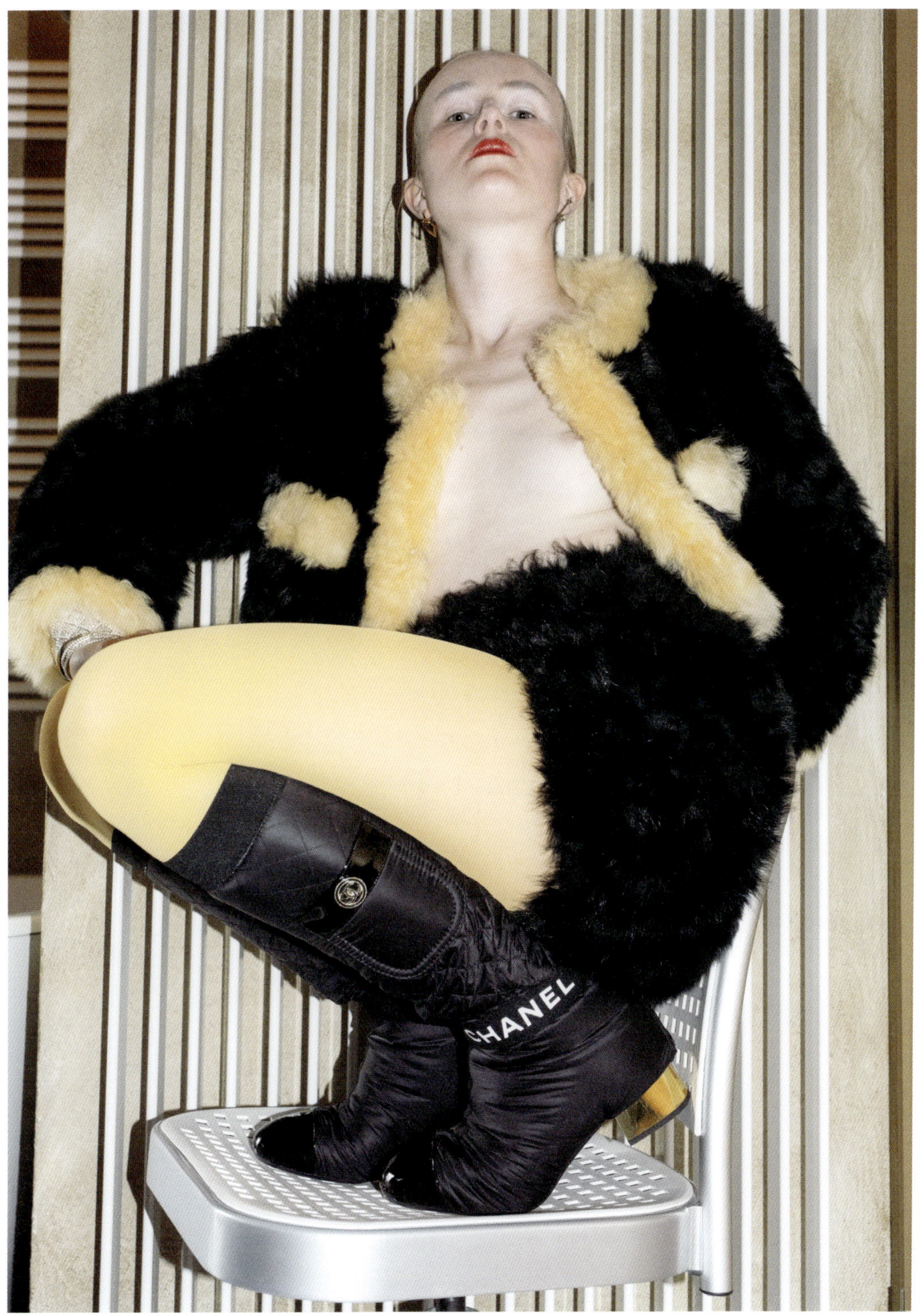

Liv Liberg
britt (chanel) [styled by Lotta Volkova], 2021
Fine art inkjet print, 42 × 30 cm
Liv Liberg

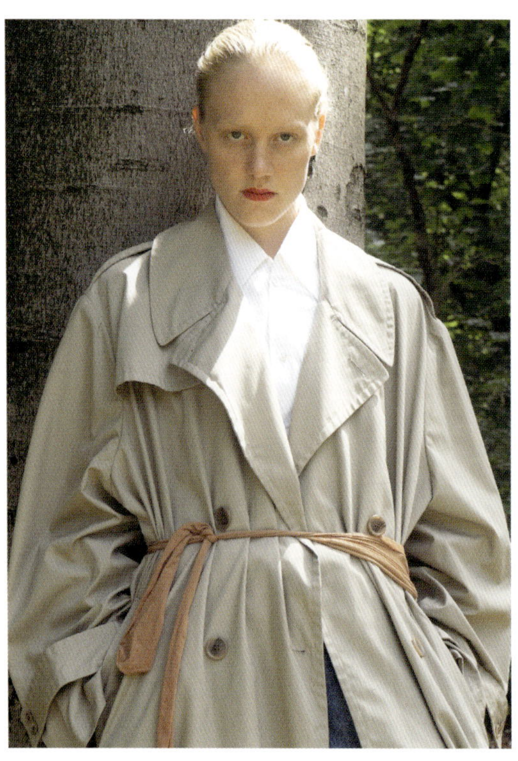

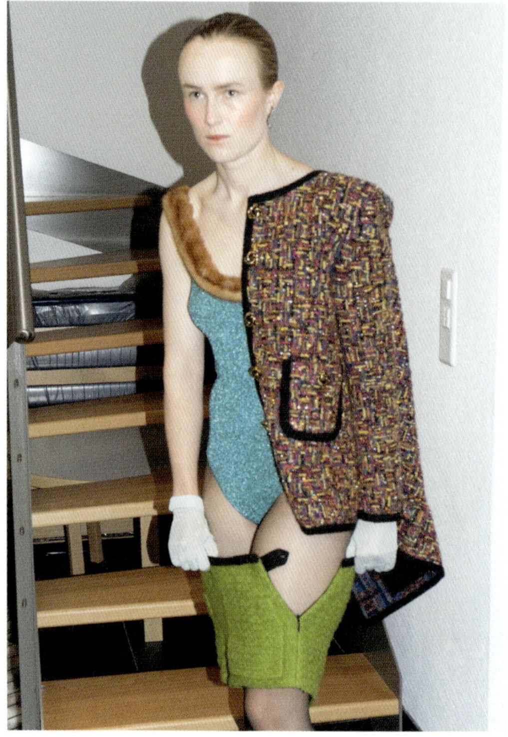

Liv Liberg
laura (tree), 2021
Fine art inkjet print, 42 × 30 cm
Liv Liberg

Liv Liberg
britt (dressed) [styled by Lotta Volkova], 2021
Fine art inkjet print, 42 × 30 cm
Liv Liberg

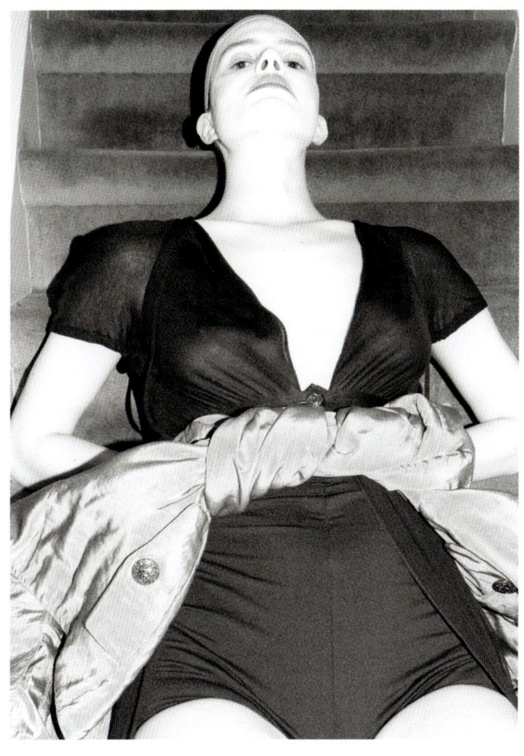

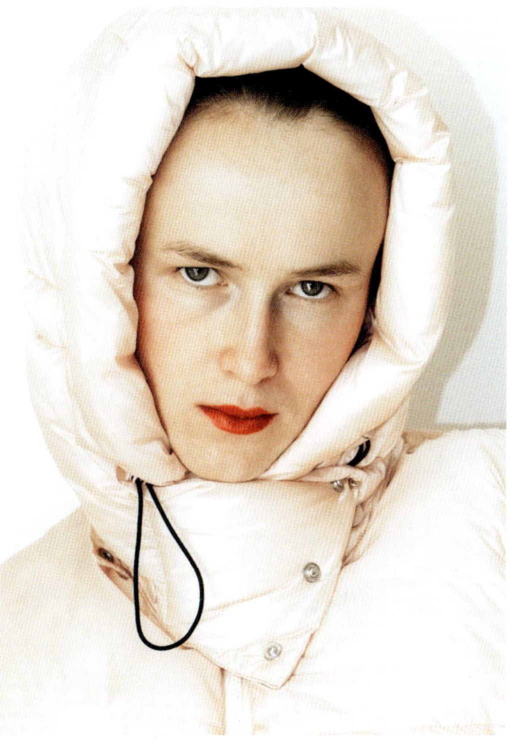

Liv Liberg
saskia (stairs), 2021
Fine art inkjet print, 42 × 30 cm
Liv Liberg

Liv Liberg
britt (hood) [styled by Isabelle Sayer], 2021
Fine art inkjet print, 42 × 30 cm
Liv Liberg

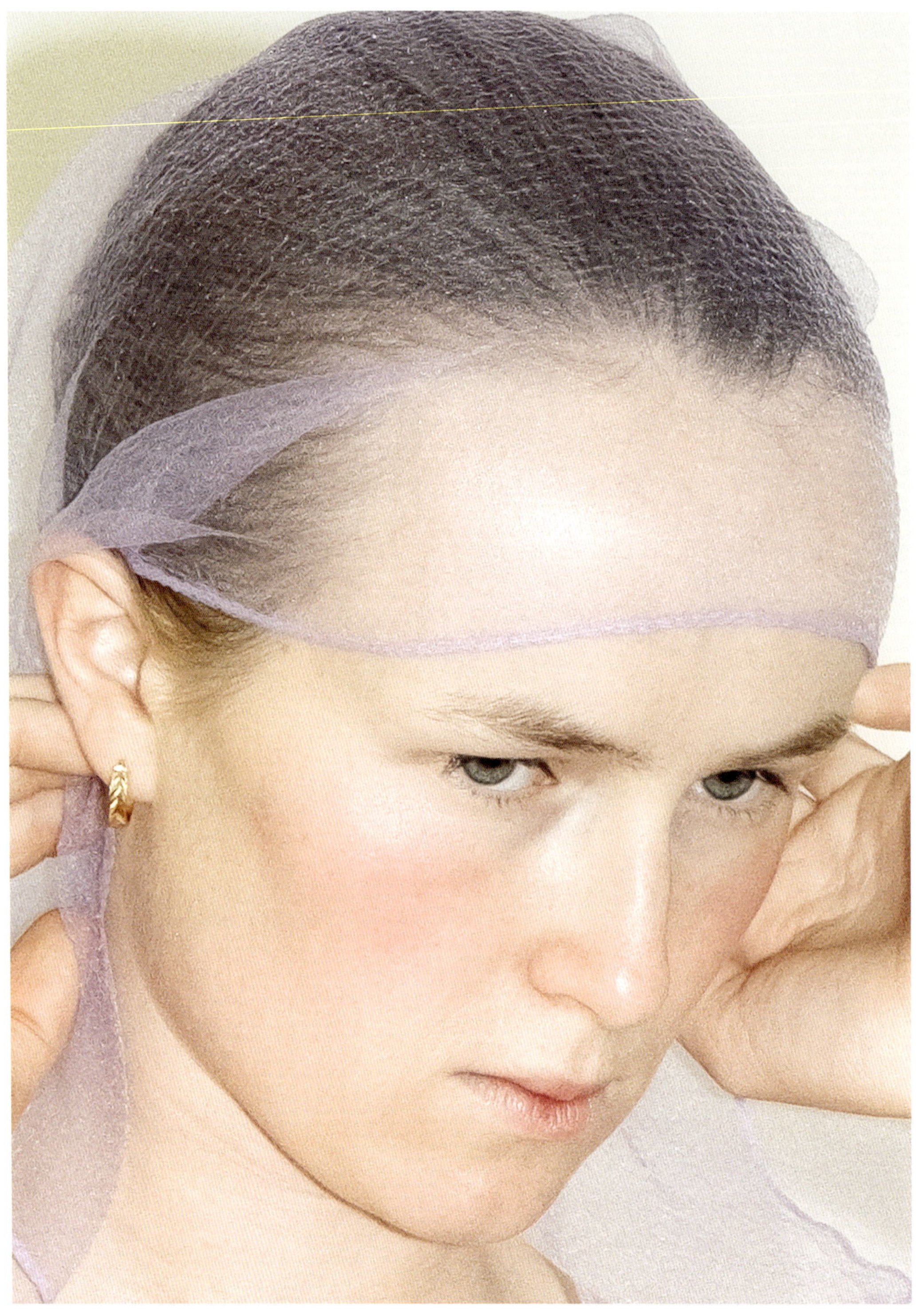

Liv Liberg
britt (mesh) [styled by Isabelle Sayer], 2021
Fine art inkjet print, 42 × 30 cm
Liv Liberg

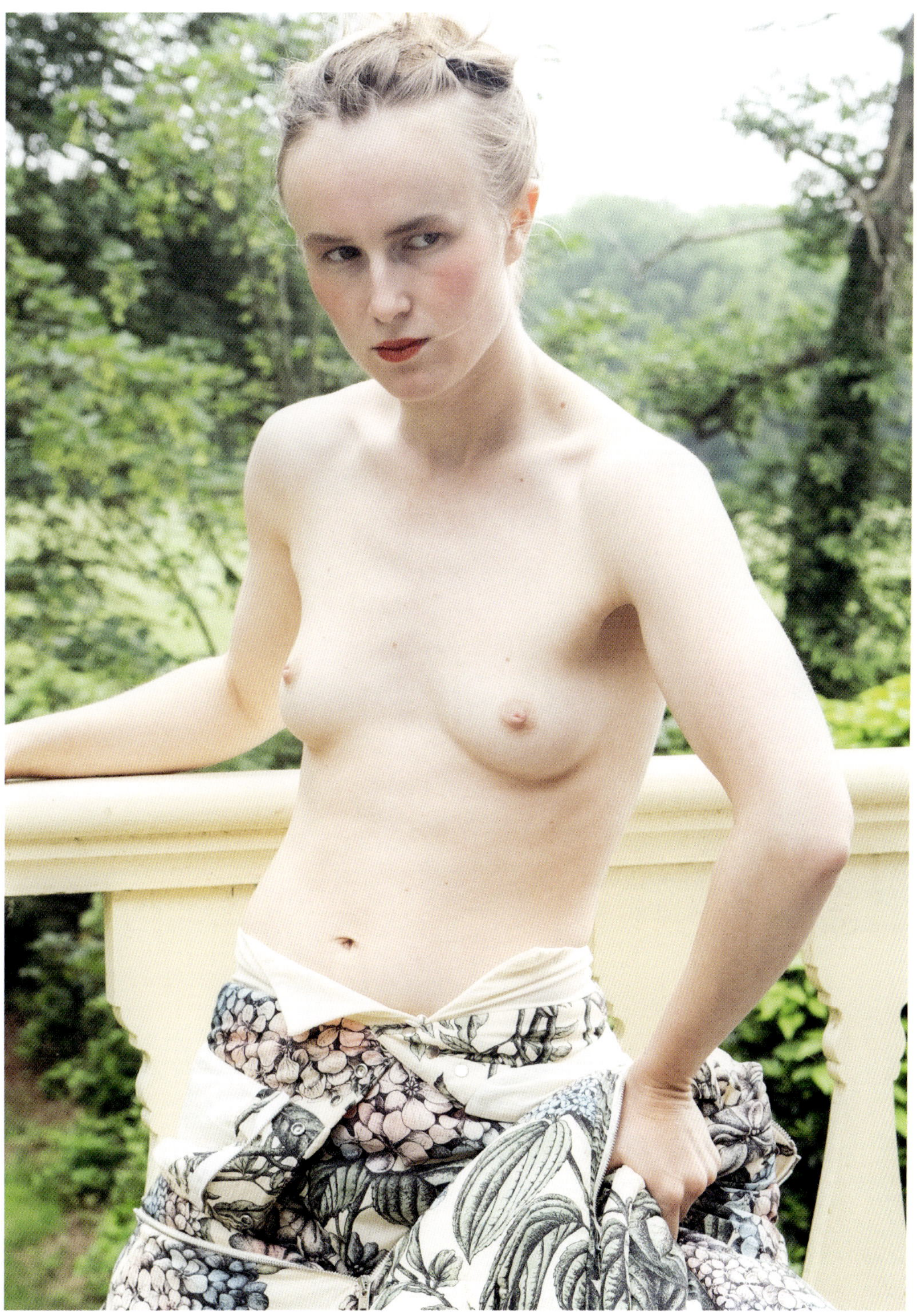

Liv Liberg
britt (summer) [styled by Isabelle Sayer], 2021
Fine art inkjet print, 42 × 30 cm
Liv Liberg

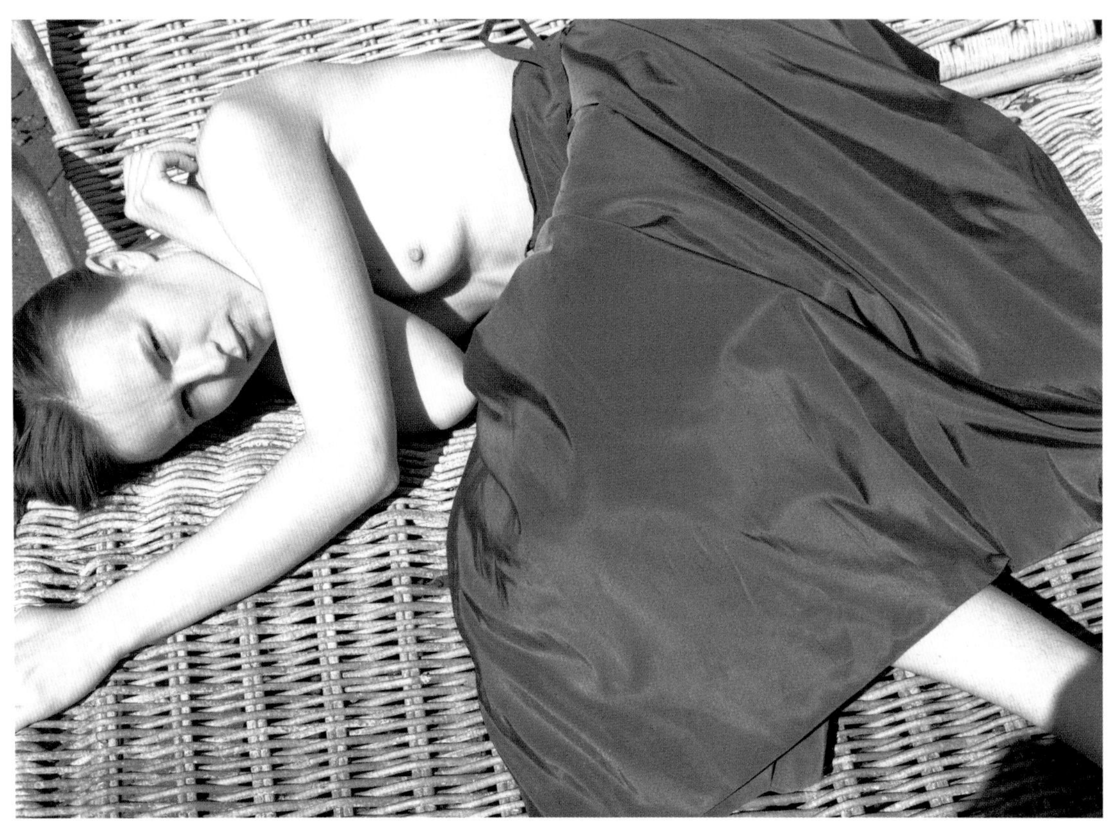

Liv Liberg
britt (laying/wicker), 2021
Fine art inkjet print, 30 × 42 cm
Liv Liberg

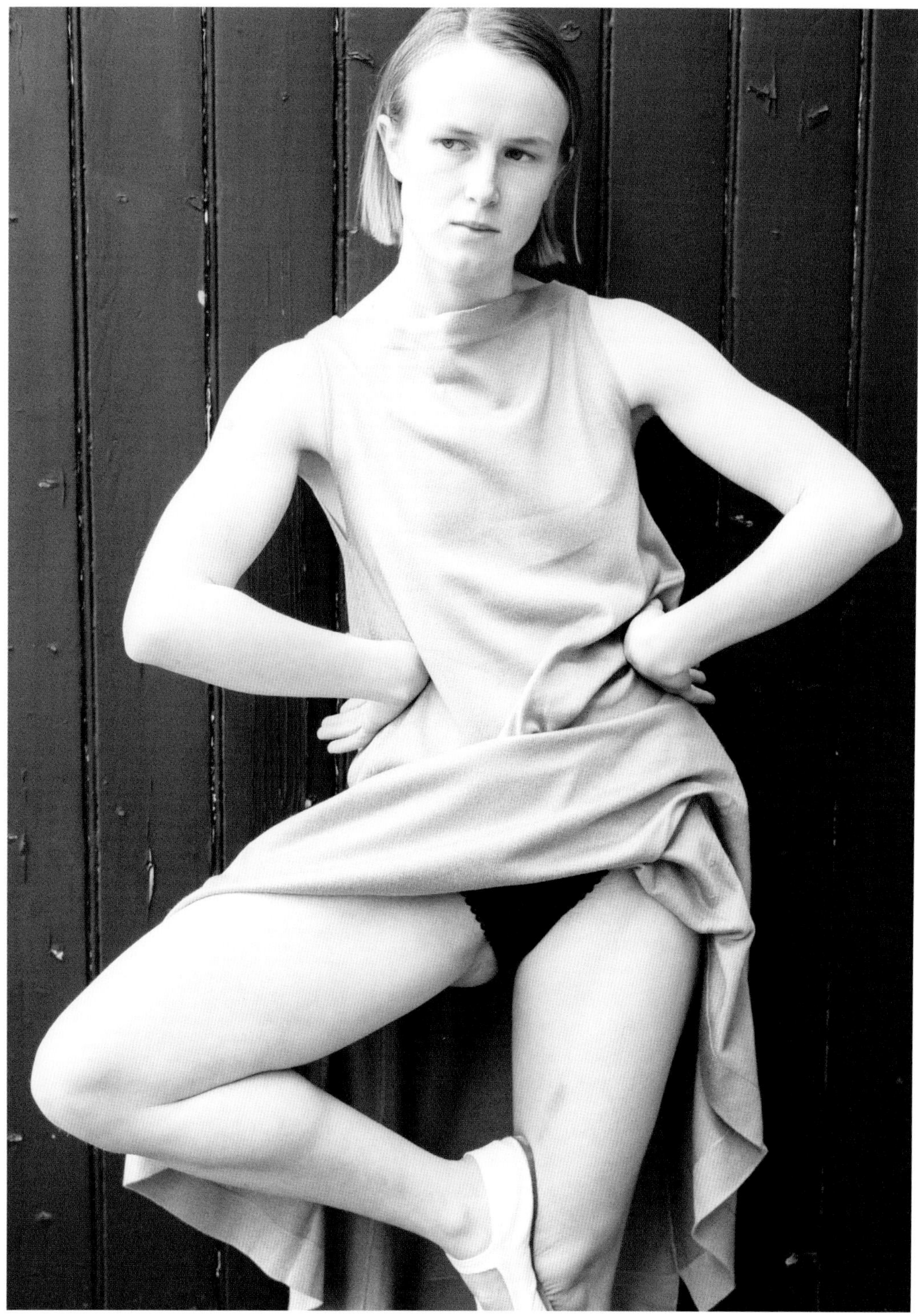

Liv Liberg
britt (pose), 2021
Fine art inkjet print, 42 × 30 cm
Liv Liberg

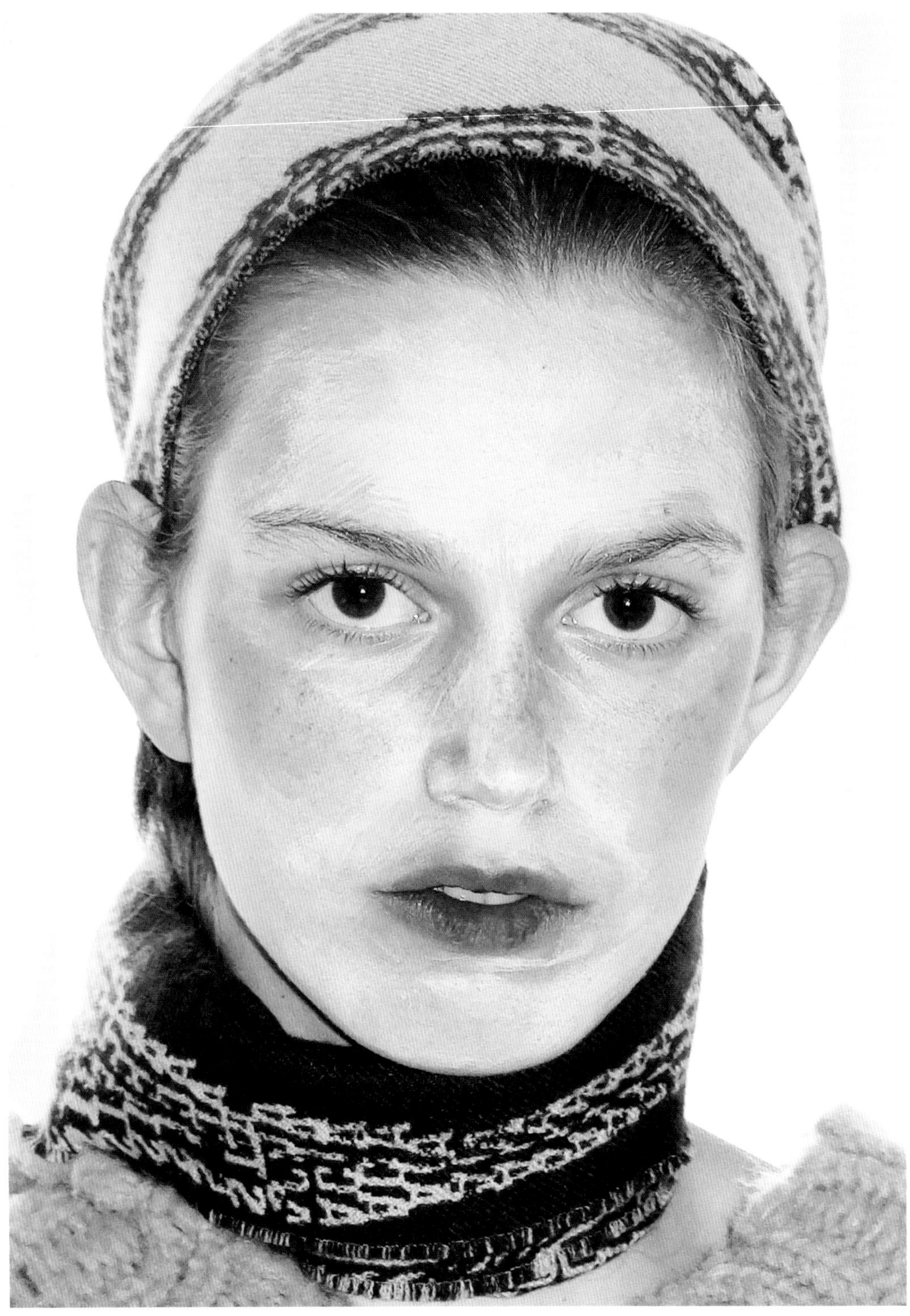

Liv Liberg
floor (scarves) #3 [for Acne Studios], 2021
Fine art inkjet print, 42 × 30 cm
Liv Liberg

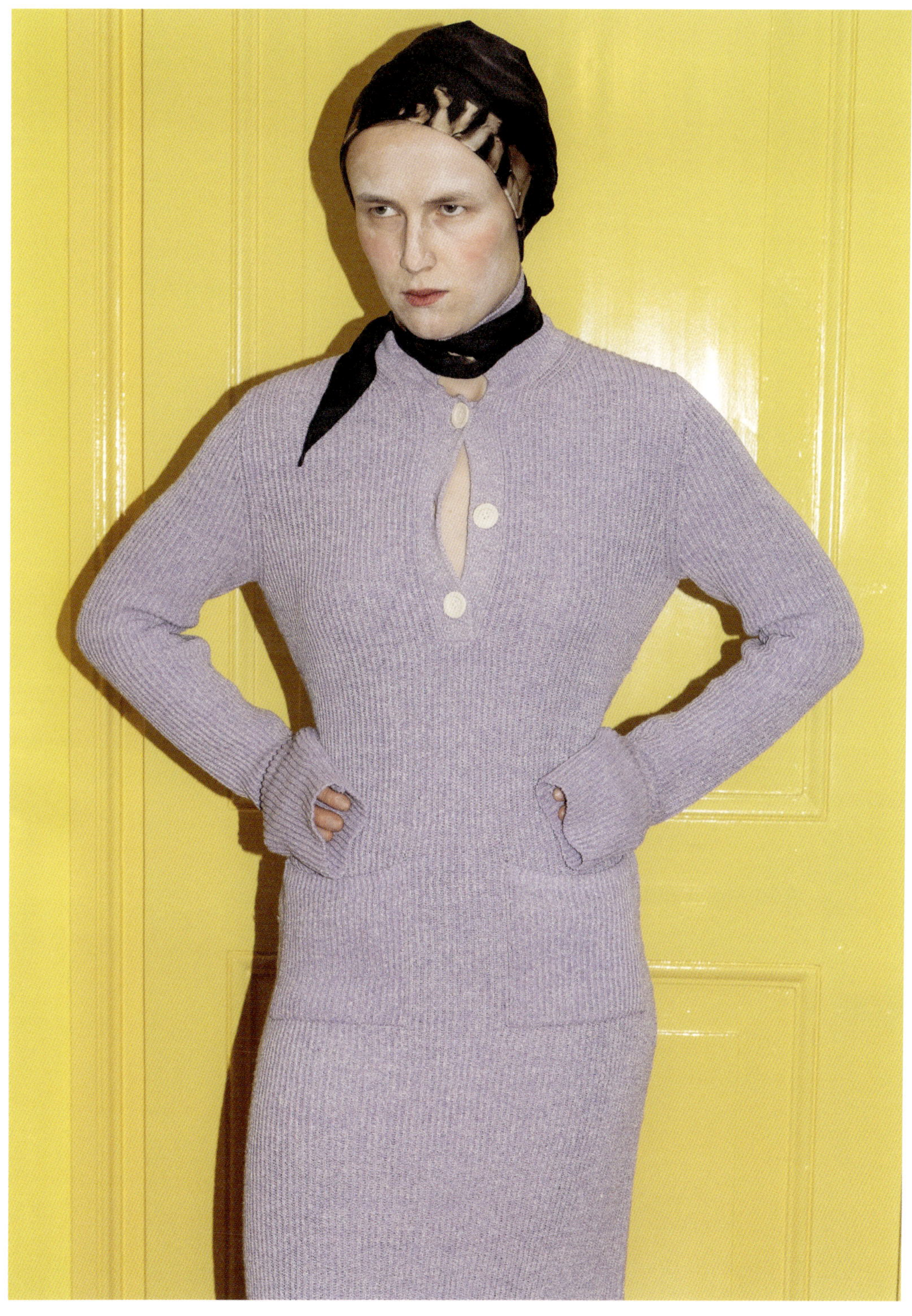

Liv Liberg
britt (yellow) [for Acne Studios], 2021
Fine art inkjet print, 42 × 30 cm
Liv Liberg

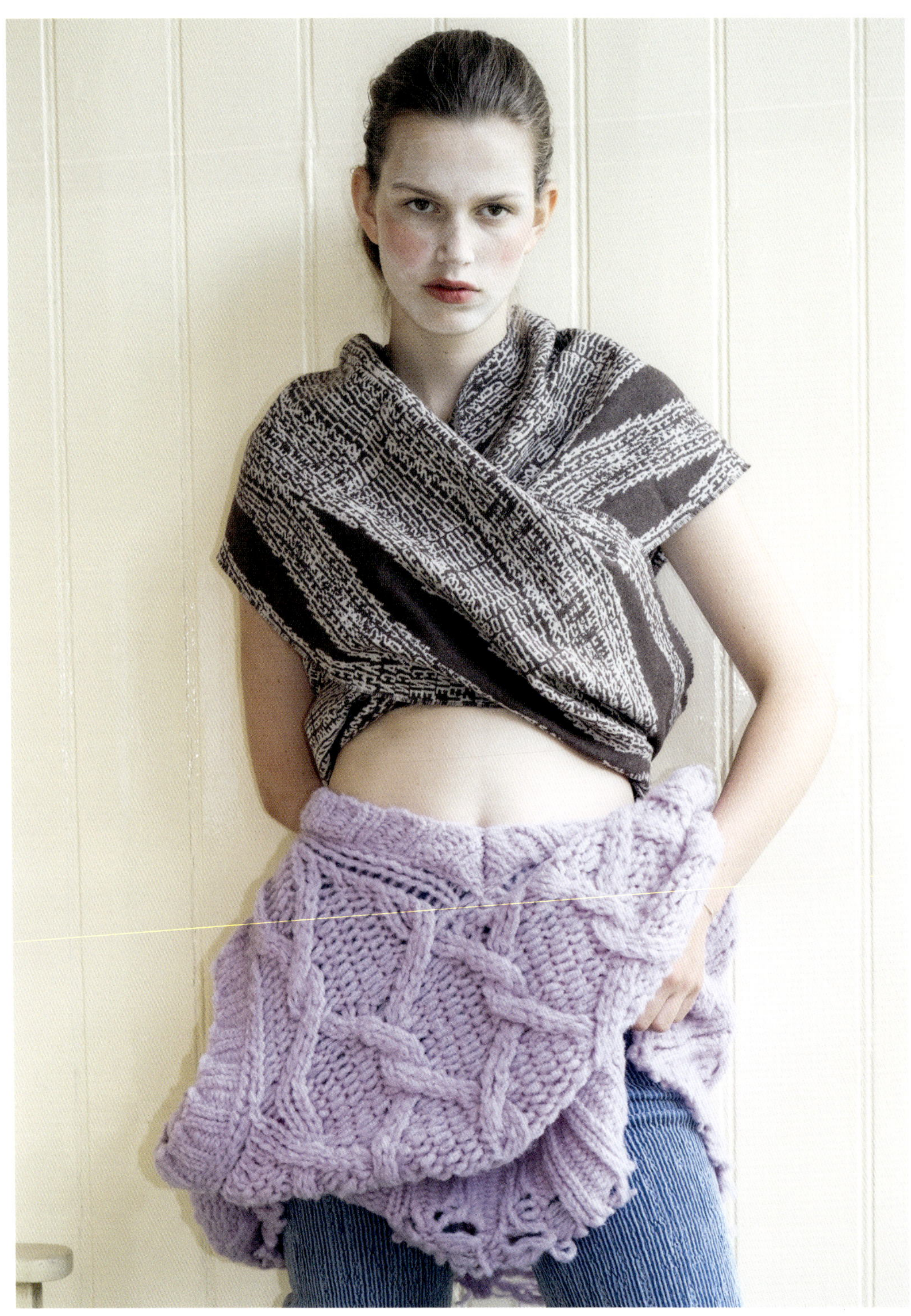

Liv Liberg
floor (cheeks) [for Acne Studios], 2021
Fine art inkjet print, 42 × 30 cm
Liv Liberg

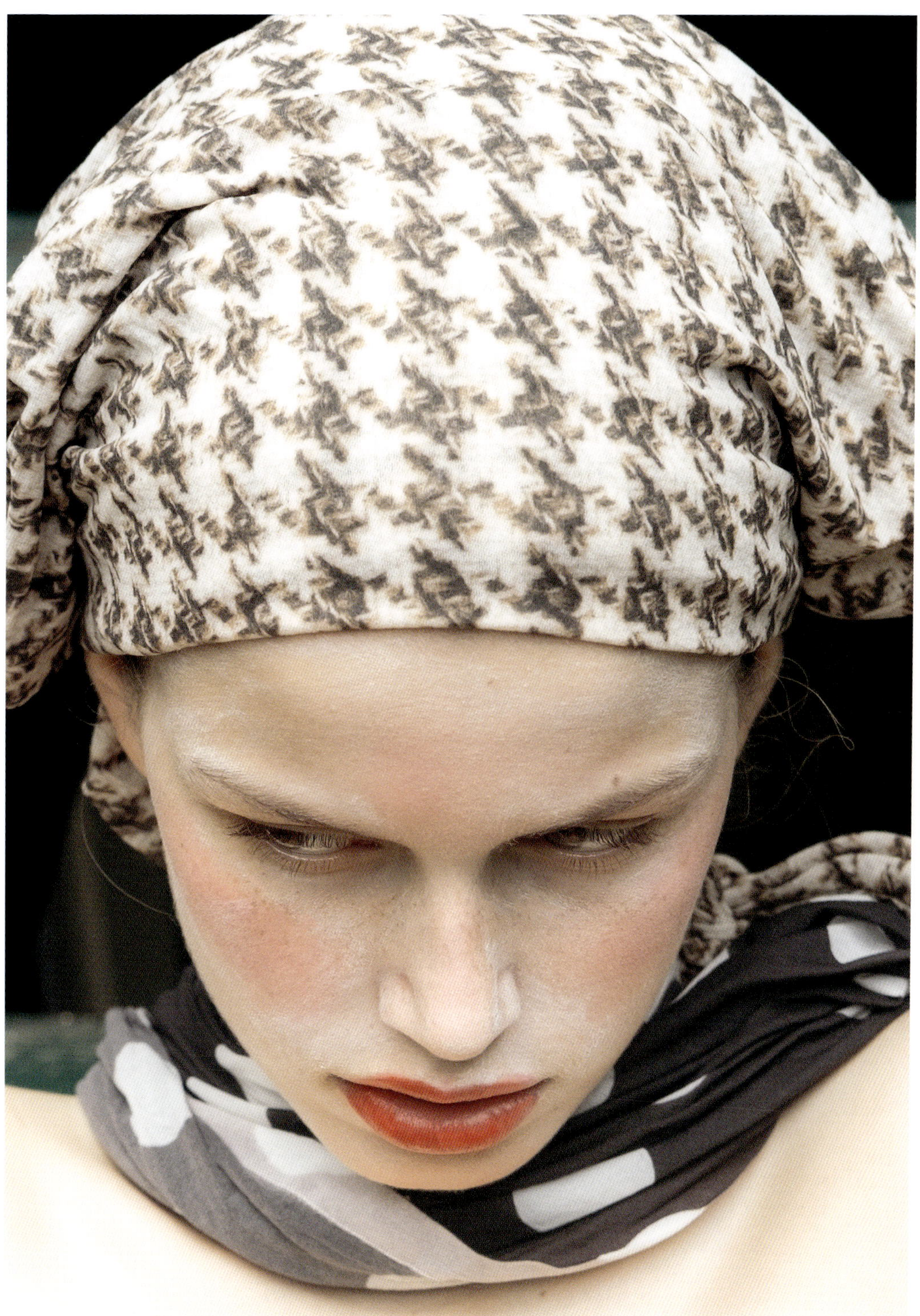

Liv Liberg
floor (scarves) #1 [for Acne Studios], 2021
Fine art inkjet print, 42 × 30 cm
Liv Liberg

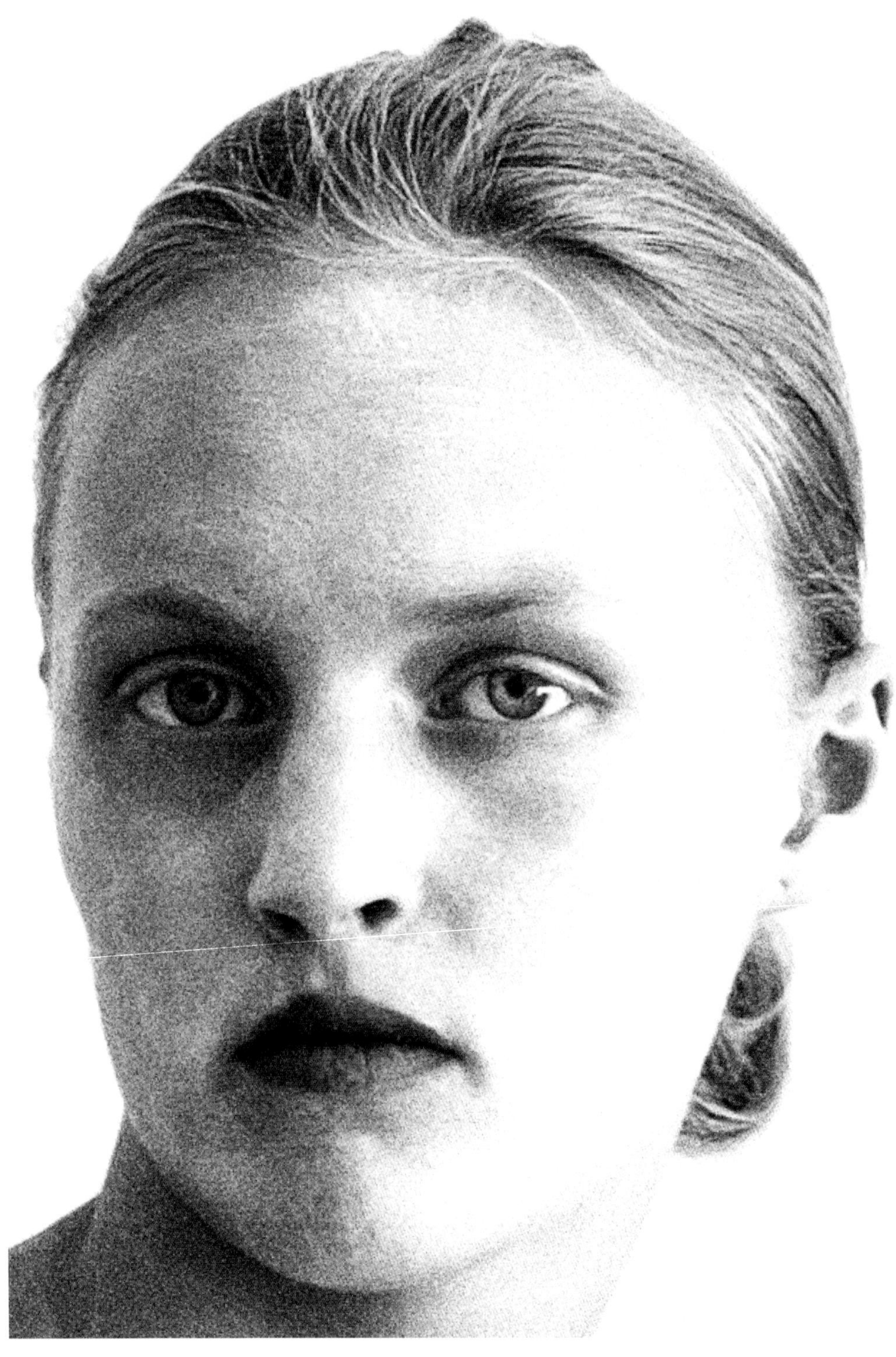

Liv Liberg
vere (face), 2021
Fine art inkjet print, 42 × 30 cm
Liv Liberg

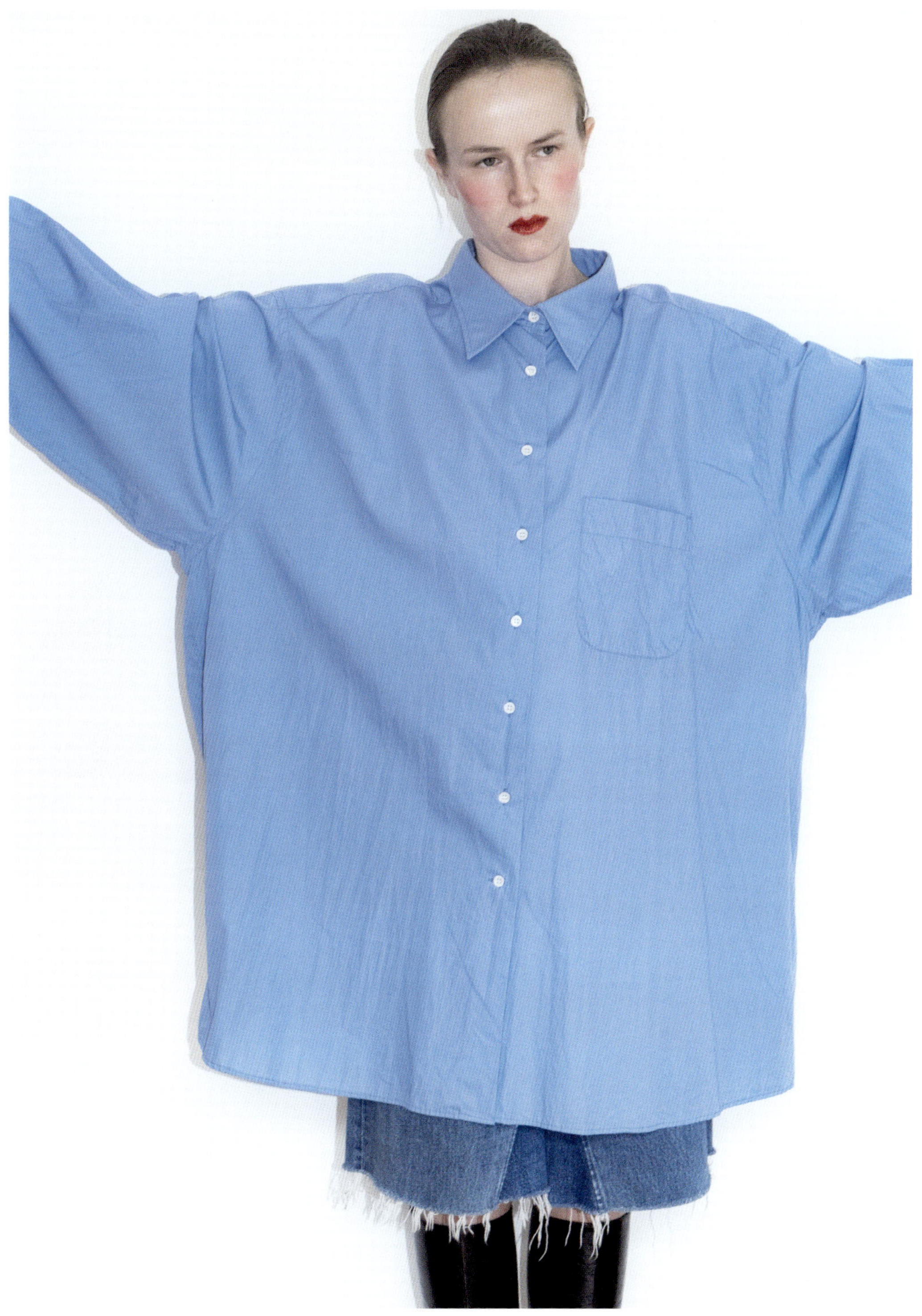

Liv Liberg
britt (shirt), 2021
Fine art inkjet print, 42 × 30 cm
Liv Liberg

Amber Pinkerton

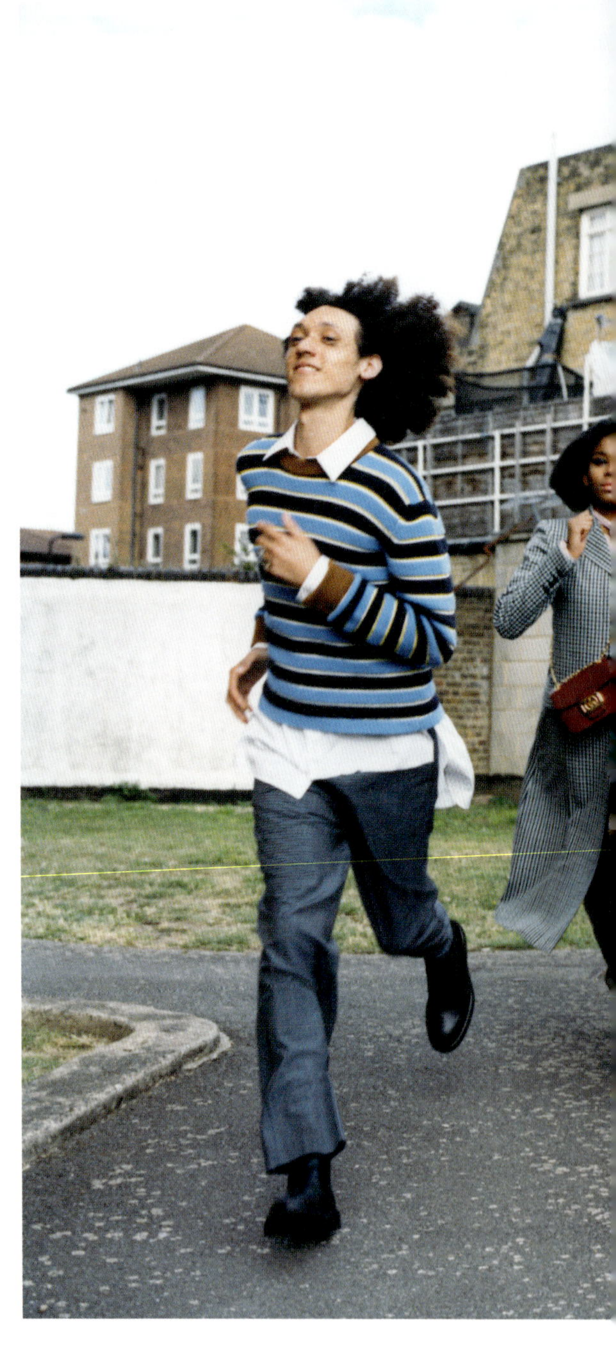

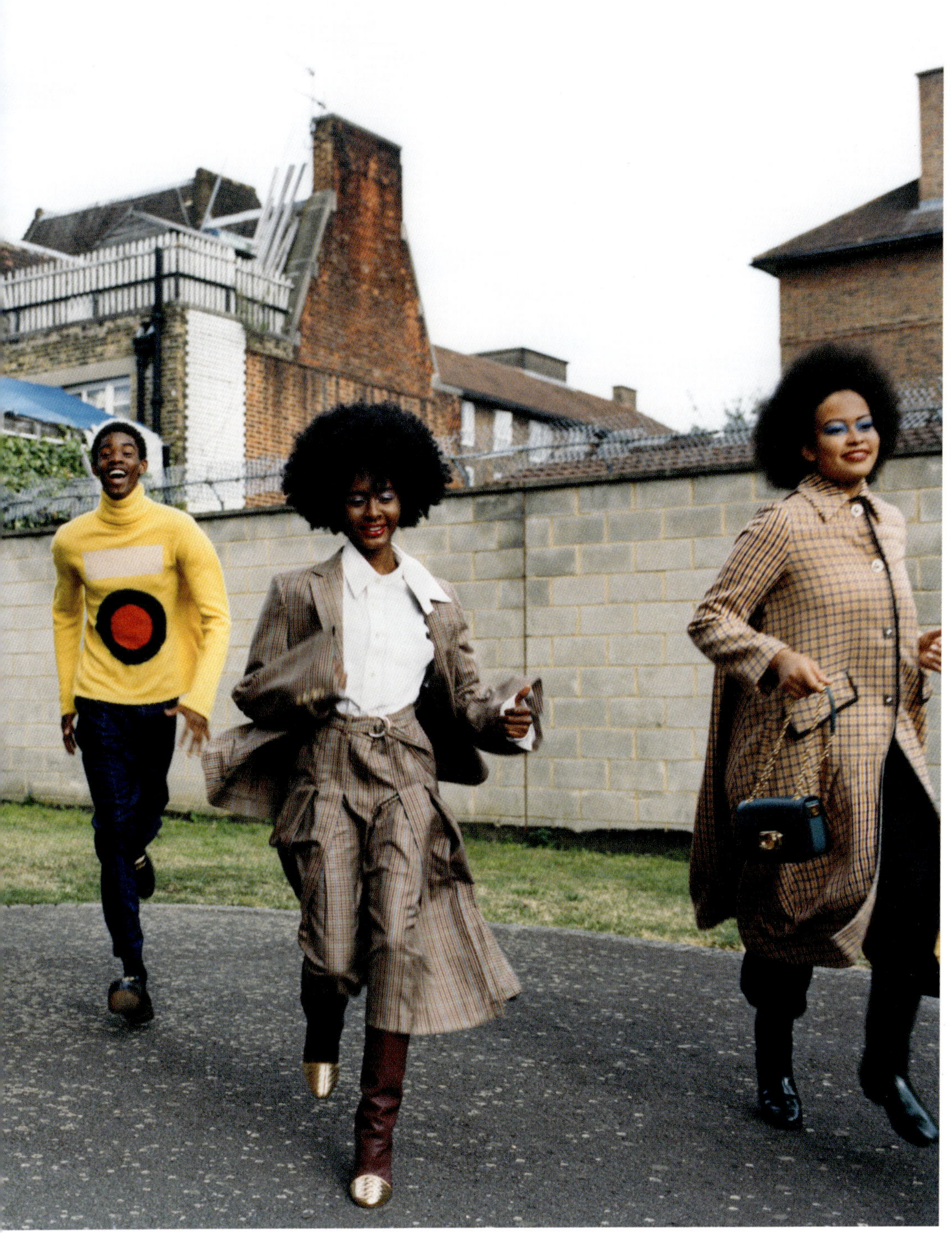

Amber Pinkerton
Youthquake: Youthquake Daydream, 2020
Digital C-type print, 33.7 × 42 cm
Alice Black Gallery

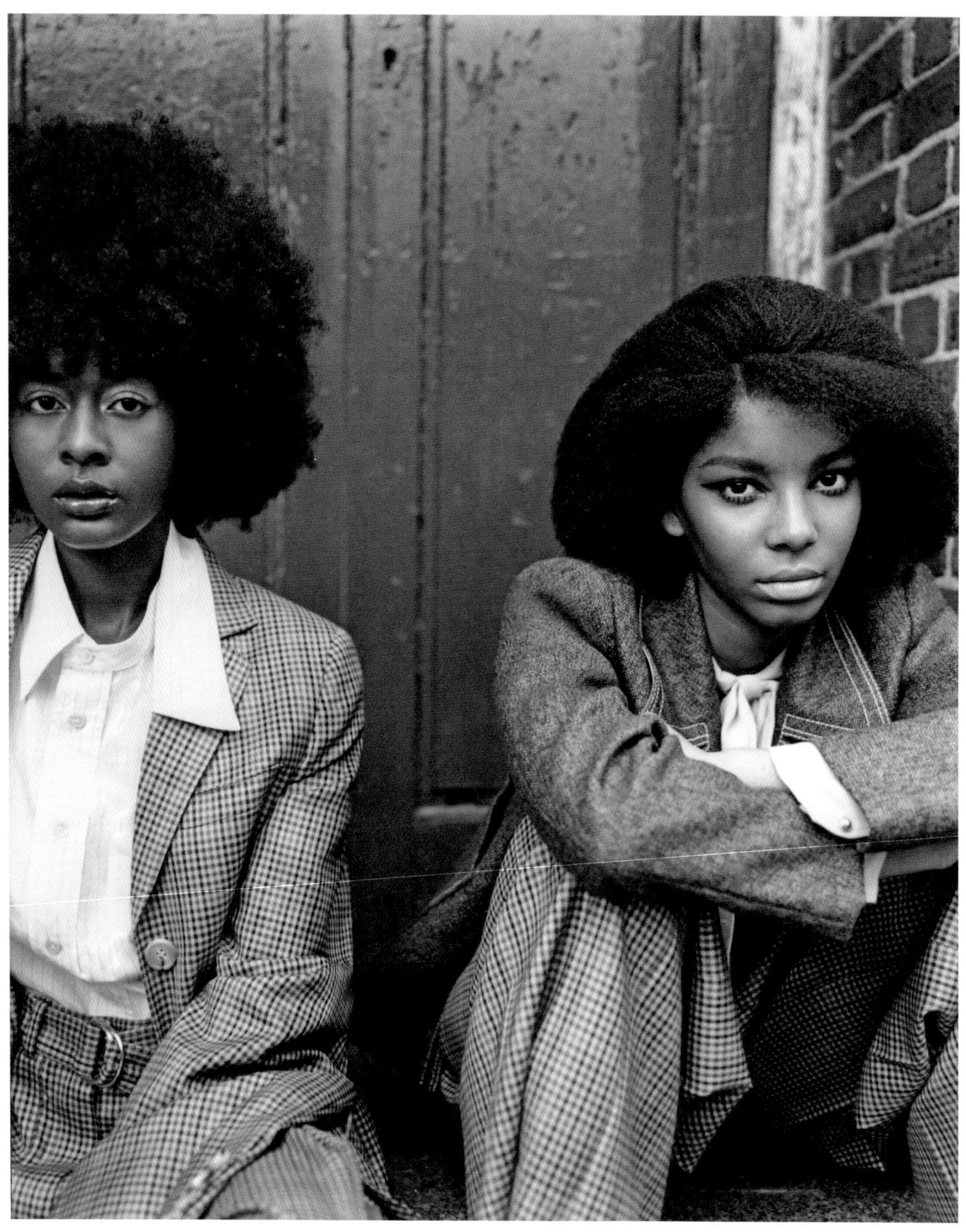

Amber Pinkerton
Kyesha & Davinya: Youthquake Daydream, 2020
Digital C-type print, 59.4 × 48 cm
Alice Black Gallery

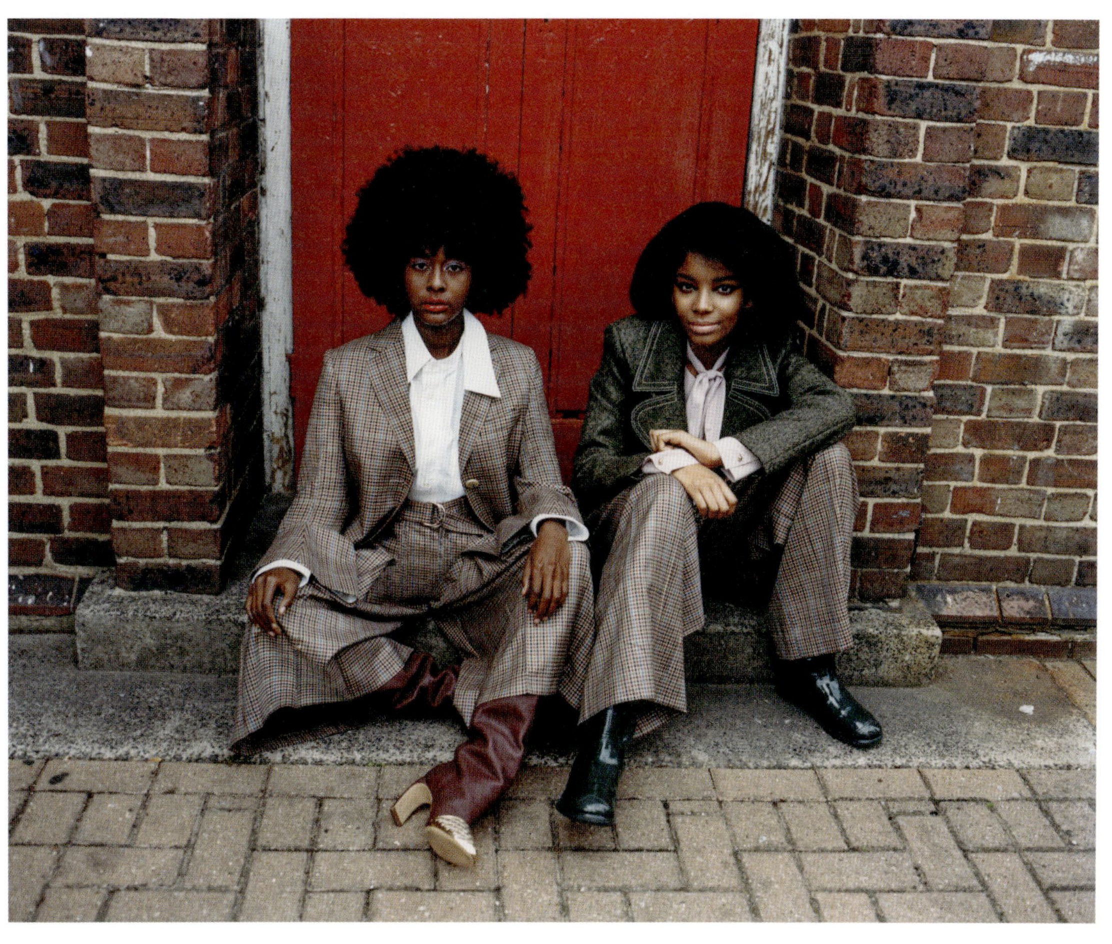

Amber Pinkerton
Davinya & Kyesha: Youthquake Daydream, 2020
Digital C-type print, 34 × 42 cm
Alice Black Gallery

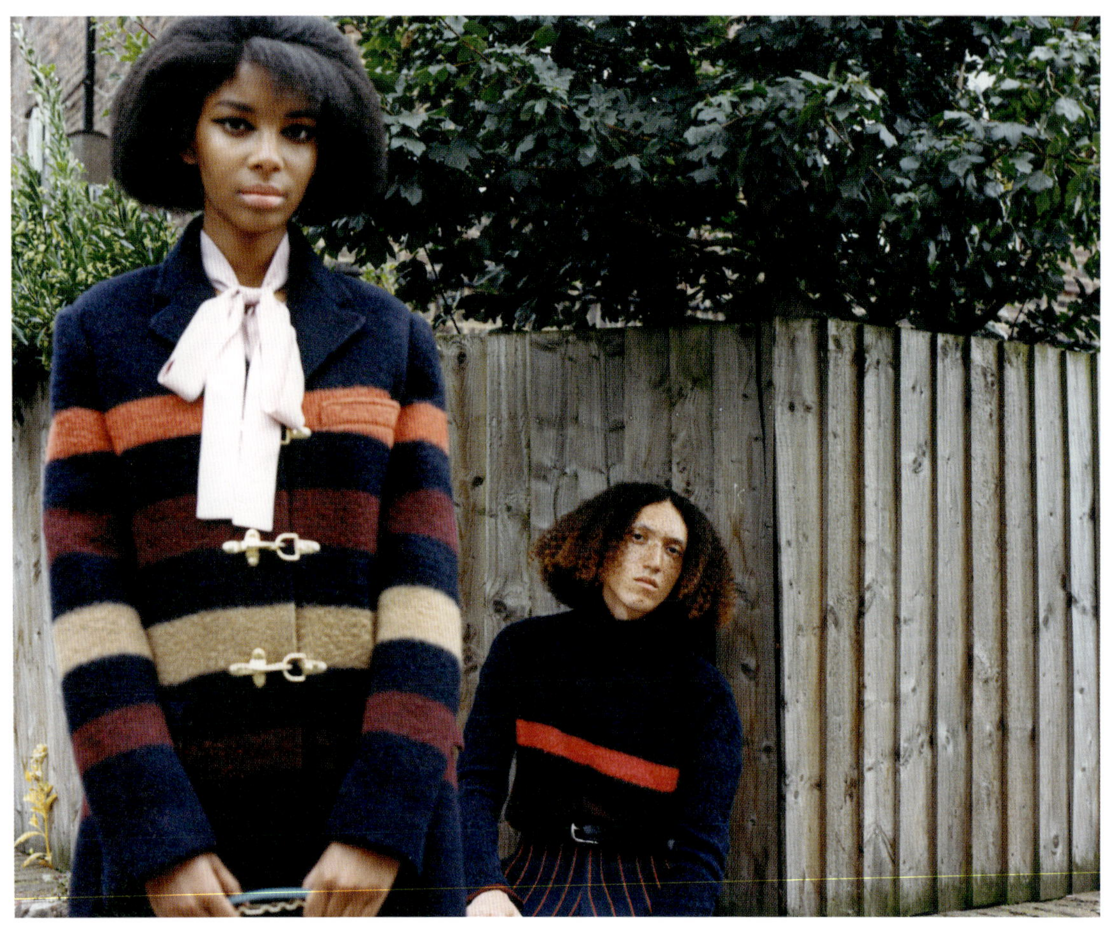

Amber Pikerton
Kyesha & Jordan: Youthquake Daydream, 2020
Digital C-type print, 34 × 42 cm
Alice Black Gallery

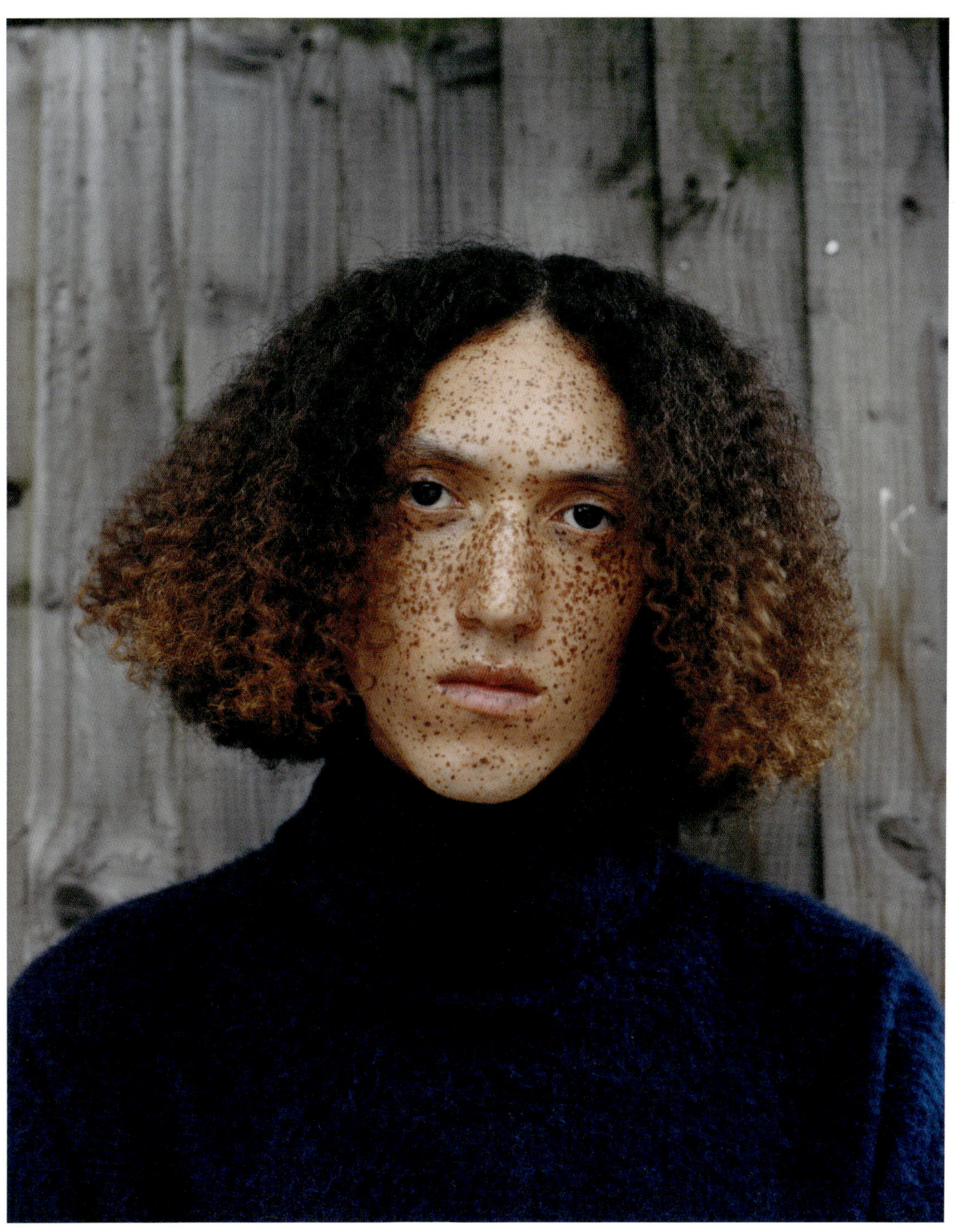

Amber Pinkerton
Jordan: Youthquake Daydream, 2020
Digital C-type print, 84.1 × 67.3 cm
Alice Black Gallery

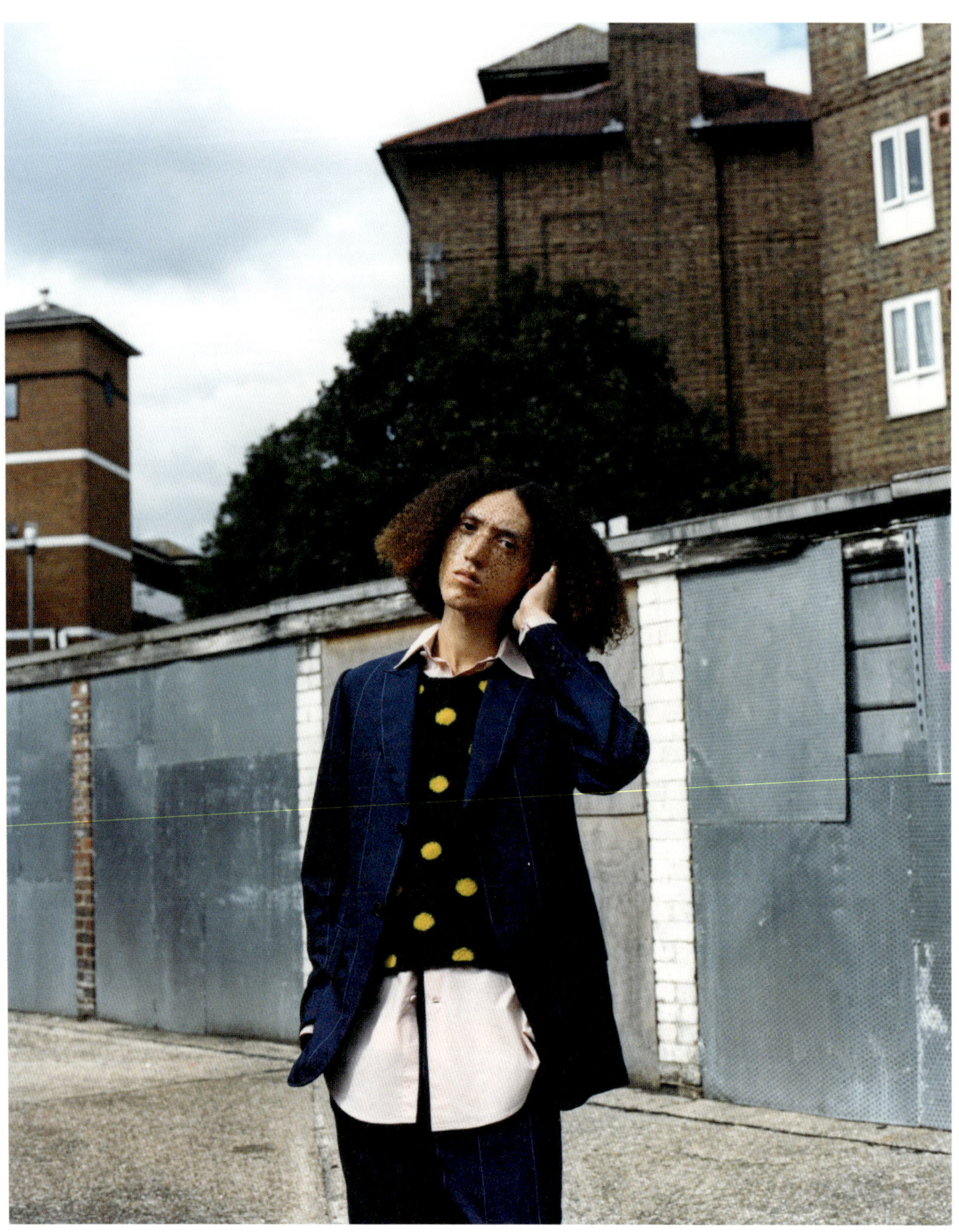

Amber Pinkerton
Jordan: Youthquake Daydream, 2020
Digital C-type print, 59.4 × 47.8 cm
Alice Black Gallery

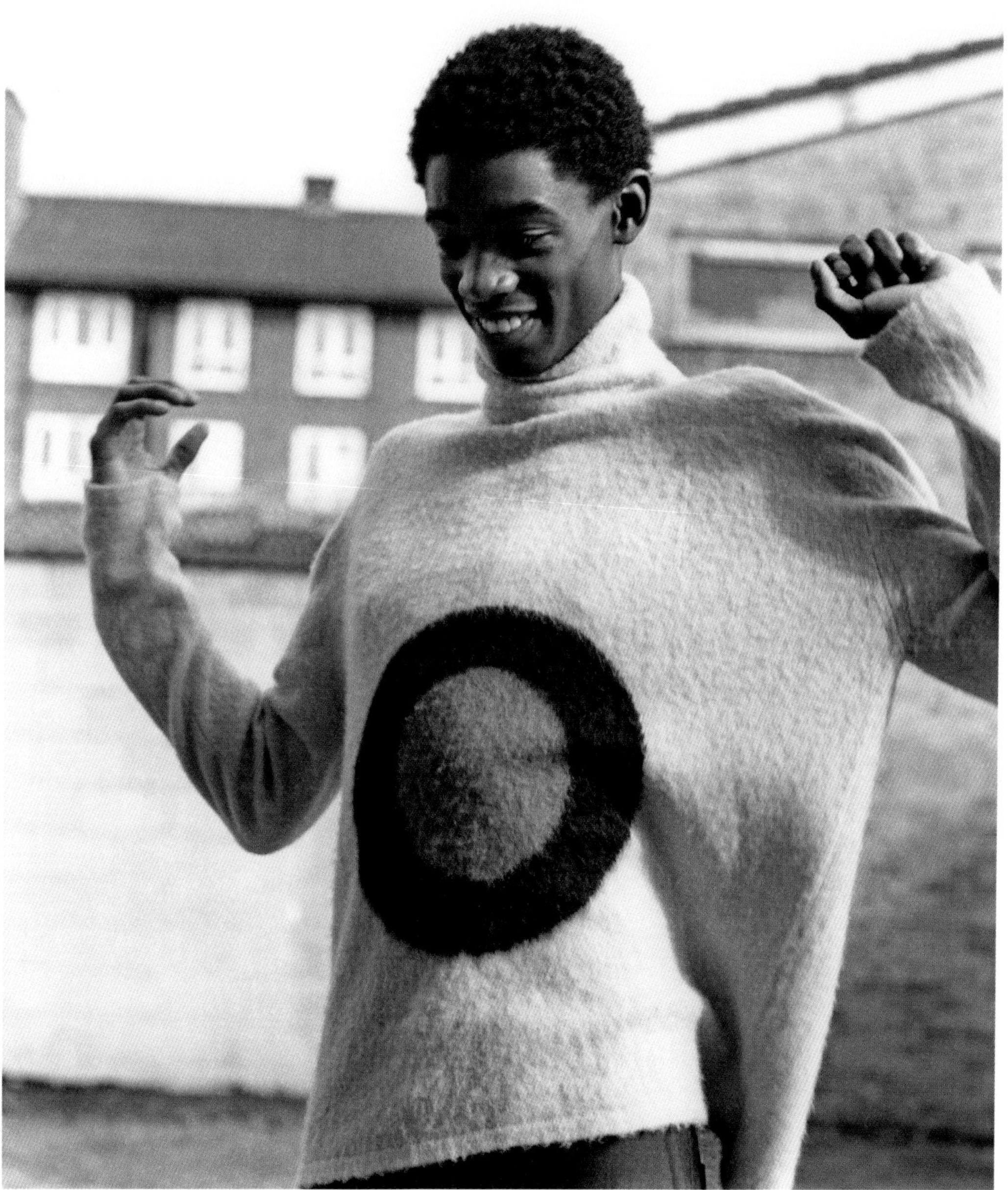

Amber Pinkerton
Glee: Youthquake Daydream, 2020
Digital C-type print, 59.4 × 47.7 cm
Alice Black Gallery

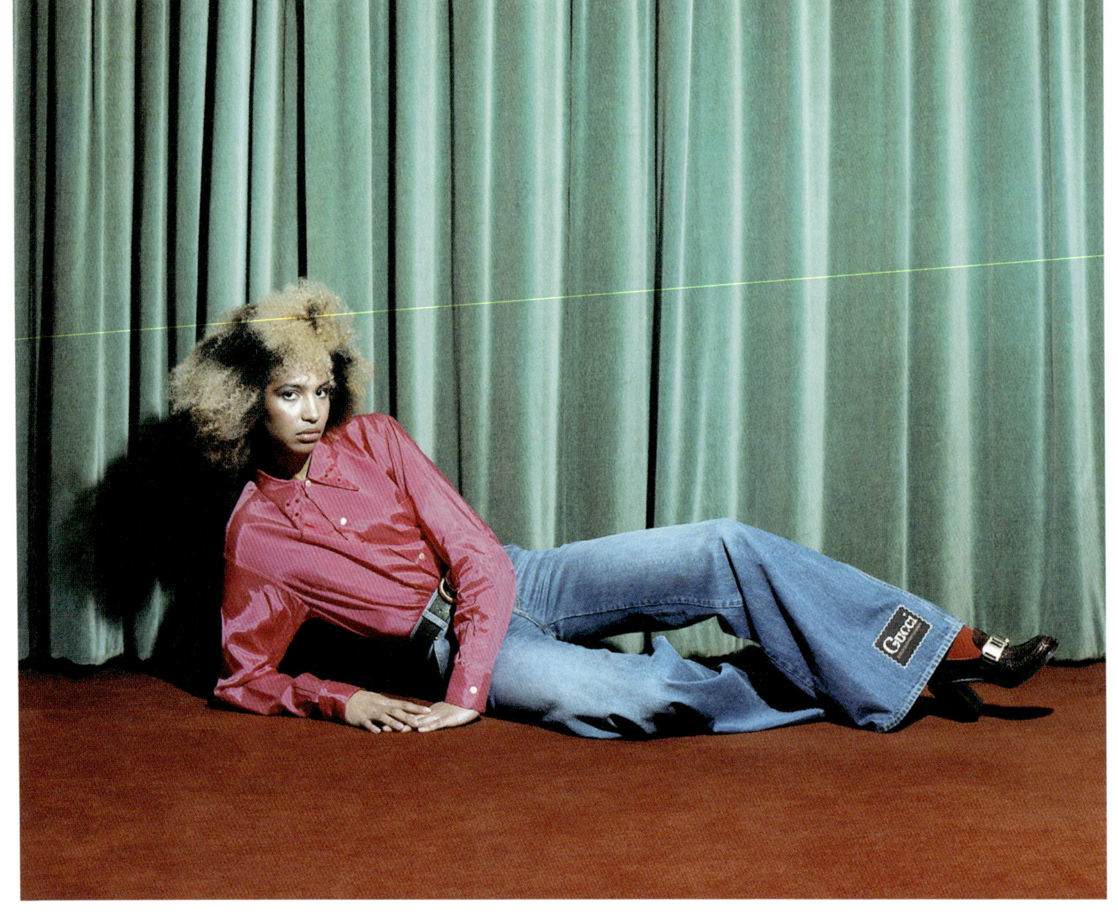

Amber Pinkerton
Nadia: Girls Next Door, 2020
Digital C-type print, 24 × 29.7 cm
Alice Black Gallery

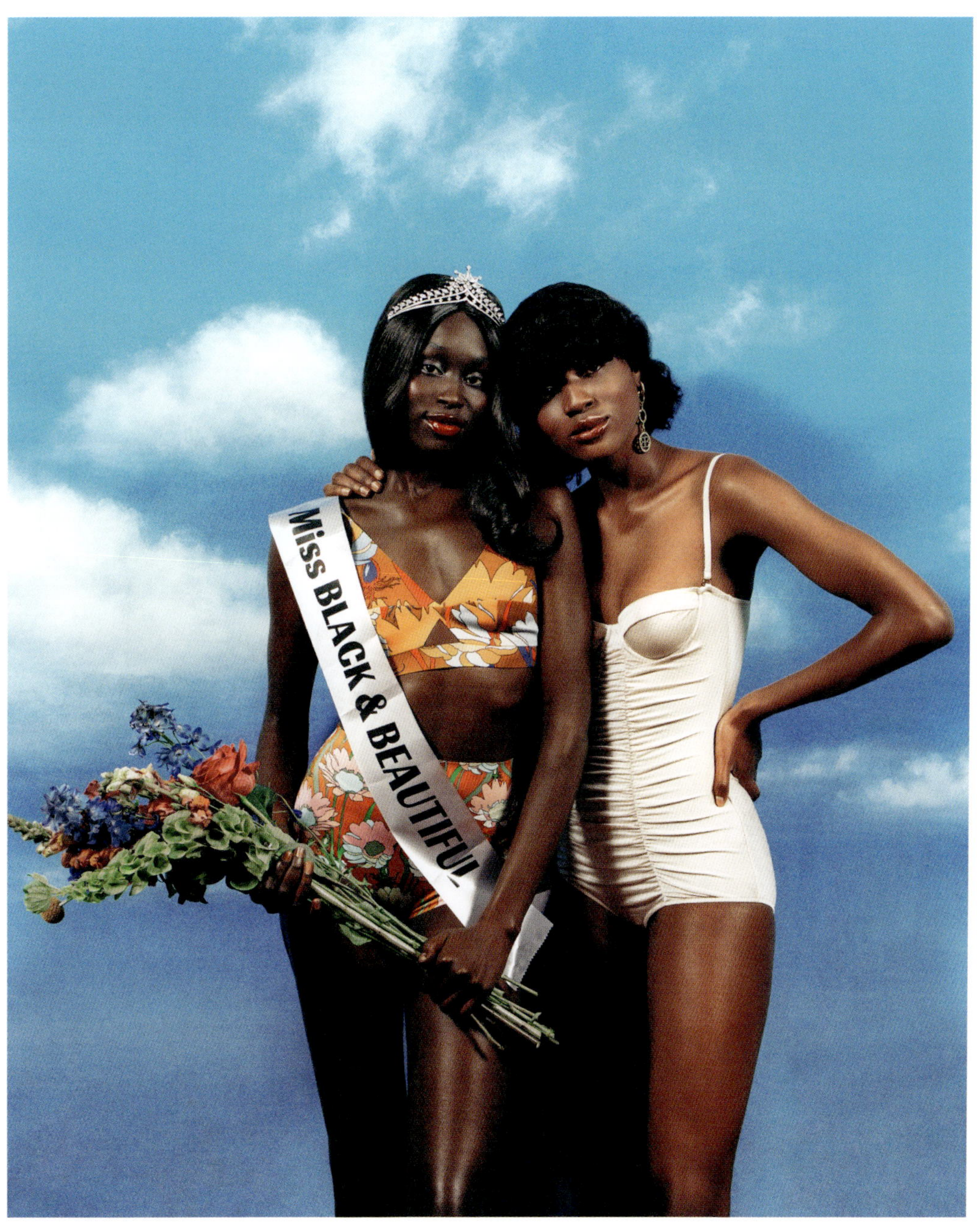

Amber Pinkerton
Sabah & Aminat: Girls Next Door, 2020
Digital C-type print, 118.9 × 97.9 cm
Alice Black Gallery

Elizaveta Porodina

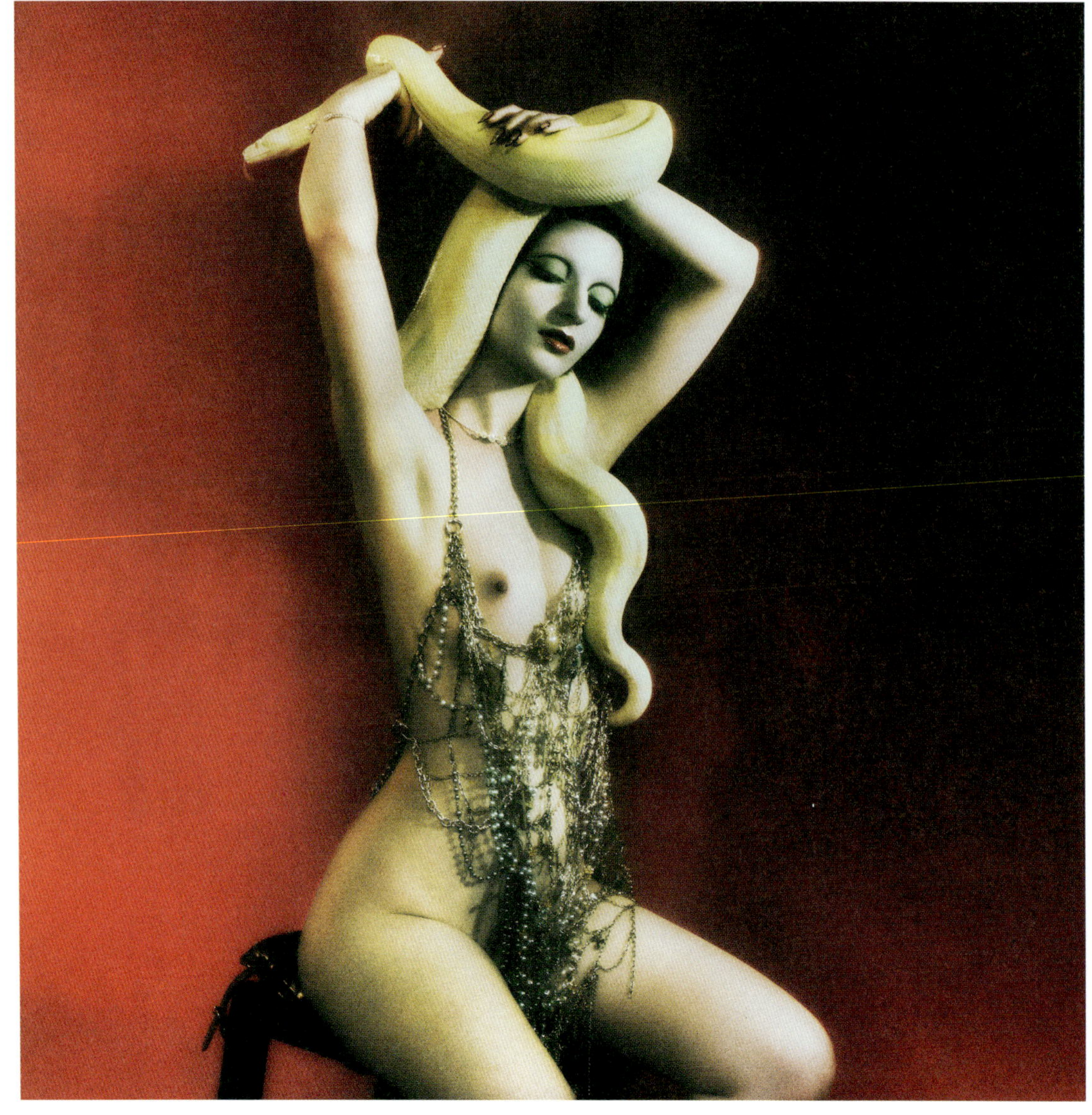

Elizaveta Porodina
Cecile and Eden, Paris, 2021
C-print, 45 × 45 cm
Elizaveta Porodina

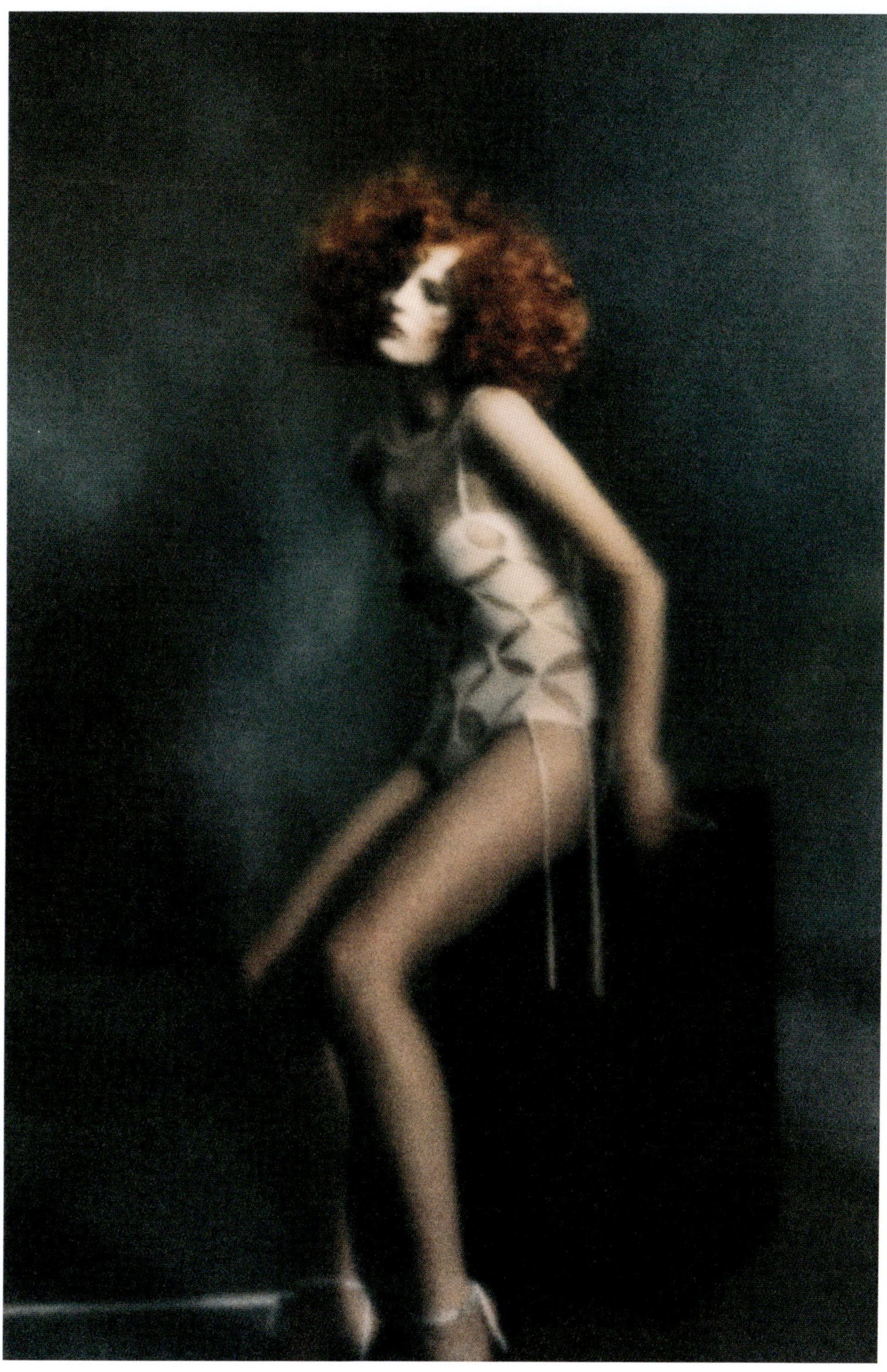

Elizaveta Porodina
Woman in Tears I, Paris, 2020
C-print, 45 × 30 cm
Elizaveta Porodina

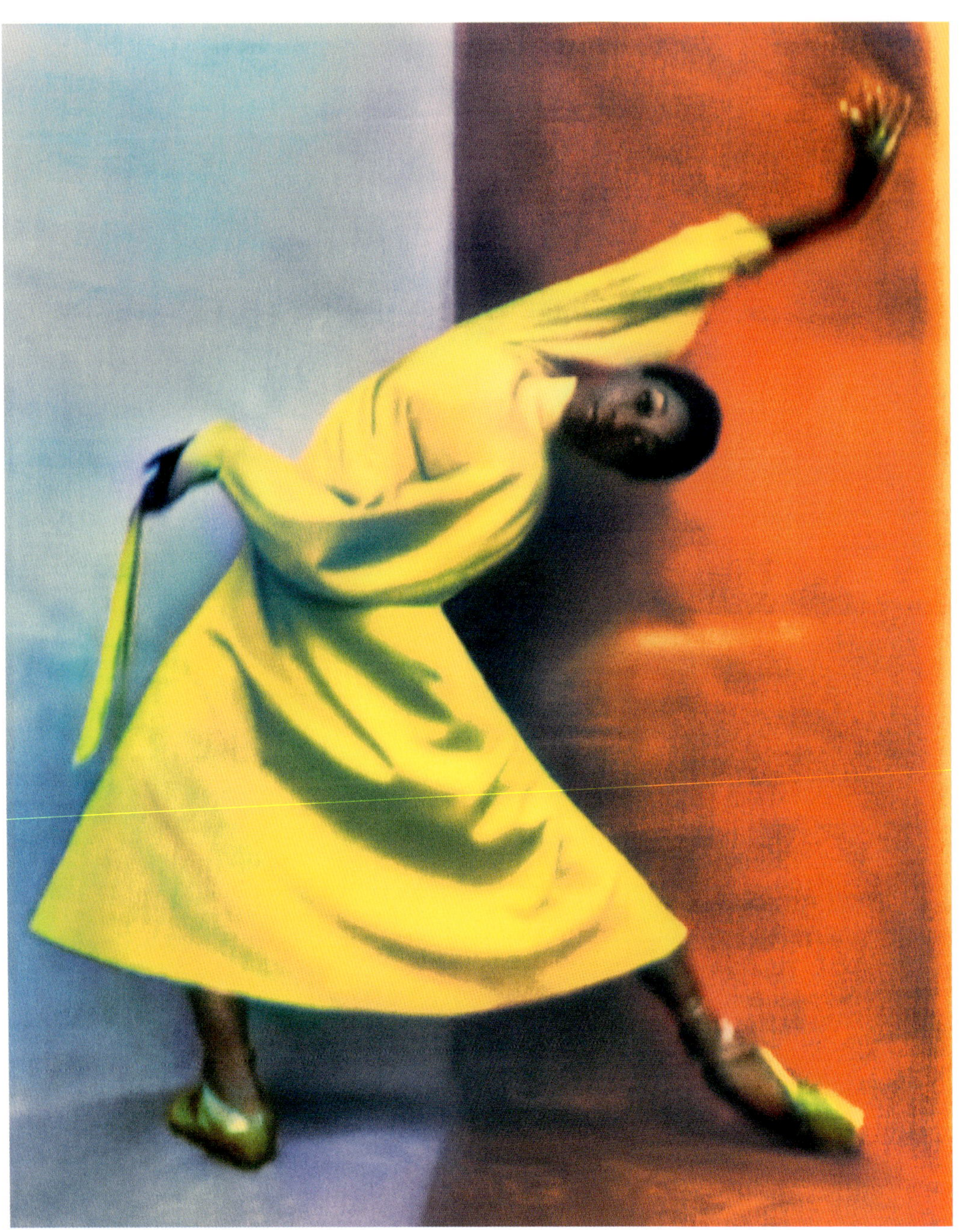

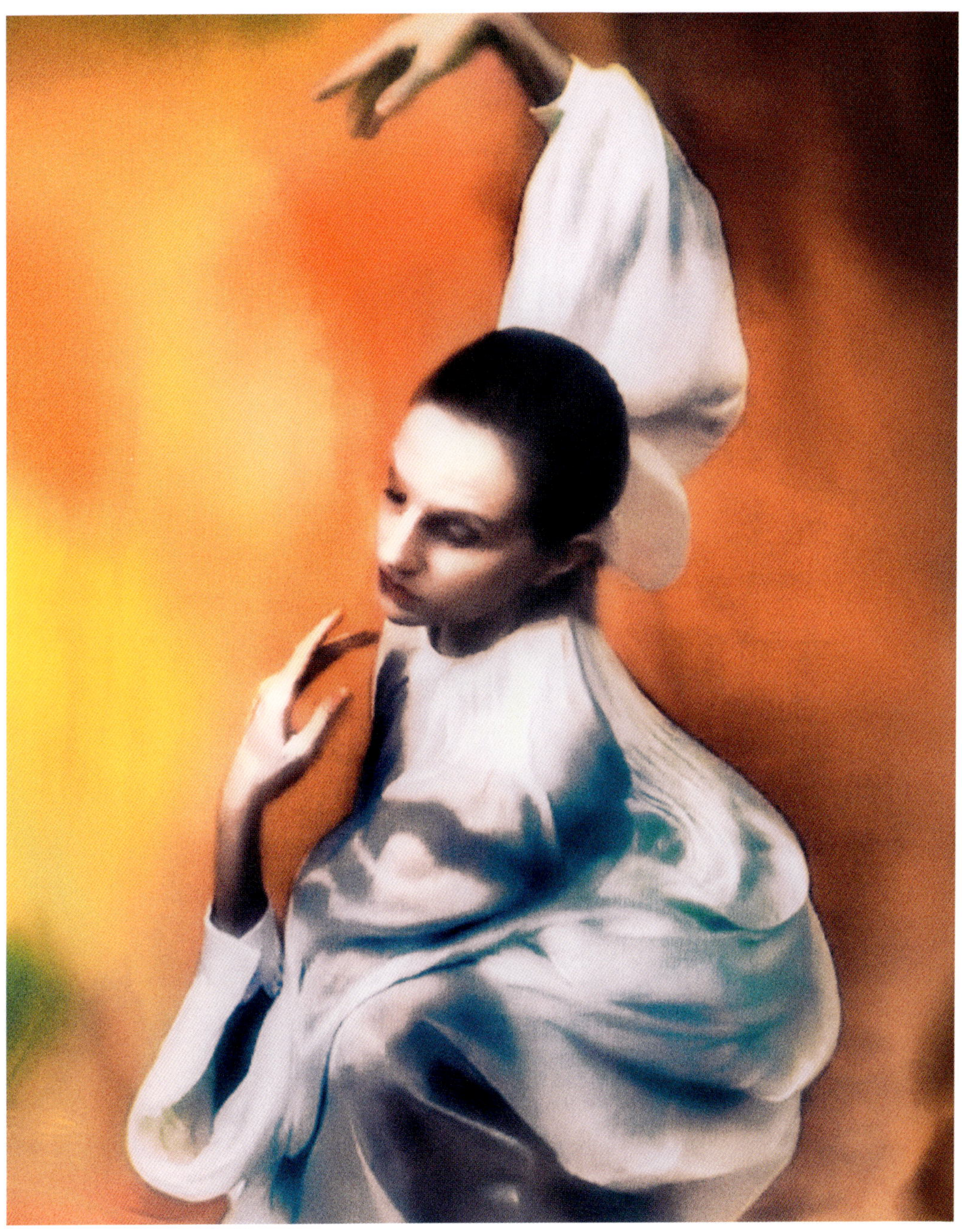

Elizaveta Porodina
Carolina Herrera I (Wendy Whelan), Zoom to New York, 2020
C-print, 40.8 × 30 cm
Elizaveta Porodina

Nadine Ijewere

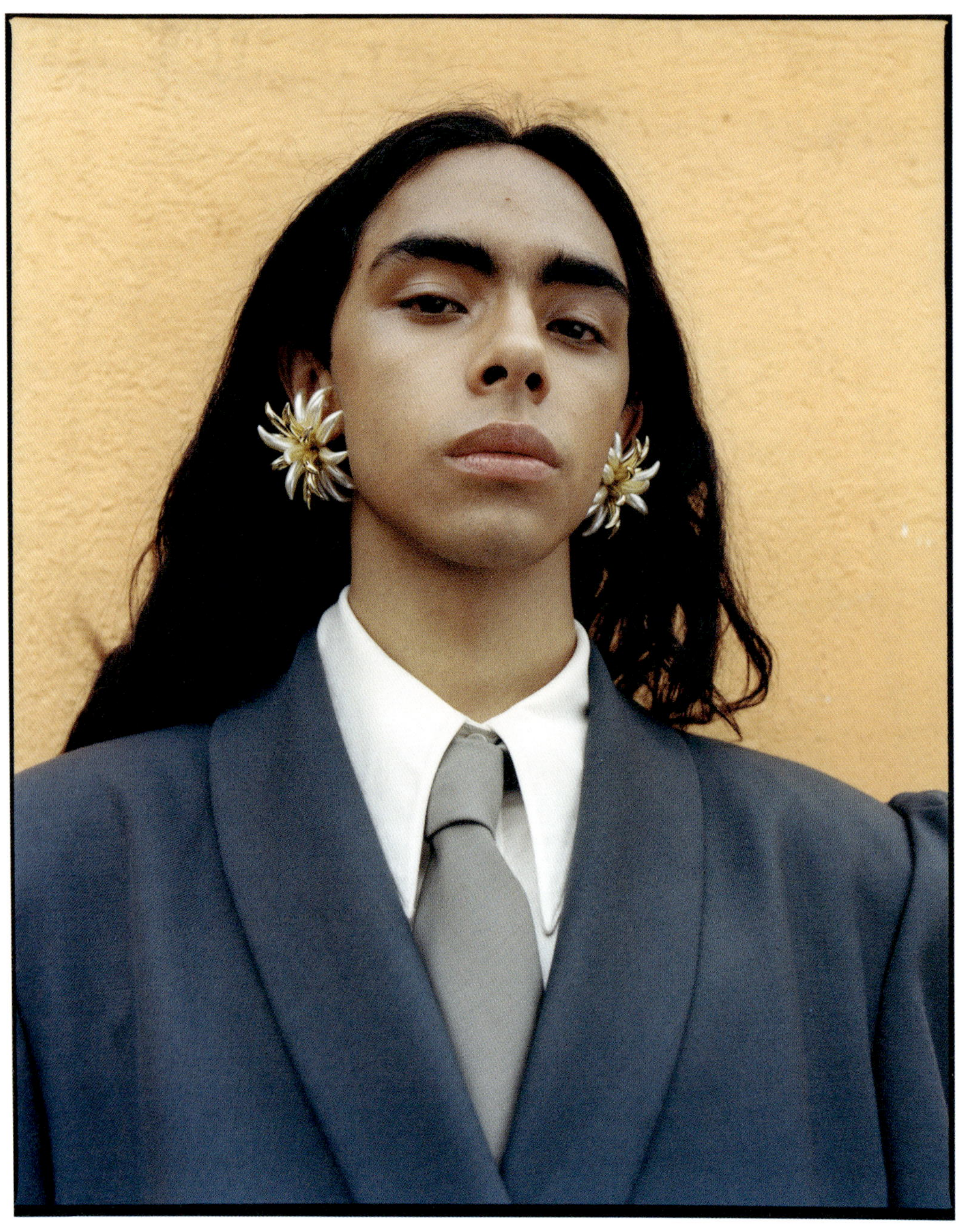

Nadine Ijewere
Flower Earrings [from the series *What's Up*], 2019
Fine art inkjet print on 305 gsm Hahnemühle Photo Rag Ultra Smooth paper, 60 × 50 cm
CLM Agency London

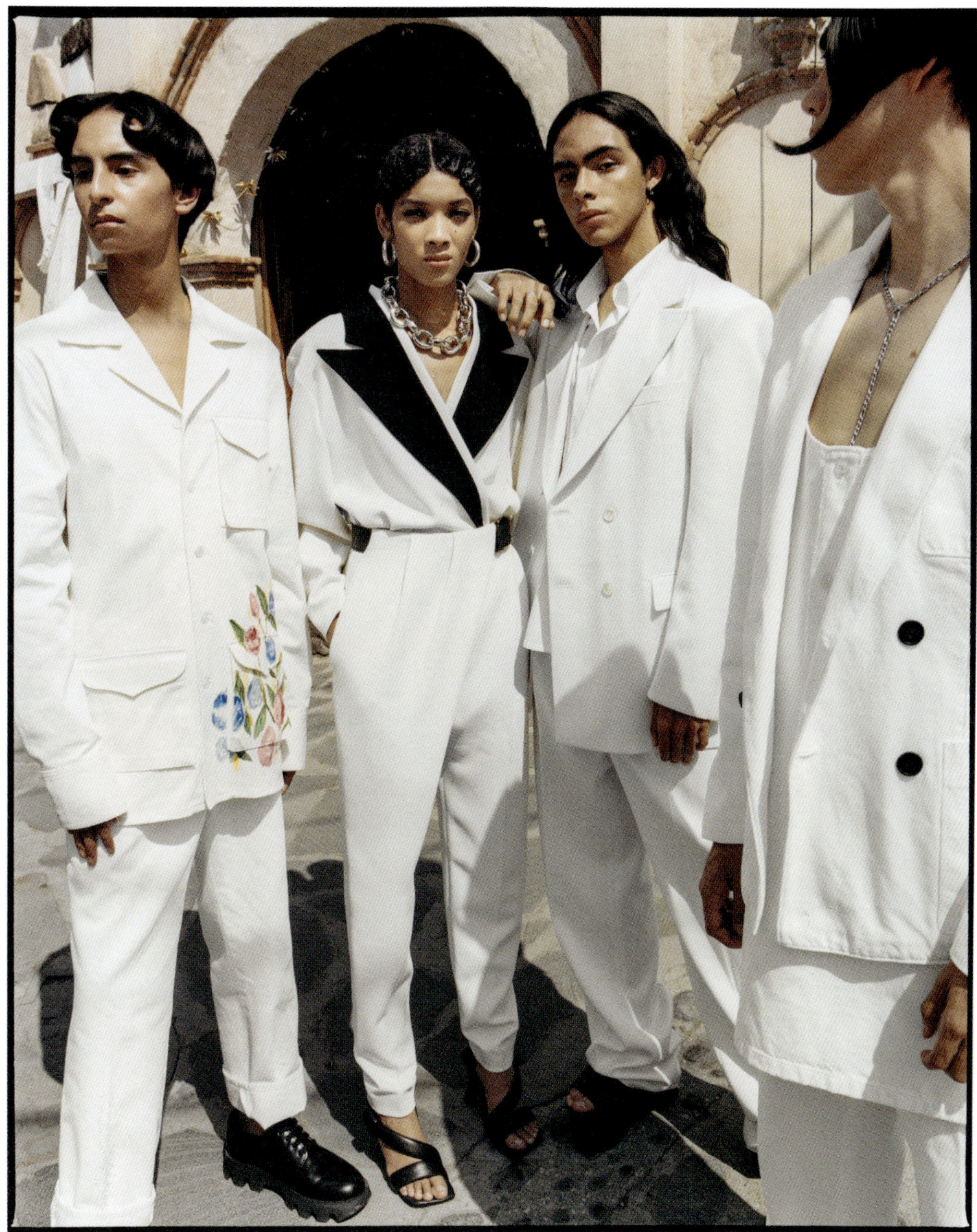

Nadine Ijewere
Untitled [from the series *What's Up*], 2019
Fine art inkjet print on 305 gsm Hahnemühle Photo Rag Ultra Smooth paper, 60 × 50 cm
CLM Agency London

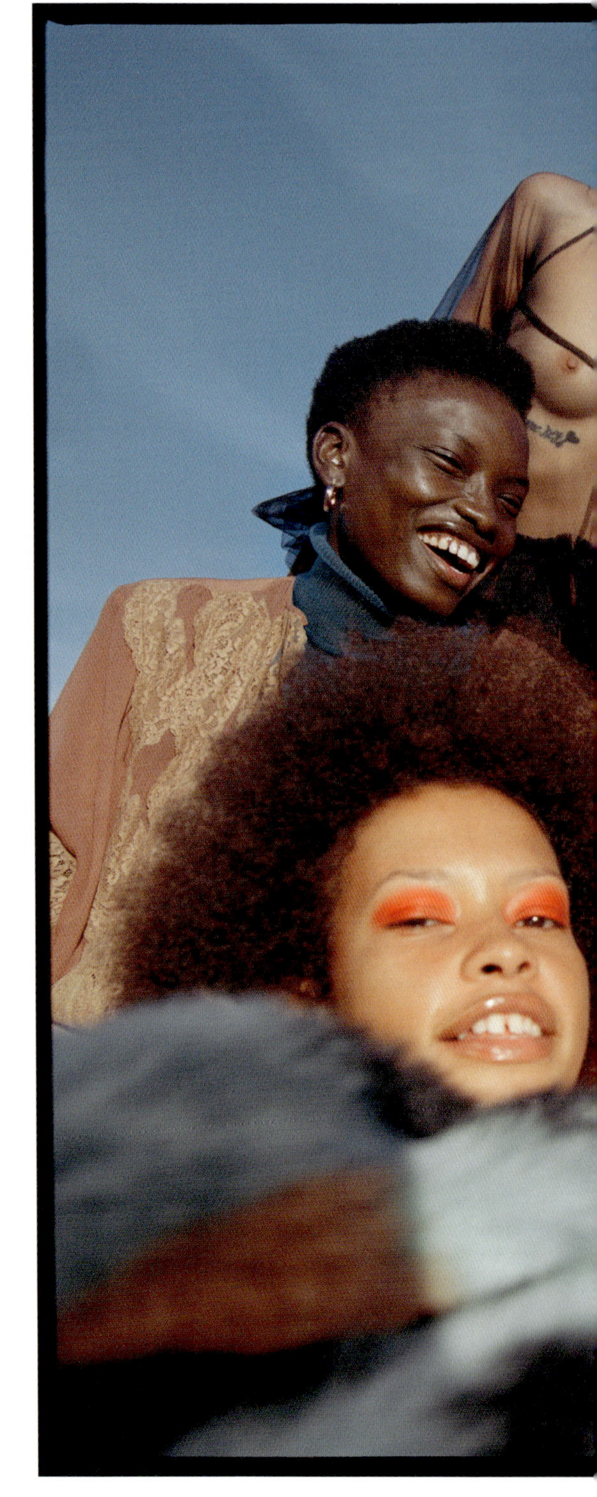

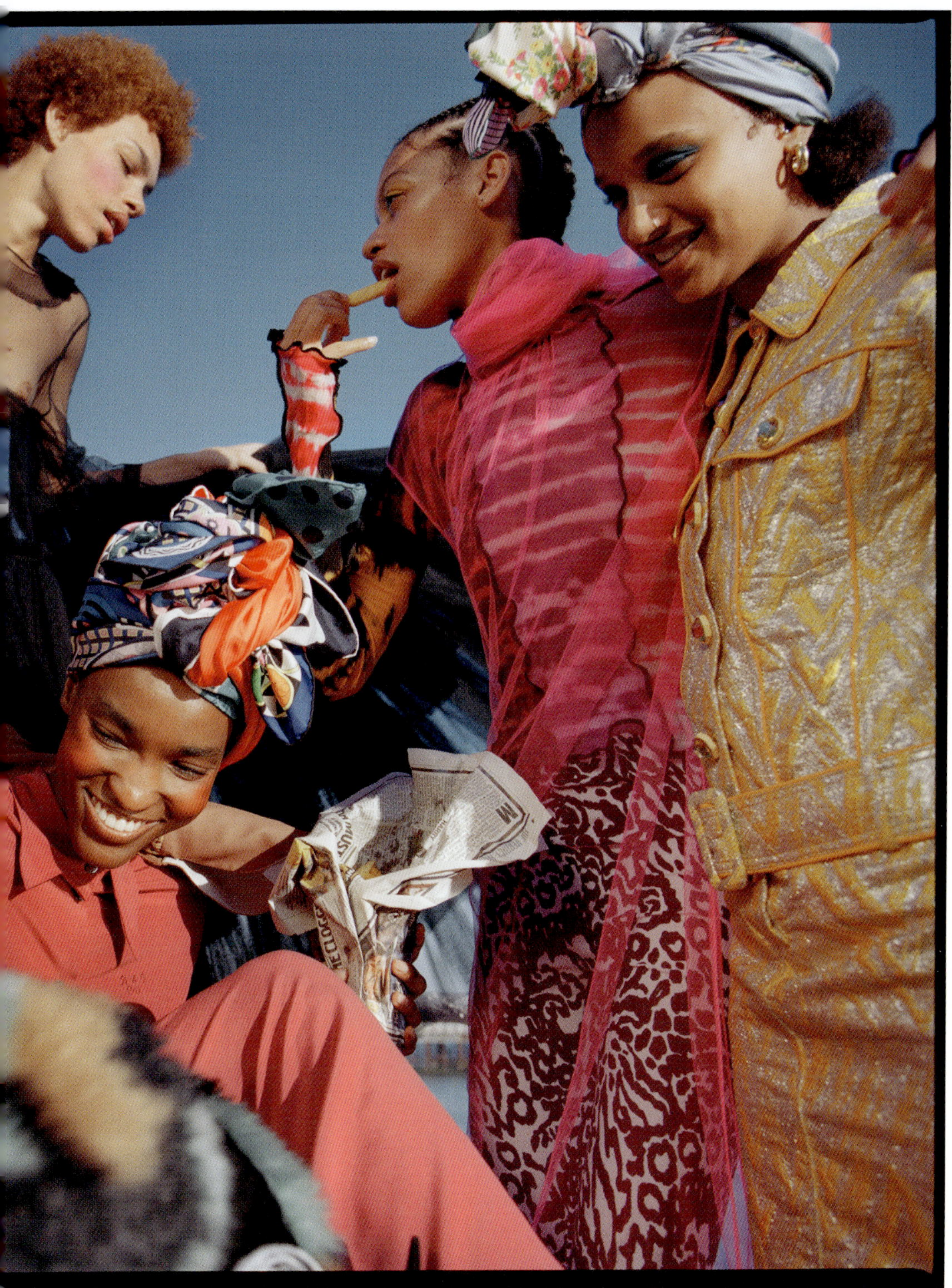

Nadine Ijewere
Untitled [from the series *Joy as an Act of Resistance*], 2018
Fine art inkjet print on 305 gsm Hahnemühle Photo Rag Ultra Smooth paper, 50 × 60 cm
CLM Agency London

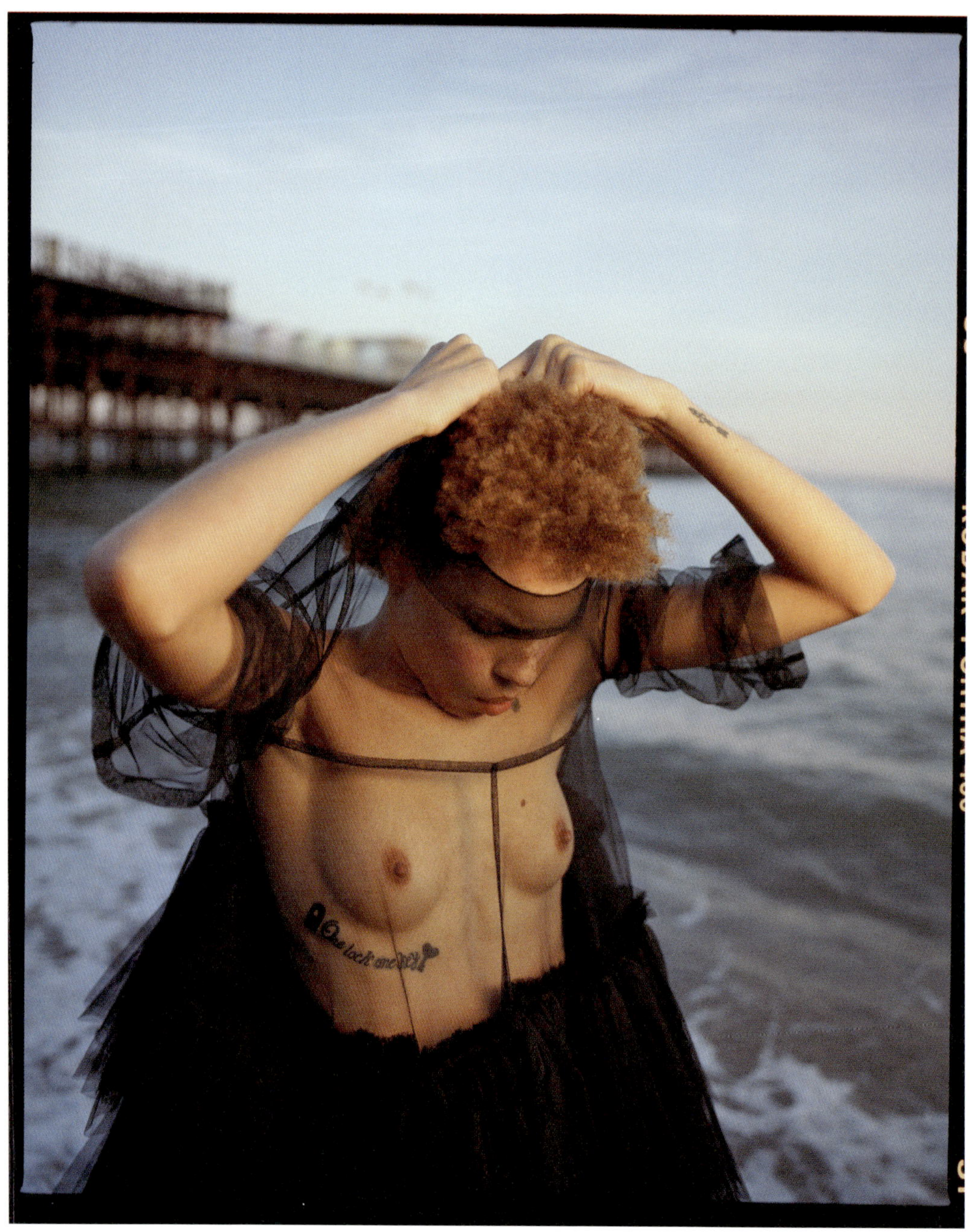

Nadine Ijewere
Untitled [from the series *Joy as an Act of Resistance*], 2018
Fine art inkjet print on 305 gsm Hahnemühle Photo Rag Ultra Smooth paper, 60 × 50 cm
CLM Agency London

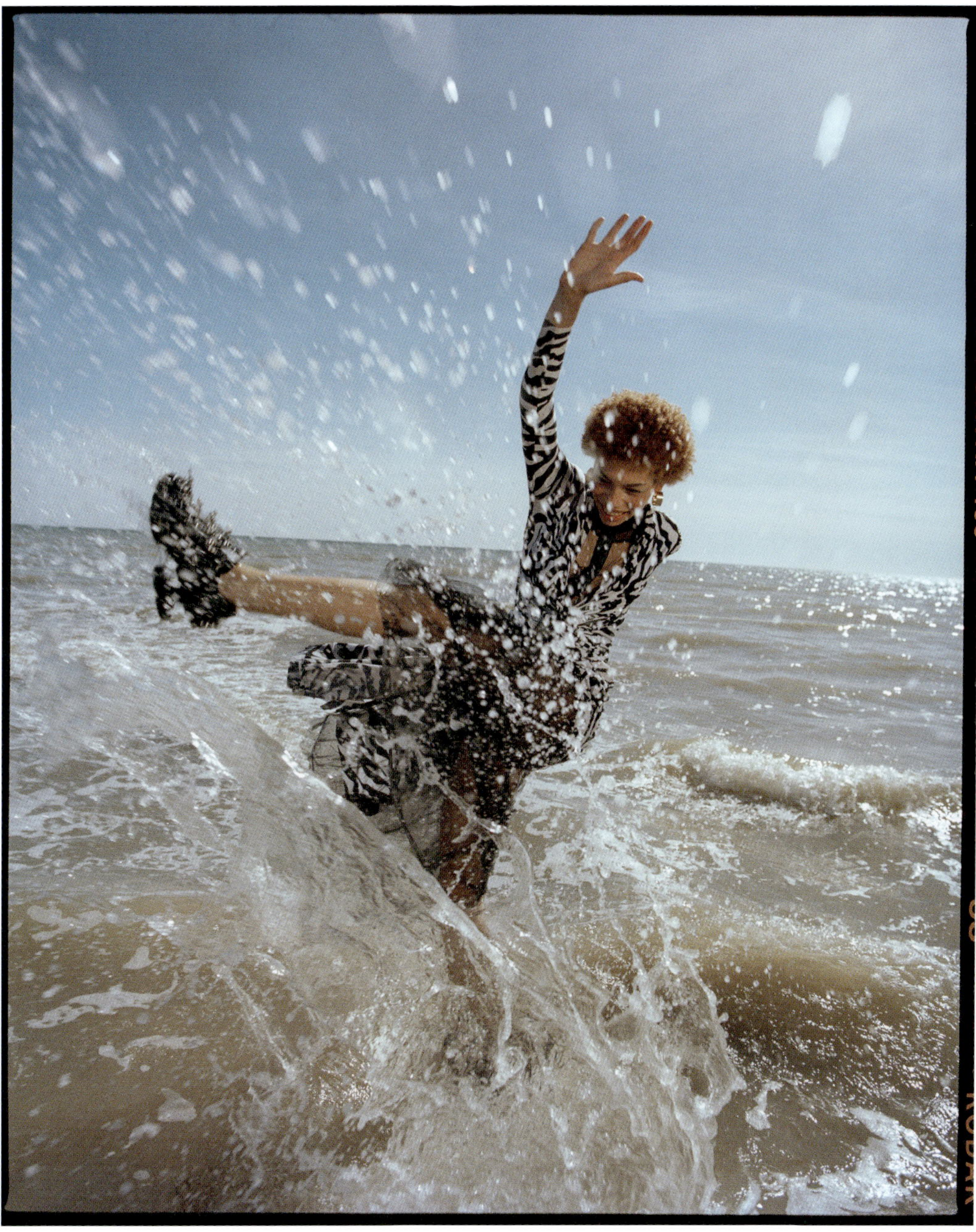

Nadine Ijewere
Untitled [from the series *Joy as an Act of Resistance*], 2018
Fine art inkjet print on 305 gsm Hahnemühle Photo Rag Ultra Smooth paper, 60 × 50 cm
CLM Agency London

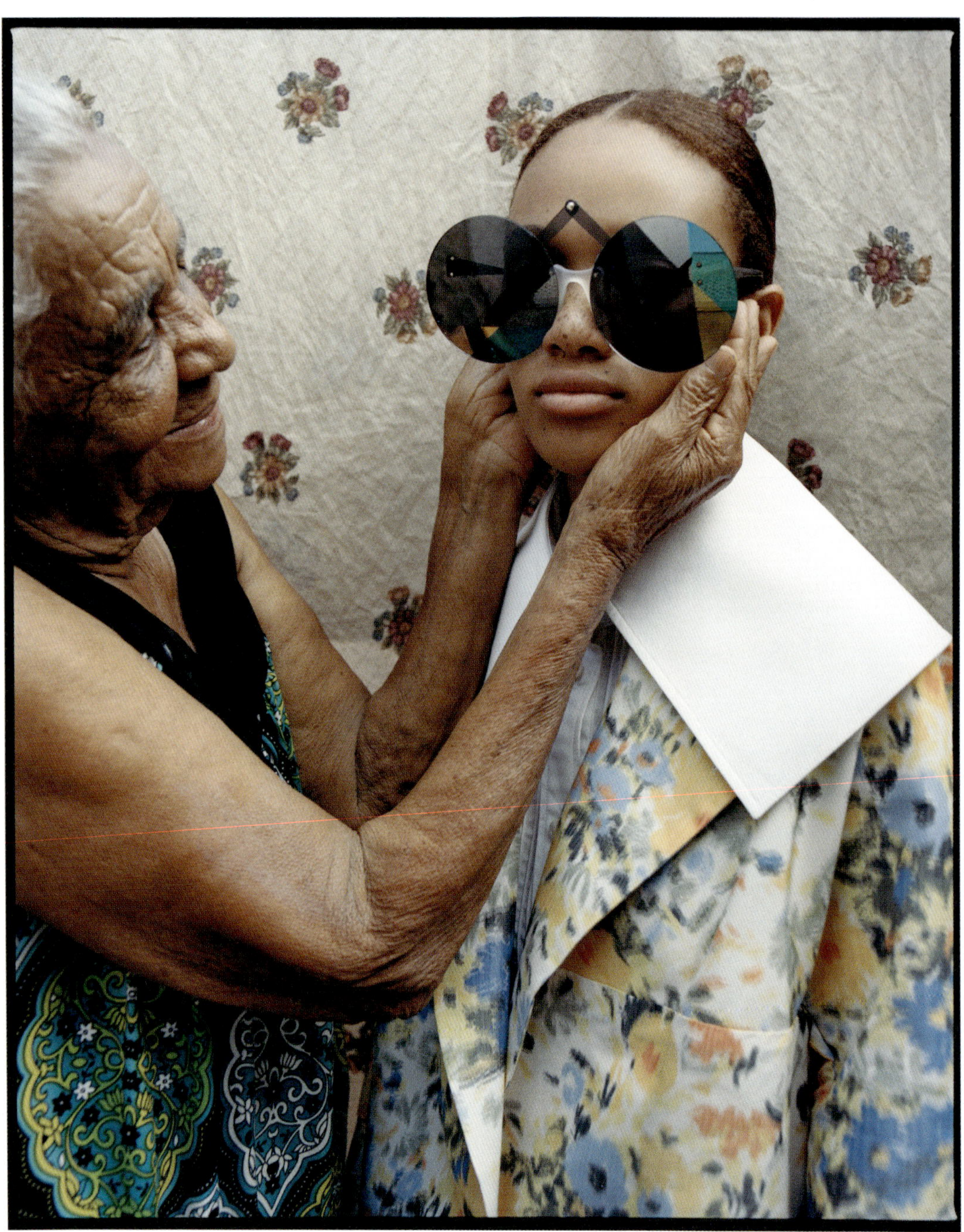

Nadine Ijewere
Untitled [for Nina Ricci], 2020
Fine art inkjet print on Hahnemühle 305 gsm Photo Rag Ultra Smooth paper, 60 × 50 cm
CLM Agency London

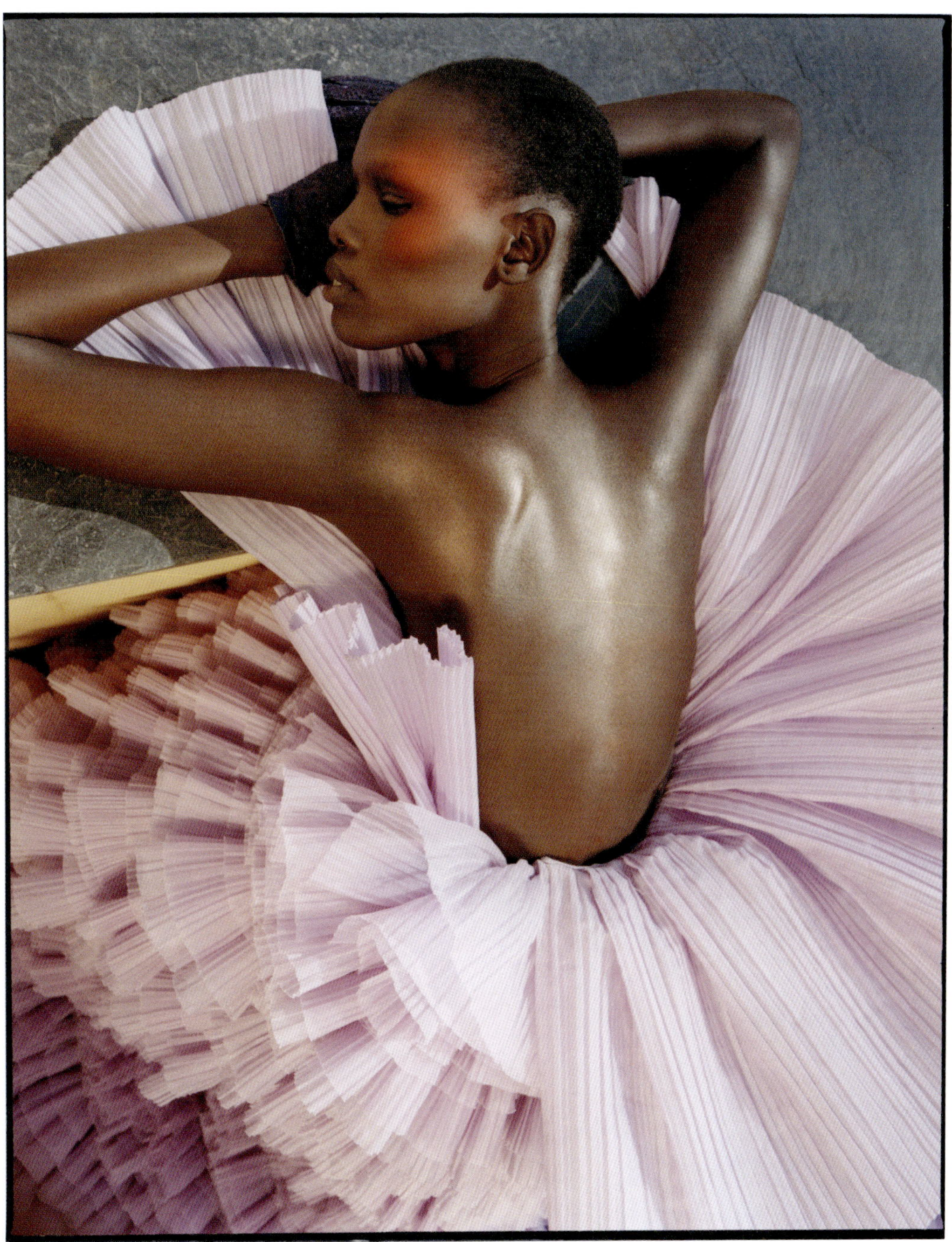

Nadine Ijewere
Fashion Swirl [from the series *Haut*], 2019
Fine art inkjet print on 305 gsm Hahnemühle Photo Rag Ultra Smooth paper, 60 × 50 cm
CLM Agency London

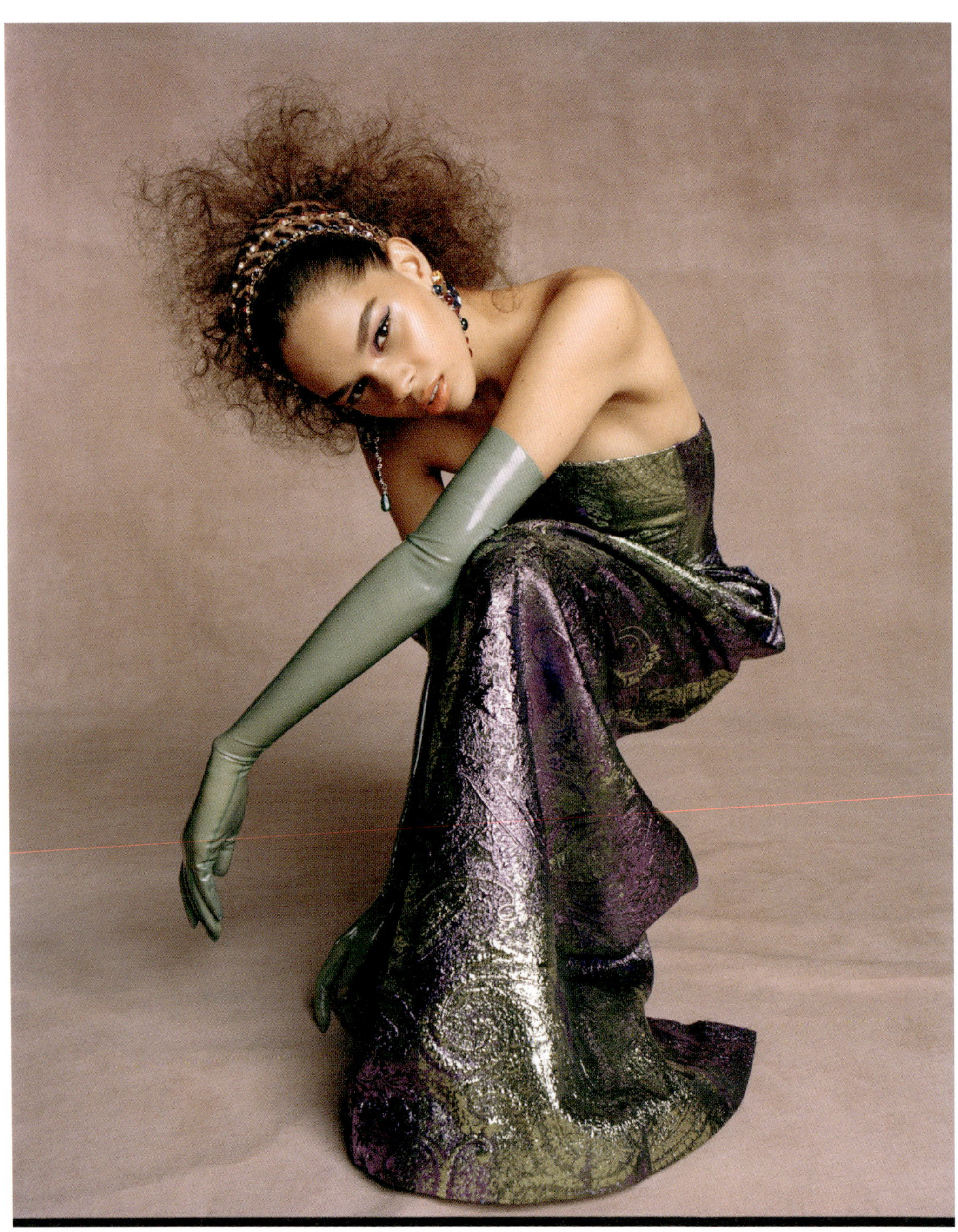

Nadine Ijewere
Untitled [from the series *Black Cotillion*], 2019
Fine art inkjet print on 305 gsm Hahnemühle Photo Rag Ultra Smooth paper, 60 × 50 cm
CLM Agency London

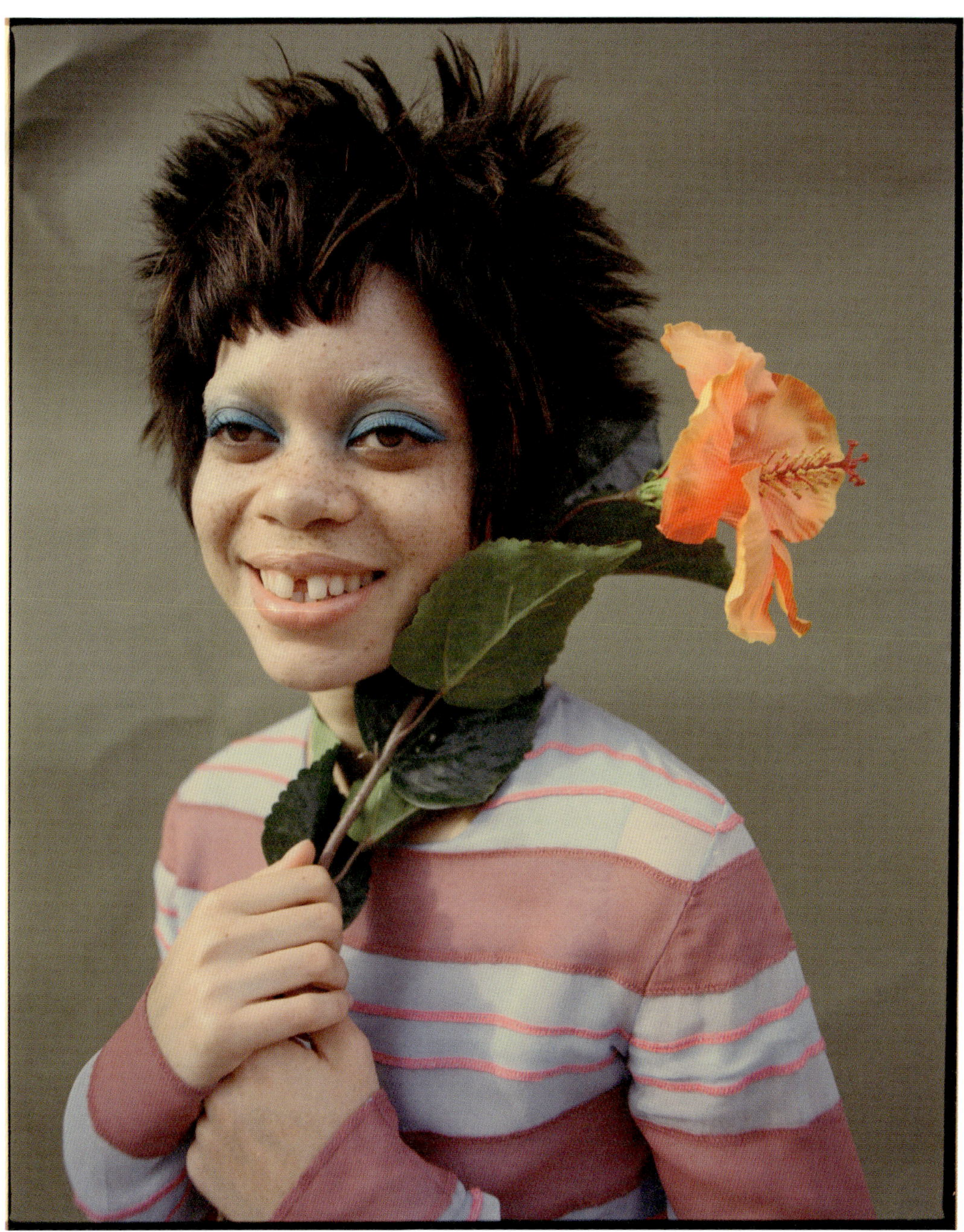

Nadine Ijewere
Seashell [from the series *Ugly*], 2017
Fine art inkjet print on 305 gsm Hahnemühle Photo Rag Ultra Smooth paper, 60 × 50 cm
CLM Agency London

Appendix

Timeline

Fashion Trends over Time

1940–1950:

· Wartime: frugal fashion; uniform, reasonable, and practical wear

· Recycling of materials

1950–1960:

· War is over: Paris resumes its role as fashion capital

· Haute Couture; Christian Dior's « New Look » revolutionises the world of fashion

· Influence of popular culture

· The bikini is born

Timeline of Women's History

1946
Trümmerfrauen: German and Austrian women who built up the bombed cities after World War II when many men were dead or prisoners of war

1949
The *Second Sex* by Simone de Beauvoir is published

1949
German Constitution of 1949 includes gender equality

1959
Barbie doll by Mattel

Historical Events

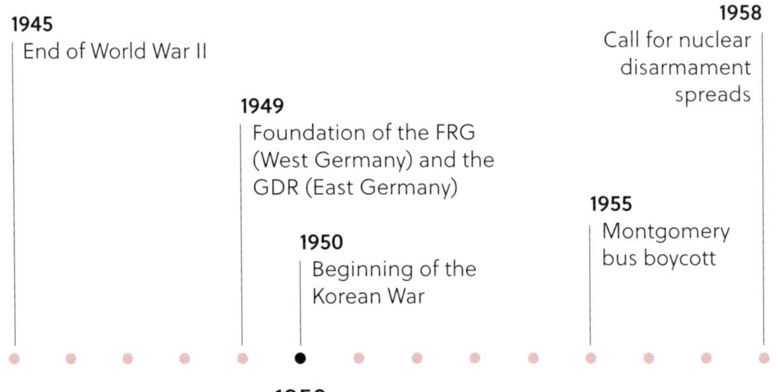

1960–1970:
· The miniskirt, the minidress
· Yves Saint Laurent's Le Smoking: the first tuxedo suit for women
· Influence of popular culture
· Spaceflight and the moon landing as inspiration for fashion
· Advent of ready-to-wear clothing

1970–1980:
· Platform shoes, flares
· Oriental, psychedelic, and flower patterns; batiks
· Punk movement with Vivienne Westwood & the Sex Pistols: tartan, torn jeans, bondage look
· Glam rock, influenced by David Bowie: androgyny, eccentricity, glamour
· Disco fashion of the late 1970s: metallic look, sequins, and neon colours

1961
First female member in the German government

1968
Second-wave feminism

1971
German magazine Stern runs cover "We've Had Abortions!": Women protest against Paragraph 218 of the German penal code

1977
First reform act of German marriage and family law

1969
The Stonewall Riots start on Christoper Street in New York. The LGBT community responds to police violence in the USA

1960s
Women's Liberation Movement, USA

1970/80s
Feminist teaching and research

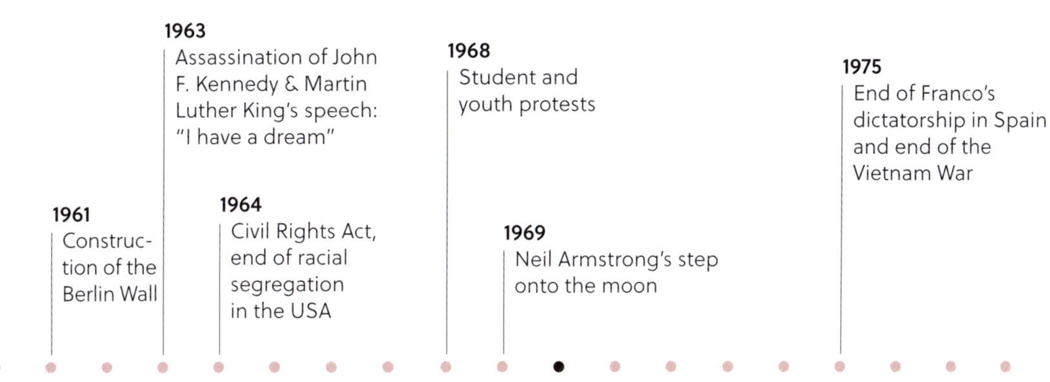

1963
Assassination of John F. Kennedy & Martin Luther King's speech: "I have a dream"

1968
Student and youth protests

1975
End of Franco's dictatorship in Spain and end of the Vietnam War

1961
Construction of the Berlin Wall

1964
Civil Rights Act, end of racial segregation in the USA

1969
Neil Armstrong's step onto the moon

1960

1970

Fashion Trends over Time

1980–1990, German Democratic Republic (GDR):
· Very limited supply
· Introduction of fully synthetic clothes
· Flares, hot pants, spiral skirts, parkas

1980–1990 In the West:
· Architectural and innovative cuts
· Japanese designers revolutionise fashion:
Comme des Garçons, Kenzo, and Yohji Yamamoto
· Blazers with padded shoulders, pantsuits
· Sports fashion: neon colours, leggings, sneakers, Lycra

1990–2000:
· Wide variety of fashions, parallel styles
· Kate Moss, Winona Rider epitomise the nineties
· Influence of hip-hop on fashion; streetwear
· Futuristic clothing with Alexander McQueen, John Galliano, Thierry Mugler
· Minimalist fashion with Ann Demeulemeester, Dries Van Noten
· Levi's 501, bodysuits, platform shoes, Doc Martens, oversize blazers and sweaters, spaghetti straps, short dresses with leather jackets

Timeline of Women's History

1980
German act on equal treatment of men and women in the workplace

1981
Women, Race and Class by the Afro-American author Angela Davis is published

Late 1980s
Kimberlé Crenshaw coins the term of intersectionality

1990
Judith Butler publishes *Gender Trouble*

1995
4th UN World Conference on Women in Peking

1999
Gender Mainstream

1970/80s
Feminist teaching and research

1980/90s
Body cult and focus on the look: era of the "supermodels"

Historical Events

1986
Chernobyl nuclear disaster

1989
Fall of the Berlin Wall

1990
German Reunification

1991
Dissolution of the Soviet Union

1992
Conclusion of the Maastricht Treaty

1994
New constitution in South Africa – End of apartheid

Genocide in Ruanda

1995
Bosnian War: Srebrenica genocide

1980

1990

2000–2010:
- Anything goes!
- Streetstyle and streetwear
- Vintage looks
- Track suits, sneakers, hoop earrings, low-waist jeans
- Ultra synthetic fibres

2010–2020:
- Comebacks of earlier fashion trends
- The impact of Instagram and social networks on fashion extends to haute couture and fashion brands
- Influencers impact fashion on social media; rapidly changing trends
- Fast fashion
- Cool and casual luxury
- A creative avant-garde mixes vintage and recycled textiles

2001
Netherlands are the first country to legalise same-sex marriage at national level

2005
Angela Merkel becomes the first female Chancellor of Germany

2014
Political transformation strategy "Care Revolution"

2017
#MeToo debate

2018
Greta Thunberg starts "Fridays for Future" movement

2000s
"It girls" and musicians set trends: Britney Spears, Paris Hilton, Destiny's Child, Lindsay Lohan, Spice Girls, Sex and the City

2010s
Star models: the sisters Gigi and Bella Hadid, Kendall Jenner, Kaia Gerber, Hailey Baldwin Bieber

2001
Terrorist attacks on World Trade Center and Pentagon

2008
Global financial crisis

2009
Barack Obama first US president of colour

2011
Fukushima nuclear disaster

2017
Donald Trump is elected president of the USA

2000

2010

Fashion Trends over Time

2020–2021:
- COVID-19: masks as fashion accessories
- Online Fashion business increases due to COVID-19 pandemic
- Social networks continue to be influential; haute couture shows take place online
- Homewear fashion
- Fast fashion leads to criticism of production conditions, ecological consequences, and lacking sustainability of the global fashion production

Timeline of Women's History

2020
Gender pay gap: Women are still being paid on average 18 % less than men

2021
Kamala Harris is the first female and woman of colour Vice President of the USA

Historical Events

2020
Beginning of the COVID pandemic, murder of George Floyd, "Black Lives Matter"

2021
United States Capitol attack and withdrawal of international troops from Afghanistan

2020

Brief Biographies

Lillian Bassman

* 1917 in New York, † 2012 in New York

From the 1940s until the 1960s, Lillian Bassman worked as a fashion photographer and became the first permanently employed female assistant for *Harper's Bazaar*. She was appointed co-art director at *Junior Bazaar*. Bassman is famous for her innovative work in the darkroom; particularly notable are her high-contrast black-and-white shots of society women, actresses, and models from the 1950s and 60s.

Sibylle Bergemann

* 1941 in Berlin, † 2010 near Gransee, Brandenburg

Sibylle Bergemann completed her photography apprenticeship with Arno Fischer. She produced fashion and portrait photos as well as documentary photographs. Bergemann was a founder member of the photographers' agency and image archive OSTKREUZ in Berlin.

Louise Dahl-Wolfe

* 1895 in San Francisco, California, † 1989 in Allendale, New Jersey

After her studies at the San Francisco Institute of Art, Louise Dahl-Wolfe first worked as a sign painter. She started with photography in 1930. Dahl-Wolfe is considered a pioneer of colour photography. She is also known for the at that time uncommon casual and everyday poses of the models in her fashion photos.

GABO

* 1961 in Hamburg, lives and works in Löwenberger Land, Brandenburg

GABO (Gabriele Oestreich) studied graphic design and worked as an international model after finishing school. She then decided to become a photographer herself and to take pictures of others from her own view. From the mid 1980s on, her works were published in various national and international magazines and periodicals (among others in *Stern*, *Vogue*, *Spiegel*, *Park Avenue*, *Playboy*, *Amica*, *L'Uomo Vogue*, *Guido*, *Barbara*).

Ingeborg Hoppe

* 1920 in Kassel, † 1983 in Stuttgart

Ingeborg Hoppe studied at the former State School of Applied Arts in Stuttgart and at the Bavarian Government Institute for Photographic Procedure in Munich. The German fashion photographer not only took commercial photos for advertising purposes, but also landscape shots, reportages, and portraits of famous personalities.

Nadine Ijewere

* 1992 in London, lives and works in London

Nadine Ijewere's works circle in on identity and diversity. She casts her models herself, frequently not complying with societal beauty norms, and she puts the focus on the representation of people who do not correspond to the mainstream. Ijewere shows beauty, even in its assumed "imperfection".

Liv Liberg

* 1992 in Utrecht, Holland, lives and works in Amsterdam

Liv Liberg studied studied photography at the Royal Academy of Art in The Hague. At the age of 10, she already started photographing her younger sister Britt, and she later published the pictures taken over 15 years in a photo book titled *Sister Sister*. She moreover works as a fashion photographer for various labels and magazines. Liberg also takes photographs specifically for distribution via social media networks such as Instagram.

Madame d'Ora

* 1881 in Vienna, Austria-Hungary, † 1963 in Frohnleiten, Austria

Madame d'Ora (Dora Kallmus) opened a photo studio in Vienna and mainly specialised in portrait photography in her early creative career. She became deeply interested in fashion photography after moving to Paris. When the Nazis occupied France in 1940, d'Ora had to flee from Paris. After the war, she increasingly engaged in documentary photography.

Ute Mahler

* 1949 in Berka near Sondershausen, Thuringia, lives and works in Oranienburg

Ute Mahler studied photography at the Academy of Fine Arts in Leipzig. She was a professor at Hamburg University of Applied Sciences and a co-founder of the photographers' agency and image archive OSTKREUZ in Berlin. Mahler documented everyday life in the German Democratic Republic in her works. She sees herself as a documentary photographer who also creates fashion images. Ute Mahler and her husband Werner have been working together closely until this day.

Charlotte March

* 1929 in Essen, † 2005 in Hamburg

In her early creative career, Charlotte March photographed her hometown Hamburg and the people living there. Later on, she became an international advertising and fashion photographer and worked for popular German magazines such as *Brigitte*.

Lee Miller

* 1907 in Poughkeepsie, New York, † 1977 in Chiddingly, England

Lee Miller is not only known for her portrait and fashion photos, but also for her documentary photographic works. As a war correspondent for *Vogue*, she accompanied the U.S. troops in World War II. After the war, she produced shocking records of the devastation in the concentration camps. Miller was a successful model herself, and she belonged to the circle of surrealists in Paris in the 1920s.

Sarah Moon

* 1941 in Vichy, France, lives and works in Paris

Sarah Moon studied visual arts in Paris, and she worked as a model prior to deciding on a career as a photographer, which she pursues as an autodidact. Her surreal, romantic, and sometimes bizarre images are internationally renowned. Moon is both a photo artist and a fashion photographer as well as a filmmaker.

Amber Pinkerton

* 1997 in Kingston, Jamaica, lives and works in London and Kingston

Amber Pinkerton studies photography at the University of Westminster in London. She is a filmmaker and known for her documentary and fashion photography. Many of her works are politically motivated. She engages in issues such as life, youth cultures, and street styles in her native country Jamaica and in London.

Elizaveta Porodina

* 1987 in Moscow, lives and works in Munich

Elizaveta Porodina is a Russian artist, photographer and psychologist known for her surrealist themes and use of symbolism. She lives and works in Germany. Her clients include Dior, Carolina Herrera, Jo Malone, Moncler, and *Vogue*, among others.

Regina Relang

* 1906 in Stuttgart, † 1989 in Munich

Regina Relang studied painting at the Stuttgart Academy of Art and the Prussian Academy of Arts in Berlin, among others. She achieved international renown with photographic travel and fashion reportages that she started producing as an autodidact. Christian Dior, Pierre Cardin, and Yves Saint Laurent are among her clients. Relang documented the haute couture in Paris for German fashion magazines and was one of the most successful photographers in Germany in the 1950s and 60s.

Bettina Rheims

* 1952 in Neuilly-sur-Seine, France, lives and works in Paris

Bettina Rheims worked as a model before she took up photography. The focus of her works is on sensual portraits of women. She wants to show the individual personality of her models. Apart from celebrities, she frequently photographs people on the fringes of society. Rheims moreover gives resonance to open and androgynous gender identities.

Charlotte Rohrbach

* 1902 in Malschöwen, East Prussia, † 1981 in Pöcking, Bavaria

Charlotte Rohrbach completed her studies at the photography department of Lette-Verein, an educational organisation for applied arts in Berlin. She worked both as a press photographer and a filmmaker. Rohrbach worked for the magazine *Film und Frau* in Hamburg, where she took architecture and fashion pictures and produced society documentaries.

Alice Springs

* 1923 in Melbourne, Australia, † 2021 in Monte-Carlo, Monaco

From 1970 on, June Newton started creating independent photographic works under the pseudonym of Alice Springs. Her complete oeuvre spans four decades and comprises advertising, fashion, and nude photography and, above all, portraits. She started taking pictures when her husband Helmut Newton contracted the flu. He explained to her how to use a camera and a light meter, and in 1970, it was she instead of the originally booked Helmut Newton who shot an advertising photo for the French cigarette brand Gitanes. The portrait of the smoking model marked the beginning of her own new career. (text: Matthias Harder)

Deborah Turbeville

* 1932 in Stoneham, Massachusetts, † 2013 in Manhattan, New York

Deborah Turbeville started as an assistant and sample model for the fashion designer Claire McCardell. Later on, she attended a six month workshop with the photographer Richard Avedon and the art director Marvin Israel. Turbeville's fashion photos are notable for their gloomy, yearning, and sometimes nostalgic atmosphere. Her pictures show pale women in forlorn places, with the fashion almost becoming secondary.

Ellen von Unwerth

* 1954 in Frankfurt am Main, lives and works in Paris

As a teenager, Ellen von Unwerth worked at a circus and was soon discovered as a model. After a number of successful years in modelling, she realised that she was happier taking pictures herself. Her photos are characterised by the sensuality with which she shows women. Ellen von Unwerth enjoys international success with the highly recognisable style she has created for her works.

Yva

* 1900 in Berlin, † 1942 in the Sobibor extermination camp, Poland

After completing her photography apprenticeship, Yva (Else Ernestine Neuländer) opened her own studio in Berlin, where she took fashion, nude, and advertising photos. She participated in the first *Biennale Internazionale d'Arte Fotografica* in Rome; other international exhibitions in Paris and London followed. In 1938 Yva was banned from working in Nazi Germany. Plans for a departure together with her husband Alfred Simon came too late. Yva was deported in 1942 and presumably murdered in the Sobibor extermination camp.

Authors

Antje-Britt Mählmann

Antje-Britt Mählmann (* 1979) studied photography and art history in Brighton, London, and Düsseldorf, where she also completed her PhD on the late work of the artist Louise Bourgeois. She worked as a freelancer at various museums and art associations (Kunstvereine) in North Rhine-Westphalia, and she completed her assistant curatorship at Kunsthalle Emden, where she stayed on as a research fellow. Mählmann has headed the Kunsthalle St. Annen in Lübeck since 2018, and she will take up the position as artistic director at Museum Schloss Moyland in Beburg-Hau in April 2022.

Nadine Barth

Nadine Barth (* 1964) is a curator and journalist. She studied philosophy, literature, and art history and for several years ran a gallery for fashion photography in Hamburg and Berlin. In 2006 she founded *barthouse culture concepts*, an agency for art and communication. She has edited over 100 publications on photography and fashion and curated numerous exhibitions at international institutions. Barth has been working as Consulting Editor for photography art books at Hatje Cantz since 2013. She lives in Berlin.

Eugenie Shinkle

Eugenie Shinkle (* 1963) is a photographer and author. She lives in in London, UK. Her works have been published both in the academic and popular press – most recently in *Foam Magazine*, *Art Journal*, and *Yale University Press*. She has contributed to numerous monographs and exhibition catalogues. Shinkle is co-editor of C4 Journal, a platform dedicated to writing about photography.

Diana Weis

Diana Weis (* 1974) studied dramatics, German, and communication science. Besides her professorship for fashion journalism, she writes on fashion theoretical issues and the sociology of the body. Her book *Modebilder* (Fashion Images) was published in 2020.

Female View exhibition, list of lenders:

Alice Black Gallery, London
CAMERA WORK, Berlin
CLM, London
Deichtorhallen Hamburg
Farleys House & Gallery LTD., Lee Miller Archives, Chiddingly (East Sussex)
GABO Photos Showroom, Löwenberger Land
F.C. Gundlach Foundation, Hamburg
Liv Liberg, Amsterdam
Ute Mahler, Oranienburg
Museum für Kunst und Gewerbe Hamburg
Helmut Newton Foundation, Berlin
Elizaveta Porodina, München
Ellen von Unwerth Studios, Paris

This book is published in conjunction with the exhibition

Female View
Female Fashion Photographers from Modernity to the Digital Age

Kunsthalle St. Annen, Lübeck
March 20–July 3, 2022

Editor
Antje-Britt Mählmann for Kunsthalle St. Annen

Concept & managing editor
Antje-Britt Mählmann

Consultant
Nadine Barth

Layout
Julia Wagner

Copy editor
Anja Hellhammer

Translation & copy editing (English)
Andrea Thode

Production
Thomas Lemaître, Hatje Cantz

Reproductions
DruckConcept, Berlin

Printing & binding
Livonia Print SIA

© 2022 Kunsthalle St. Annen, Lübeck, Hatje Cantz Verlag, Berlin, and authors

Picture credits
For the reproduced works by the artists Louise Dahl-Wolfe, Sarah Moon, and Bettina Rheims © VG Bild-Kunst, Bonn 2022
For the reproduced works by:
Lillian Bassman © Estate of Lillian Bassman; Sibylle Bergemann © Estate of Sibylle Bergemann, OSTKREUZ; Sibylle Bergemann (Katharina Reinwald) © Estate of Sibylle Bergemann, OSTKREUZ, Courtesy Loock Galerie, Berlin, Costume: Angelika Kroker, Allerleirauh; Madame d'Ora © Estate of Madame d'Ora, Museum für Kunst und Gewerbe Hamburg; GABO © the artist; Ingeborg Hoppe © Estate of Ingeborg Hoppe, Matthias Mangold; Nadine Ijewere © the artist; Liv Liberg © the artist; Ute Mahler © the artist, OSTKREUZ; Charlotte March © Estate of Charlotte March; Lee Miller © Lee Miller Archives, England 2022; Amber Pinkerton © the artist, courtesy Alice Black Gallery; Elizaveta Porodina © the artist; Regina Relang © Münchner Stadtmuseum, Sammlung Fotografie, Archiv Relang; Charlotte Rohrbach © Estate of Charlotte Rohrbach; Alice Springs © Estate of Alice Springs, courtesy Helmut Newton Foundation; Deborah Turbeville © Estate of Deborah Turbeville; courtesy Deborah Bell Photographs, New York, and Staley-Wise Gallery, New York; Ellen von Unwerth © the artist; Yva © Museum für Kunst und Gewerbe Hamburg (Public Domain)

Photo credits
Lillian Bassman, Sibylle Bergemann, Louise Dahl-Wolfe, Ingeborg Hoppe, Sarah Moon, Deborah Turbeville, Yva (S. 46–51) © Deichtorhallen Hamburg, Christoph Irrgang; Charlotte March, Regina Relang (S. 72/73), Madame d'Ora, Yva (S. 43–45) © Museum für Kunst und Gewerbe Hamburg; Regina Relang (S. 66–71), Charlotte Rohrbach © Stiftung F.C. Gundlach; Alice Springs © Helmut Newton Foundation
The assertion of claims pursuant to § 60h UrhG for the reproduction of images of the exhibits / inventory works is carried out by VG Bild-Kunst.
Despite intensive research, it was not possible to locate the rightholders of the images in all cases. Legitimate claims will be settled within the framework of the usual agreements.

Published by
Hatje Cantz Verlag GmbH
Mommsenstrasse 27
10629 Berlin
www.hatjecantz.com

Bibliographic information published by the Deutsche Nationalbibliothek: The Deutsche Nationalbibliothek lists this publication in the Deutsche Nationalbibliografie; detailed bibliographic data are available on the Internet at http://dnb.d-nb.de.

ISBN: 978-3-7757-5184-1

Printed in Europe

Cover illustration
Lillian Bassman, *Barbara Mullen*, c. 1952

Back cover illustration
Ellen von Unwerth, *Lana del Rey*, 2012

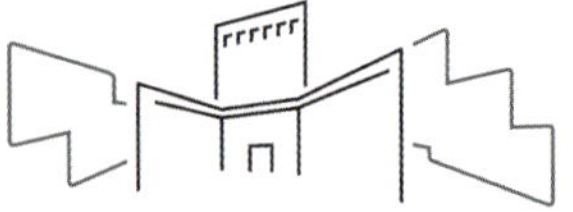

Kunsthalle St. Annen

Exhibition

Kunsthalle St. Annen
St.-Annen-Straße 15
23552 Lübeck
Germany
Tel.: +49 (0)451 122 4137 (Cash register)
Fax: +49 (0)451 122 4183
mq@luebeck.de
www.kunsthalle-st-annen.de

Museum director & exhibition curator
Antje-Britt Mählmann

Assistant curators
Emma-Louise Arcade, Ann-Kristin Jürgensen

Cultural volunteers
Benita Martis, Irma Rüb

Administration
Elke Krüger, Andrea Schwarz

Press relations
CAB Artis – Thomas Spindler

Conservators
Donat Klafs, Susanne Schöning

Technical support
Roger Grimm, Helmut Langer, Andreas Meyer,
Dominik Steinhagen, Klaus Weller

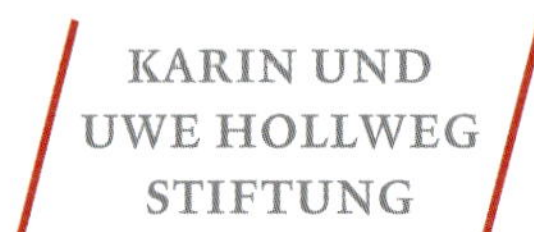

Von Keller-Stiftung Lübeck

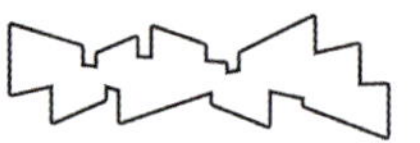

Kulturstiftung Hansestadt Lübeck
Die LÜBECKER MUSEEN
Schildstraße 12
23552 Lübeck
Germany
Tel.: +49 (0)451 122 4192
Fax: +49 (0)451 122 4106
museen@luebeck.de
www.die-luebecker-museen.de

Executive director
Hans Wißkirchen

Commercial management
Arndt Brücker

Administration
Bernadett Braun

Event manager
Helene Hoffmann

Education & communication
Helena Ruff

Press & marketing
Thomas Neubert, Diana Wenninger

Shop
Ines Bohnsack

This exhibition was made possible through the support of

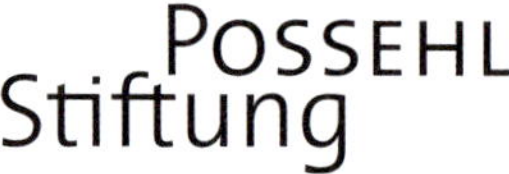

Friedrich Bluhme und Else Jebsen-Stiftung